Weekends with
Daisy

Weekends with

Daisy

Sharron Kahn Luttrell

G

GALLERY BOOKS

New York London Toronto Sydney New Delhi

G

Gallery Books
A Division of Simon & Schuster, Inc.
1230 Avenue of the Americas
New York, NY 10020

First Gallery Books hardcover edition September 2013

GALLERY BOOKS and colophon are registered trademarks of Simon & Schuster, Inc.

For information about special discounts for bulk purchases,
please contact Simon & Schuster Special Sales at 1-866-506-1949
or business@simonandschuster.com

The Simon & Schuster Speakers Bureau can bring authors to your live event. For
more information or to book an event contact the Simon & Schuster Speakers
Bureau at 1-866-248-3049 or visit our website at www.simonspeakers.com.

Designed by Davina Mock-Maniscalco

Manufactured in the United States of America

10   9   8   7   6   5   4   3   2   1

Library of Congress Cataloging-in-Publication Data is avalaible.

ISBN 978-1-4516-8623-4
ISBN 978-1-4516-8624-1 (ebook)

To the loves of my life: Marty, Aviva, and Josh

Introduction

SOMEWHERE BETWEEN THE pickles and the olives I found exactly what I was looking for: a dog. It was Mother's Day and we were returning from a visit to my in-laws. The entire family was together—a minor miracle given my husband's schedule and the fact that the older of our two children preferred to be anywhere but with us. We made a quick stop at the supermarket to buy something to grill for dinner. My husband and my son took off toward the meat counter while I headed down the condiments aisle with our teenage daughter. That's when I spotted the dog. Or rather its tail end, rounding the corner.

In the two years since Tucker, our German shepherd, had died I'd developed a full-blown case of Canine Deficit Disorder. The primary symptoms were a preoccupation with dogs and a total loss of inhibition when near one. Friends had nicknamed our home Camp Luttrell because that's where they would send their dogs every time they went away. If I drove past someone walking a dog, I would slow the car for a closer look while my children slouched in their seats with embarrassment.

So, seeing a dog in a supermarket, of all places, sprung my mania into overdrive. "Oh my God," I whispered as I held out my hand to stop my daughter. "That . . . was a dog."

"Mom, don't," she pleaded, but I was already speed-walking up the aisle and skidding around the endcap. And there it was. A small yellow Labrador retriever was keeping pace alongside a young man holding a basket of groceries. They stepped into a checkout line, the dog waiting serenely for their next move. It wore a bright blue vest with the words "NEADS Puppy-in-Training."

This is where the story begins.

Get It

MY DAUGHTER SAYS I threw myself at the man with the yellow Lab, but she tends to be overly dramatic. I distinctly remember keeping a respectful distance as he described his role as a volunteer puppy raiser, even if it did require I clasp my hands behind my back to physically restrain myself from patting the dog.

If it had been a few years earlier—when Tucker was still alive, the kids little, and my in-laws healthy—I wouldn't have reacted so strongly to the sight of the dog. Sure, I would have been curious, but my mild social anxiety would have kept me from speaking up. Instead, I would have strolled by as many times as it took to make out the words on the dog's vest before retreating back to my shopping list. But on that day, I was feeling desperate. I should have been content. I had a husband who loved me, a good job, two healthy, relatively happy children. But

I couldn't enjoy being with my family that day because the fact that the four of us were together only underscored how rare an occurrence that had become. Our kids were growing out of childhood and pulling me grudgingly along with them. Soon enough, they would be grown and gone, and with them, much of what defined me for the past decade and a half. Without them, I'd have to somehow figure out who I would be next. The sight of the dog offered if not the answer to my fears of the future, a pleasant diversion from them. And at the very least, a possible cure for my CDD.

The man unloaded his groceries onto the belt as he described the National Education for Assistance Dog Services (NEADS), which trains service dogs. I'd heard of NEADS, had even covered one of its graduations years earlier when I was a newspaper reporter. But back then, NEADS only trained dogs to alert their hearing-impaired owners to sounds like alarm clocks and crying babies. I hadn't realized that in the years since, it had expanded its mission to train dogs to assist with a range of disabilities: multiple sclerosis, spina bifida, autism, post-traumatic stress disorder. There really was no limit to whom the dogs could help.

These days, most of their puppies are trained by inmates in prisons and released on weekends to volunteers like the man in the supermarket, who by now had pulled out his wallet to pay the cashier. I said good-bye and he urged me to visit the NEADS website to learn more. I returned to my daughter, who was lurking two lanes away, pretending to study the cover of *Diabetic Living*.

———

THAT EVENING AFTER dinner, I settled in front of my computer and clicked around on the NEADS website until I found the page for the Prison Pup Partnership. I learned that NEADS places puppies in select prisons throughout New England, where inmates train them to be assistance dogs. The inmate dog handlers have the most coveted job in prison. In exchange for raising and training a puppy, they get three dollars a day and their own cell to share with their dog. Over the course of twelve months or so, these specially chosen inmates are responsible for housebreaking their puppies and teaching them basic obedience before moving on to more specialized tasks with help from a professional trainer: teaching their dogs to pick up dropped coins, turn light switches on and off, push elevator buttons with their noses, get the phone when it rings, open and close doors, and fetch items from a refrigerator. Because inmates have all the time in the world to devote to their jobs, they're able to train their dogs in about half the time it would take a professional dog trainer, and at significantly reduced cost.

There is one problem, though, and it's kind of a big one. Assistance dogs go everywhere with their owners, so they need to be confident in all situations. If all a dog knows is prison, it won't be able to function in the outside world. Things we take for granted—such as phones ringing, couples hugging, cars, and kids—are likely to send the dog into a barking frenzy or scrambling for the nearest hiding place. This is where weekend puppy raisers come in. On Friday afternoons, each puppy is furloughed into the custody of a volunteer who brings the dog along on errands and outings all weekend long, exposing it to new situations and continuing its training until Sunday evening, when the volunteer returns the puppy to prison.

The application to be a weekend puppy raiser was on the website. I skimmed the questions, looking for anything that might immediately disqualify me. There weren't any requests for documentation of an advanced degree in canine behavior modification, no trick questions asking whether I'd interrupt my dinner to reward a begging puppy with (a) table scraps or (b) a slab of deli meat from the fridge. The questions were straight-forward. How many adults in your household? (Two, if you count me.) How many children and what are their ages? (Fifteen and eleven, but growing up too fast. Sometimes not fast enough.) Any pets? (Two bunnies that live in a hutch outside.) NEADS wanted to know about our house and yard. I described our location in a semirural Massachusetts suburb, emphasizing the total lack of traffic on our cul-de-sac. Then I came to the question "Why do you want to raise a NEADS puppy?"

I closed my eyes and thought about it. Long before Tucker was our dog, she was my aspiration. As a kid, I'd begged for a dog, threatened to run away if I didn't get one, bargained, cajoled, and whined (a lot). My mother's answer was always the same: "When you have your own house, you can have a dog."

It was worth the wait. Marty and I moved into our first home in the month of June and took Tucker, a pudgy eight-week-old puppy with an outsize personality, home in September. We found her in the classifieds of the local newspaper, the product of a secret rendezvous between neighboring German shepherds.

Tucker lived for nearly fifteen years. During that time, I had two babies and figured out how to be a mother. The Tucker years coincided with—and influenced—all of those thrilling firsts: first steps (my daughter was a late walker because of the constant threat of being knocked off her feet); first words ("Tu" for both of my kids); the first day of kindergarten (Tucker rode in the backseat while I followed the school bus at what I hoped was a discreet distance). There isn't a home video from those years that doesn't include at least one furry eclipse or scene-blocking shot of Tucker's snout and an off-camera voice yelling, "Tucker! Move!"

Throughout the changes wrought by parenthood, Tucker was a reassuring constant. She kept us anchored to routine amid the chaos of kids and work. Every morning, Tucker and I went together for a forty-minute walk through the woods behind our house. I'd stand in the kitchen and call out, "Where are my boots?" running the words together so they came out as a single burst of sound. Tucker would push her snout through the kitty door to the basement, trying to reach the ledge by the stairs where I kept my shoes. She would dart forward, pretend-biting my hands while I sat on the floor to lace them up, and race back and forth through the kitchen until I opened the back door. Then she'd streak outside, disappear through the trees, and wait on the path until I caught up. We did this every day, even when our walk was a slog through rain or snow or I had to wrap a scarf around my face to keep my skin from freezing in the cold.

I felt safe with Tucker. I worked for a newspaper, and when I was transferred to the early-morning copy desk and we had to start our walks in the predawn darkness, Tucker would stay close to me while I focused the beam of the flashlight downward to illuminate roots and rocks, feeling as much as seeing the shadows pulse inward on either side of us. I'd draw comfort from Tucker's steady panting and the sound of twigs snapping beneath our feet, feeling protected by my dog and the noise we made together.

When I was a teenager, I brought three things with me

whenever I had to walk anywhere alone: a jackknife that I discovered half-buried in the dirt outside my school; a rock that fit in the palm of my hand but was heavy enough to use against an attacker; and a small, carved wooden lion that my mother gave me after my father moved out and which she said would give me strength. There was no specific reason for me to be fearful, just an awareness that sometimes awful things happened and one should be prepared as best she could. It didn't help that I was small. Even now I'm sometimes mistaken for an eleven-year-old from behind. With Tucker, I didn't need a rock or a knife or a wooden lion. She was my talisman, my weapon, and my protector. But mostly, she was my dog.

As the kids grew up, Tucker grew old. The moment of her death was quick and painless, but the months leading up to it were excruciating for her and for us. Our dog, who in her younger years had so much energy that I suspected someone had secretly implanted springs in her feet, would struggle to stand up, then collapse as her legs buckled under her weight. She was incontinent and, I'm pretty sure, heartbreakingly ashamed of it.

Every night I'd kiss the top of her head right between her ears, and in the morning I'd reach over the side of the bed and touch her body lightly with my hand until I felt it rise and fall with her breath. My relief at having my dog still with me would fade, though, at the thought of her suffering through another day.

Eventually, Marty and I accepted that it was up to us to stop Tucker's suffering. She was at the end of her life. We had to let her go. I called the vet and arranged to bring Tucker after the weekend, on a Monday. That gave me time to tell her everything I needed to say to her. For those three days, I'd lie on the floor next to her and reminisce about her puppyhood, my panic on the first ride home when she wouldn't stop yelping and crying because she missed her mother and siblings, how lucky we felt to find her, out of all the dogs in the world. I thanked her for preparing me and Marty to be parents, for protecting me and the children, for being our dog.

Marty came home from work early that Monday and we gave the kids time to say good-bye. They cried a little, then drifted off to read or play. Tucker was their parents' dog more than theirs.

At the vet, Tucker used her last bit of strength to snap at the technician. I was silently proud that my dog was going out fighting. Plus, it was entirely in character for her. Tucker loved going to the vet but hated the exam table. Every time we took her there for shots or a physical, she would race up the steps into the waiting room and greet everyone there with her tail wagging, but the moment we got her on the table, she'd transform from Dr. Jekyll to Mr. Hyde and start snarling and nipping—and out would come the muzzle. This time would be no different. The vet, a stony-faced but kind woman, apologized when she handed us the blue cloth muzzle and waited while Marty slipped it over Tucker's nose. While the vet injected our dog with pentobarbital, Marty and I took turns whispering into Tucker's ear that she was a good dog, a smart dog, the best pal ever, until the vet removed the muzzle so that, in those last moments, we could stroke Tucker's nose and kiss the spot between her eyes and scratch behind her ears, which we did until we realized there was no longer life beneath our touch.

Marty, whose decades as a journalist taught him the value of gallows humor in times of tragedy, took a long, wavering breath and said between sobs, "Oh, Tucker! You always knew this place would be the death of you." The vet's expression didn't change but the technician laughed nervously. I put my arms around Marty, shaking from laughter and sobs.

Back home, I washed Tucker's dishes and stored them in the basement. I used pliers to pry the tags from her collar, then attached them to a long chain and wore them around my neck. The following weekend, Marty and I picked out new carpet. I allowed myself to appreciate the luxury of not worrying about getting home in time to let the dog out even as I hated opening the door to an empty house.

Friends wanted to know when we were going to adopt another dog. We'd tell them maybe someday, but for now we wanted to enjoy our new carpets. Of course that was a lie. Marty always worried about our tight finances and wanted a break from the vet bills. And I didn't want to start over with a new pet because a dog's limited years on earth were an uncomfortable reminder of our own. As all endings do, Tucker's death forced me to look back on my past and forward to my future. Behind me was a life that spilled over with the busyness of a growing family. In front of me, I saw that same family getting older until, in less than half the span of a dog's natural life, the kids would be off on their own, and it would be just me and Marty left at home.

Oh, crap. I was crying. I swiped my eyes and stared at the question on the computer screen. Why did I want to raise a NEADS puppy? Because I didn't want a dog who would grow old and die. But that's not what I wrote. Instead, I typed: *I know firsthand how much a dog can enrich a person's life—my dog was enormously important to me. And I suspect that for a person dealing with the emotional and physical challenges of a disability, a specially trained service dog enhances his or her quality of life even* more. NEADS *performs an invaluable service and I'd like to be part of it.*

I read over what I'd written and, satisfied, saved the application to my hard drive. The NEADS weekend puppy-raiser program, I naively thought, would be an ideal cure for my Canine Deficit Disorder—pick up a puppy on Friday night, return it on Sunday night, a new puppy every year, no strings attached. I couldn't have been more wrong.

MARTY WAS IN our bedroom, working out a Neil Young song on his beat-up old Yamaha guitar. His face was partially hidden behind a harmonica stand looped around his neck. Marty's more than a decade older than I am and was already going gray when we met twenty years earlier, but he has a boyish quality that leaves people unsure of his age.

He blew a final note into the harmonica. "Thank you very much. You've been a wonderful audience," he said, deepening his voice to a Johnny Cash twang.

I clapped and settled onto the bed. "Okay, so, you know that dog we saw in the supermarket?"

He unhooked the harmonica holder from around his neck and placed it on his guitar case. "Okaaay . . ." He drew out the word. I noticed he didn't meet my eyes. Marty is the opposite of spontaneous. He needs time to warm up to new ideas, especially those that might bring extra cost or complication into our lives.

"So, I'm thinking we should do it. What do you think? We'd have a puppy on weekends. They supply the food; we wouldn't have to pay for anything. And it would be for a good cause."

Marty pulled the strap over his head and leaned forward to lay the guitar back in its case. I figured he was remembering the recent Saturday afternoon he spent in the Laundromat when one of our canine houseguests snapped at him and peed on our down comforter. "Well, I'm not crazy about it," he said.

I brightened. He had said the same exact words to me when I was eight months pregnant and asked how he felt about naming our daughter in memory of my cousin Aviva. Fifteen years later, he couldn't imagine calling her anything else.

"I'll send you the link so you can check out the program yourself. That way at least you'll know more about it," I told him.

"Yeah, do that. I'll take a look at it tomorrow if I have time."

I was pretty sure he wouldn't find the time. Or if he did, he'd choose to spend it some other way. But that didn't matter because I knew he'd be mulling it over. Eighteen years of marriage had taught me that.

The next night, when the kids were in bed, I draped myself over Marty's lap for a back rub while he sat on the couch watching the eleven o'clock news. He pressed his fingers into the area beside my right shoulder blade and kneaded the muscle that's chronically tight from working the computer mouse.

I turned my head and looked up at him. "Have you had a chance to look at the link I sent you about puppy raising?"

This time he met my eye. "I haven't. Tell me about it again?"

Marty rubbed my back mechanically while I told him about the program. When I finished, he was quiet for a long time. Before I knew him well, I'd think he was ignoring me, or forgot we were having a conversation. Eventually I realized that he's just never felt the need to fill silences. A commercial came on and he patted my back, signaling that the back rub was over. I sat up and looked at him.

"Well, if it's that important to you, let's go ahead and do it." I smiled.

A FEW DAYS after I submitted the application, the phone rang. When I saw "NEADS" pop up on caller ID I felt a surge of excitement. This immediately triggered a countersurge of cynicism—a sort of self-defense mechanism I deploy to protect myself from disappointment, like an indoor sprinkler system reacting to a spike in building temperature.

I picked up the phone, bracing for a fund-raising appeal.

"Hi. Is this [pause] Sharron?"

"It is," I said, keeping my voice polite but noncommittal.

"This is Kerry Lemerise. I'm the foster family coordinator for NEADS, I work with the weekend puppy raisers."

"*Hi!*" I said, a little too loudly.

"Um. Hi!" Kerry said, gamely trying to match my tone. "We received your application."

Kerry and I spent about twenty minutes on the phone. I learned there was a long waiting list of weekend puppy raisers at the two prisons closest to me, but not enough volunteers at the medium-security prison in Cranston, Rhode Island. I'd never been to Cranston. I didn't know where it was, but I was beginning to feel a little panicky about missing out on a puppy, so I flipped through my brain for mental evidence that Cranston was within reasonable driving distance of my home. The Rhode Island state line is five miles from my house. Providence is only about thirty-five minutes away from me. "Is Cranston anywhere near Providence?" I asked Kerry. She thought it might be.

Gas prices were edging upward to four dollars a gallon. I—like every other driver in the nation—was cutting back on road trips, not adding them. Still, I wanted so badly to be part of the NEADS program that I did a quick calculation in my head and immediately began rationalizing: I was lucky to have a job that allowed me to work from home and drive in to the office in Boston only once a week. Even if Cranston was farther away than Providence (which it turned out it was, but only by three or four miles), I'd still be better off than if I had to commute into Boston five days a week for my job. I know one has nothing to do with the other, but I was desperate, and a desperate mind can rationalize just about anything.

"Rhode Island's a small state. How far could it be? I'll do it," I said.

"You're sure, now?" I could tell Kerry needed confirmation that I was in this for real.

I pushed all doubt from my voice. "Absolutely!" I told her.

We made arrangements for me to attend an upcoming puppy-raiser orientation at NEADS. There I'd get an overview of the prison-pup partnership and learn what to expect as a puppy raiser. Once I completed the orientation, I'd be eligible for my own puppy. Before we got off the phone, Kerry asked whether I had any questions. I did.

"How do the puppies go to the bathroom if they're locked in a cell?" It had been eating at me since I met the puppy raiser in the supermarket.

Kerry told me the dogs were in minimum- and medium-security prisons where the inmates had plenty of time outside the cells and with complete access to the prison yard. Clearly I had a lot to learn about the prison system. And, as I was soon to find out, about dog training, too.

———————

AT THE NEADS orientation, there were nine prospective puppy raisers sitting around a large conference table. A few were women around my age, but there was also a teenage girl there with her boyfriend and her mother, and a young couple who were new to Massachusetts. Most of us wore the blank but polite expressions people paste on their faces when they want to make a good impression but are running through their grocery lists or visiting foreign lands in their heads. Or, in our particular case, thinking about playing with puppies. The first few hours of PowerPoint slides and tips on how to read a dog's body language were seriously fascinating, and Kerry, who led the orientation, had an easy humor that made us like her instantly. But that morning she'd hinted that we'd get to practice some training techniques on real live puppies after the lecture, and, judging from the yips and barks on the other side of the door, that moment was about to arrive.

The puppies had been walked over from the Early Learning Center (better known as the puppy house), a 1950s-style Cape at the entrance to the NEADS property. We were in the main building on the NEADS "campus," an eighteen-acre spread carved into the woods of the rural town of Princeton, Massachusetts. The main building houses kennels, offices, and training rooms, all with the purpose of transforming puppies into service dogs and placing them with people who need them. Across the parking lot is a two-story farmhouse where the clients live with their new service dogs for two weeks of intense training.

The three-hour orientation was total dog immersion. We learned that NEADS service dogs are almost always Labrador and golden retrievers. The breeds tend to be eager to please, intelligent, and adaptable, which makes them easy to train and excellent helpers. NEADS also trains standard poodles and labradoodles for clients who are allergic to dog hair; and smooth-coated collies, which tend to be tall, so function nicely as "balance dogs" for people who have difficulty walking without support.

We also learned about the Americans with Disabilities Act. The ADA doesn't distinguish between service animals or between different types of devices disabled people need, like a wheelchair or an oxygen tank. By law, public places have to grant service dogs access. However, it's up to individual states to decide whether to allow animals public access when they're still in training. Fortunately, in both Massachusetts and Rhode Island people with puppies in training have the same rights as those with full service dogs.

Finally, Kerry switched off the projector and announced it was time to meet some puppies. I capped my pen and leaped to my feet, but I wasn't fast enough. By the time I reached the doorway, at least half my classmates were already in the next room and on the floor, melting into human puddles. When I broke through the crowd and saw four potbellied, tail-wagging black Labs and a fluffy golden retriever named Sutton, I let out a little cry and collapsed into an oozing mess right along with my fellow trainees.

We followed Kerry and the puppies outside to a grassy area

near the main building. She distributed the dogs by handing us the ends of their leashes like she was dealing a deck of cards. I was secretly pleased to end up with Sutton because he was, I thought, the cutest of the group. He and the other puppies were bolting around, happy to be outside chasing insects and rolling in the grass while we humans at the ends of their leashes looked on helplessly. Kerry grabbed a black Lab midpounce and showed us how to fashion a makeshift harness from the leash by threading it behind the puppy's front legs and looping it back up through the collar. She led the chunky little puppy around like that, and while the setup did keep him from lunging on the lead, it also caused him to lift his front legs unnaturally high, like an awkwardly prancing horse. We all practiced harnessing our puppies. Then we worked on "object exchanges." Kerry handed around nuggets of kibble, then pulled an assortment of chew toys and balls from a net bag and tossed them to the ground, one in front of each puppy. When the puppy grabbed its toy, we were to grasp one end, say "Give," and offer it the kibble. Over time, the puppies would learn to give up an object on command.

We learned a few more basic training tips, but the highlight was toward the end of the session when we got to practice puppy-handling exercises. I hauled Sutton onto my lap and played with his paws, flopped his ears back and forth, pried open his mouth and felt around inside, all while feeding him treats so he'd form positive associations with being handled. For someone like me, who had been in the throes of dog withdrawal for twenty-four months, the puppy-handling exercise was morphine. It's a wonder the NEADS folks didn't have to mop me up with a sponge when we were through.

———————

AT THE END of the session, we were told that we'd get a call as soon as a puppy was ready. I didn't have to wait long. Less than one month later, I was assigned my first prison puppy. Except Jones wasn't a puppy. He was a fourteen-month-old black standard poodle. Poodles need more socialization than most service breeds, so Jones had spent the first year of his life living with a full-time puppy raiser in Maine before being transferred to a prison for more focused training. The Maine raiser's task had been to teach Jones basic obedience and expose him to as many situations and people as possible so he wouldn't develop, well, let's just say poodle-like tendencies. Poodles are highly intelligent, finely tuned animals, and for these reasons can make excellent service dogs, but they are different from Labs or golden retrievers in a few key ways. Labs are forgiving; poodles are not. If you had a standard poodle and accidentally poked him in the nose while spoon-feeding him his nightly dinner of liver pâté, he would never touch a spoon, chopped liver, or you again. Poodles, like German shepherds, bond closely with their person and tend to be skittish around unusual sights and sounds and suspicious of people. That's why they need tons of socialization.

So when Kerry called to tell me my experience as a German shepherd owner would prepare me for a poodle and they had the perfect one for me to start with, my heart sank. But I kept quiet. My kids didn't.

"A poodle! No *way!*" Aviva wailed when I broke the news.

"I thought we were getting a *cute* dog!" Josh said.

"Yeah, me, too" is what I *didn't* say. Instead, I told them in the infuriatingly sanctimonious voice I use when I have the moral upper hand that we weren't volunteering with NEADS so we could have a cute dog, we were doing it to help others. Truthfully, I needed the reminder as much as my children did.

————————

KERRY HAD GIVEN me the phone number for the prison captain in charge of the puppy program at the J. J. Moran medium-security facility in Cranston with instructions to let him know I was a new puppy raiser and would be taking Jones out that upcoming Friday. I had already sent in my vitals—name, birth date, social security number—and I had passed the criminal background check. Never one to let a teachable moment pass, I let my kids know that it pays to stay on the right side of the law, because I wouldn't be allowed in the prison if I'd had a felony conviction in my past. They nodded their heads solemnly, having learned to humor their mother.

I dialed the number and got the NEADS liaison, Captain Nelson Lefebvre, on the phone.

I was pleased to find that he was talkative. Not in a genial, storytelling, "I got a million of 'em" kind of way. He was just very thorough. I doodled floppy-eared cartoon puppies in a notebook while he gave me some background on the program. He had helped to bring the first pair of prison puppies to Rhode Island three years earlier, and now there were a dozen puppy-inmate teams between Moran and the state's other medium-security prison. I liked Captain Lefebvre's voice. It had a pleasant, gauzy quality, like it was filtered through a layer of muslin. I decided I liked him, too, after he asked whether I'd ever visited the puppy house on the NEADS campus. When I told him I hadn't, that we'd only spent time with five puppies as part of orientation, he urged me to go sometime. "I'll tell you, Sharron, when things are getting to be a little too hectic and stressful around here, I'll go up there and just play with the puppies. That's my therapy." I stifled laughter as I imagined a burly, hardened prison captain rolling in the grass, giggling while a litter of puppies pounced and licked his face.

He asked whether I'd been in a prison before and I told him just once, when I was a reporter, but it was a prerelease center and the inmates were all out on work release. It looked like a college dorm.

"Yeah, this is different," he said. "Do you have a pen? I'll describe exactly how to get here and how to get inside." He gave me directions to the prison and told me that once I got there, I would check in at the reception building, which was separated from the main prison by a courtyard. The guard on duty would pick up his phone and call the guards in A-block, where the dogs and their handlers lived.

I'd be admitted to the courtyard through a set of double doors and gates, enter the main building through a large lobby, and wait to be buzzed in to an area called "shift command," which was where the prison lieutenants and captains went about the business of running a prison. That's where the puppy exchange would take place, monitored at all times by the officers on duty. The inmate would come down with the dog, a report to fill out, and food for two days. If I had any leftover food at the end of the weekend, I was to keep it. Puppy raisers are not allowed to give inmates anything except the dog and the paperwork. I scribbled frantically in my notebook, trying to form a map of the route in my head but coming up only with images from the movies—Alcatraz perched on its rocky island, Tim Robbins digging his way out of Shawshank—except in my version, there were puppies.

I hung up feeling reassured, but on Friday, when it was time for me to actually go to the prison to pick up Jones for the first time, I was jumpy and nervous. I tend to feel uneasy when I'm doing something new for the first time, and in this case, that was compounded by the fact that I was about to bring home a fully grown male dog, who had somehow merged in my mind with the prison, leaving me feeling like I was bringing a convict into my house. (As it turns out, I wasn't too far off.) I fretted, too, about meeting the inmate, whom I pictured as a skinhead with roughly hewn prison tattoos and a dangerous leer—perhaps to counteract the prissy French poodle on the end of his leash.

When I turned off the main road, the complex of state buildings where the prison was located did not help my state of mind.

J. J. Moran Medium Security Facility sits at the edge of a dead-end road, the last stop on what I came to regard as a scenic tour through human despair. One of the first buildings off the main road is the juvenile detention center, its tiny exercise yard enclosed by a chain-link fence that arcs inward to keep the young inmates from climbing over it. The state psychiatric hospital is a couple of doors down, across the street from a homeless shelter. Great clouds of steam billowed from an underground vent in front of the shelter, shrouding its crumbling redbrick edifice and partially obscuring the shabbily dressed figures who waited on the steps for the doors to open for the night. The final turn took me past the state's minimum-security prison, an ancient towering facility with windows large enough, perhaps, for a man to fit through. On this day, an inmate pressed his face to the bars of one of them, dangling his arms outside, touching freedom.

By comparison, Moran isn't that bad. There is no mistaking it's a prison—it's surrounded by double and triple rows of high fences and razor wire—but it's one of the newer buildings, constructed in the early 1990s, and it sprawls across twenty-nine acres, which gives it an open, airy feel. At least from a visitor's perspective.

I found a parking spot and sat in the car for a moment, considering my pocketbook on the passenger seat. I hadn't asked Captain Lefebvre about carrying a purse into the prison and he hadn't mentioned anything, but somehow it didn't seem right. It seemed too . . . I don't know, breezy, to waltz into a prison with a flower-embroidered purse slung over my shoulder, like I was going shopping. I scanned the area to make sure no one was watching, then stuffed the pocketbook under the passenger seat.

I forced my mind to go blank as I picked my way toward the entrance. It's a trick I learned as a newspaper reporter, when I'd be sent to knock on the door of an alleged mobster or to interview the family of a crime victim. As long as I don't think, I can function.

It took a second for my eyes to adjust to the gloom inside. A skinny man with gray hair and a handsome face was sitting behind the desk.

"Hi. I'm here for a dog. He's a poodle?"

The guard reached for a phone on his desk and looked back up at me. "What's the dog's name?"

"Jones."

"What?"

"Jones," I repeated.

The guard stared back at me a long moment before chuckling and shaking his head. "Who names these dogs, anyway?" Before I could answer, he was talking loudly into the phone: "I need the handler for canine Jones," he said, drawing out the name like a game-show announcer. "Send him over to the brass's office." He clicked the receiver button and pressed another number. This time his tone was professional, respectful: "Captain, dog handler on the way." He hung up and looked at me. I looked back.

"Umm, I don't know where to go."

He gestured for me to pass behind his desk to a set of steel and glass doors.

"Do I have to walk through that?" There was a metal detector positioned off to one side.

"No, no. We don't make the dog people do that. You guys are special."

I relaxed a bit. His jokey tone was familiar from my time spent in police and fire stations. I took a lot of ribbing back then for being a female reporter who dared pierce the inner sanctum of the uniformed male. And for being short. Guys think that's hilarious for some reason.

The officer leaned over some paperwork while I walked past him and to the door. When I turned the knob and pushed, nothing happened.

"Ummm. It won't open," I said, my level of comfort starting to plummet.

"He has to buzz you through." The officer pointed to the

next room, where I could see an older man watching me through tinted glass. I heard a buzz. "Now you can open it," he said. I pushed, but again, nothing happened.

"You missed it. Wait for the buzz and try again." I heard the buzz, paused, then pushed. Again, the door refused to yield. It reminded me of trying to unlock the car door as someone is lifting the handle to open it. The guard behind the glass held up his finger. I waited, my hand poised on the knob, feeling more foolish by the second. I heard a faint buzz and leaned my weight against the door. It opened. "Got it!" I said a little too triumphantly as I stepped through and let the door slam heavily behind me. I was standing in a vestibule before another door identical to the first and had to go through the entire process again, only this time I made sure to push the door as soon as I heard the buzz. When I stepped through, I was back outside, facing a set of towering gates, beyond which lay the rest of the prison. Stretching out on either side and in front of me was a double row of nineteen-foot fences. Coils of razor wire bulged from the bottom up to the height of a tall man and again at the top, encircling the rim of the fence. When a bird landed delicately between the blades, I flinched reflexively.

The inmates at J. J. Moran live in cell blocks and by the clock. There are six low concrete buildings housing two tiers of cells each, which from the ground floor look like rows of numbered broom closets, except each has a tiny window. Segments of time are announced through a PA system that snakes through the prison complex, emerging here and there through perforated metal plates bolted to the walls. If you happen to be standing next to one of the speakers during an announcement, it will rattle the teeth in your head.

The day starts at seven fifteen, when inmates are let out of their cells for breakfast. If you don't like what they're serving and you have money in your account, you can eat ramen noodles or a foil pouch of tuna fish, but only if you planned ahead and ordered them from the commissary. Some of the inmates have jobs to report to after breakfast. But they have to be done before lockdown, which happens twice a day.

The day ends at eight forty-five with lights-out. If you're a dog handler with a young puppy, you can flick your cell lights on at ten thirty to signal the correctional officer on duty that you need a final trip outside before being locked up for the night. But that's the most variety your day will have.

For someone who's used to hurrying headlong through life, always late for one thing or another, the process of getting into the shift command offices where the dog waited was agonizingly slow. All of the doors and gates at Moran come in pairs; you have to wait for the first one to close behind you before the second one opens, like the airlock to a space station, or a butterfly garden. Which is exactly what I had blurted out on the phone to Captain Lefebvre during our conversation when he described the double-secure exit and entry procedure to me. He was silent for a moment, possibly processing the image of monarchs and swallowtails beating their wings against the locked steel doors. Finally he simply said, "I'd never thought of it that way."

The first gate slid open and I stepped inside to face the second one. For a few uncomfortable moments after the gate shut behind me, I was caged between the two, like an animal caught in a Havahart trap. Then the second gate slid open to a wide manicured courtyard bisected by a concrete path and lined on either side by mulched beds. If not for the barbed wire on either side of me, I could have been on a college campus. The courtyard led to a vast, echoey tiled hall that smelled faintly of an indoor swimming pool. At the far end were two doors separated by a span of tinted glass, one marked "visiting." I headed toward the unmarked door on the left, remembering Captain Lefebvre's instructions. The door slid open before I reached it.

The journey into shift command made me feel simultaneously overly trusting for allowing a successive series of doors and gates to lock behind me as I ventured deeper into the prison, and incredibly important for being granted access to such a protected space.

A dark-haired, teddy-bearish man in a dusky blue uniform was waiting when I stepped through the final door. He was about my age and had kind brown eyes. "Sharron?" I recognized Captain Lefebvre's voice. He held out his hand and I shook it, hoping my palms weren't too sweaty. "Come on in. The inmate's on his way now." Captain Lefebvre led me down a short hallway that widened slightly into a vestibule that looked out onto the prison yard. A photocopy of a *New York Times* article about prison dogs was pinned to a bulletin board.

He invited me to take a seat in his office, a small room with pale yellow cinder-block walls and spare furnishings. I sat on a rolling desk chair, planting my feet firmly so it wouldn't skitter out from under me on the tile floor while we chatted about my drive to the prison. I thanked him again for giving me such detailed directions. He was about to answer when a short buzz broke through our conversation. "Here he is. Come meet your dog." I followed Captain Lefebvre's broad back into the vestibule, where a large man in khaki-colored prison scrubs was leading a black poodle through the door. The inmate bounded over, a wide grin on his round, boyish face, and grabbed my hand in a warm handshake. "Hi! I'm Lance. And this is Jones." He stepped back and gestured proudly at the dog. Jones was as skinny as a licorice stick, his body so long that the blue NEADS vest covered only his shoulders. It looked like he was wearing a fashionable woman's shrug. Jones considered me coolly from beneath his curly pompadour while Lance described in rapid-fire speech the commands Jones knew, his feeding schedule, his quirks. He probably would have gone on to tell me about Jones's favorite television shows if Captain Lefebvre, who stood by with his arms folded tightly across his barrel chest, hadn't stepped forward to catch Lance's eye and nod toward the door. Lance handed me Jones's leash and his food for the weekend. When I turned to leave, Lance called out, "Oh, I almost forgot. Jones has a very strong prey drive, so keep an eye on that."

Prey drive? I didn't know what that meant and considered possible interpretations as I said good-bye to Captain Lefebvre, then waited with Jones for the first series of doors to slide open. The looming metal fences seemed less intimidating on the way back, although that could have been because I was distracted by Jones, who jogged through the courtyard while I skidded along behind, turning over the phrase "prey drive" in my head. Maybe it was prison slang. We waited before the final set of locked doors. Jones whipped his head toward a leaf skittering by on the wind. When the buzz sounded I pulled hard on the knob and pulled him along beside me into the vestibule. The officer in the reception area swiveled in his chair and watched us through the glass. When the second door buzzed open and we stepped inside, he let his jaw drop in exaggerated shock. "Whoa! What is that thing? A horse?" He shifted his gaze from Jones to me. "You could ride him out of here!"

"Next time I'll bring a saddle," I called over my shoulder as Jones led me out of the building. When we reached the parking lot, we scared up a flock of small birds. Jones, who stood higher than my waist and was over half my weight in solid muscle, launched himself into the air after them, nearly carrying me with him into flight. The clear plastic food bag spilled to the ground as the dog lunged and dipped and dove and lunged again while I clung to the end of the leash, attempting to land him like a kite in a hurricane. Eventually I managed to reel Jones in hand-over-hand until his collar was within reach. I grabbed tight, yanking him along as I hopped over to the spot where the food bag lay, thankfully unbroken. Then, afraid another bird would land within view, I hustled Jones to the car, where I stuffed him into the backseat and slammed the door before he could muscle his way back out. Now I knew what prey drive meant.

I hesitated before starting my car but drove home with Jones anyway.

Jones demonstrated his prey drive again and again over the next two days. When I got him home, he behaved like an unruly child fresh off a Skittles and Mountain Dew binge. He pranced from room to room, hopping on the furniture and standing on his hind legs to get a better look out the windows. On a sweep through the living room, he scattered a Lincoln Logs housing development that Josh had under construction, then stole a small green bear from a toy box and carried it around the house while Josh complained loudly and I deployed the object-exchange strategy to extract it from his mouth. My eyes were spinning in my head, trying to keep up with him. Tucker never behaved like that. *None* of the dogs we'd had in our house did. I wanted to put Jones in a time-out. Or hold him down and force-feed him Ritalin.

Marty, who always looks for the positive angle of any situation, complimented Jones's spirit. However, much later he confessed to me that Jones reminded him of Mombo, a standard poodle from his childhood who would ambush him on his way home from school and try to eat his face.

Josh tried to avoid Jones and Aviva thought he was the ugliest thing she'd ever seen, but at some point during the weekend she asked to take him outside on the leash. She aborted her plans about three seconds in, though, when he tried to drag her into the woods and up a tree after a squirrel. Walks were great fun for Jones, miserable for me. Jones would start out on high alert, plumed tail held high, eyes darting back and forth. I quickly learned to distract him with treats when we approached known trouble spots, which started the moment we stepped onto the sidewalk. To our left, tethered to the neighbor's railing on a long cord, was Peekaboo, a declawed cat. To our right was a yellow Lab mix named Bailey, and next door to her was Amy, a Jack Russell terrier. Jones would take the treats I held out, snapping hard at my fingers while I rushed him straight ahead through the gauntlet of known distractions. But I couldn't avoid the surprises, and there were plenty of them. There were wild rabbits that turned suicidal in the presence of Jones, hurtling out of the underbrush and across our path. Chipmunks would race across the sidewalk like tiny remote control cars, their tails pointing straight up like antennae. Jones would bolt after each one, dragging me along with him or ripping the leash out of my grasp, leaving painful red rashes on the palms of my hands. Jones went after two-legged and wheeled creatures, too: joggers, skateboarders, cyclists, fast-moving children—he didn't discriminate.

On the second day of Jones's second weekend with us, I decided to walk him only after the sun went down, when it was too dark for either of us to see anything. This solved the problem of walking Jones, but his overactive prey drive kicked in at other times, as it did when Aviva brought the two little girls she was babysitting over to our house. I had left Aviva to introduce the girls to Jones when I heard screaming. I ran in to find Jones leaping happily on the four-year-old, who was shrieking and desperately trying to cover her face with her hands. Aviva was grabbing at Jones's collar, trying to pull him off, while the girl's older sister pummeled his back and head with her fists. I yanked Jones away and into the dog crate, sliding the latch in place behind him. Jones was too tall for the crate. He stood hunched over like a jackal, his curly bouffant sticking out the top between the grates, panting through an openmouthed smile.

Later, when Aviva returned from delivering her charges safely home, she faced me, hands on her hips. "Mom, you've got to get rid of that dog." Her tone sliced through me, releasing the vast reserve of doubt I harbored about my parenting skills.

I went on the defense in an attempt to quench the guilt. "I made a commitment."

"Mom! That dog tried to kill Claire!"

"Well, I wouldn't say he was trying to kill her . . ." Aviva drew in a breath, but before she could strike again, I told her I would call NEADS. "Don't worry. I've got it under control." Those were familiar and, I was afraid, hollow words to my children because it was clear that I had very little under control. Other families ate together each night and planned fun vacations and educational activities. In ours, dinnertime snuck up and surprised me each night like it had never visited our house before, and I'd rush to throw together something that the kids would eat (Marty, wisely, came home late). For entertainment, I'd open the front door and point the kids outside so I could have some peace and quiet. It's the way I grew up. My own family was more a fractured collection of individuals than a cohesive unit. Then it broke apart completely when my father packed up and moved out and my older brothers left for college. I just didn't know how to run a family, and here I was, wrecking things again by bringing a killer poodle into the house.

I called the NEADS coordinator, Kerry.

THE NEXT WEEK, Kerry was standing in my kitchen while I rooted through the deli drawer in my refrigerator for a plastic-encased stick of string cheese to use as dog bait. Her plan? To train Jones to ignore his killing instinct. Her method? Teaching Jones to play the children's game Mother May I?

We spent the next half hour or so in the backyard facing Aviva's two bunny rabbits, Snoopy and Malted Milk Ball. Kerry would lead Jones twenty feet from the bunny hutch and ask him to sit. He would obey but lock in on the bunnies, every nerve in his body ready to spring toward them. Then Kerry would tell Jones, "Let's go," and they would take a few steps toward the bunnies, stop, and Jones would sit. Kerry tore off a piece of cheese and fed it to Jones each time he was able to move toward the bunnies without straining on the leash. When he failed, they would return to the "start line" and repeat the process. Before Kerry left, she told me to practice with the bunnies every day that I had Jones. I did. And all I can say is, I'm glad those bunnies were safely caged, because each game of Mother May I? invariably ended with me peeling Jones off the hutch.

That feeling of dread I had the first time I went to the prison? It didn't go away as I became more accustomed to the weekend routine. In fact, it got worse (encouraged, of course, by Jones). During our first phone conversation, Captain Lefebvre told me that some puppy raisers show up for the first time, then never return again. I could see why.

After a while, hallelujah, Kerry was forced to accept the depth of Jones's prey drive. She and another NEADS trainer furloughed Jones and two or three puppies to a city park. All of the dogs were interested in the pigeons but Jones would not, could not, be distracted from them.

Her voice was somber over the phone: "We've decided to release Jones from the program."

"Release? What does that mean?"

"We're taking him out of the program." A friend of the family who fostered Jones for the first fourteen months of his life would be adopting him, and Kerry assured me that Jones would be much happier living his life as a pet dog.

I silently cheered.

"He'll be up at NEADS for a few days, though, if you'd like to come visit him, or say good-bye."

"No, that's okay. I'm good."

_____

I'M THE KIND of person who doesn't give up easily, but only if people are watching. Otherwise, I abandon all sorts of projects. Somewhere, stuffed deep in a bag in the basement, a needle and thread still dangles from an *A* in an embroidery sampler I began when I was pregnant with Aviva. The first *A* in her name, not the second one. If not for my unwillingness to let Kerry down, I would have conceded to Marty that he was right, our lives were chaotic enough without bringing an untamed convict dog into it. And who knows? Maybe I would have quit anyway if I'd had longer to think about it. But the leash burns on my hands had barely healed when Kerry sent me an e-mail request to take a three-month-old puppy named Daisy. Not sure I wanted to try this again, I clicked on the attachment anyway, and there she was—a tiny yellow Lab the color of buttered toast, looking straight into the camera. I felt a smile spreading across my face as I took in the wrinkled brow, the tiny black nose. Now *this* was more like it.

2

Let's Go

I COULD HAVE THROWN up, that's how nervous I was about going into the prison to meet Daisy for the first time. You know that feeling when you're getting ready for a first date or going to a job interview? That sensation of excitement spiked with dread, like someone has injected ginger ale into your central nervous system? Well, that sickly brew had worked its way down to my knees and up into my throat by the time I pulled into the parking lot of J. J. Moran. I swallowed it down and stepped out of my car.

Everything felt new and off-kilter. Labor Day had just passed; it was the start of a new school year. I hadn't been to the prison for a nearly a month—not since I'd returned Jones for the final (blessed) time. I calmed myself by noting what was familiar. There was that faded cutout of a cartoon police officer leaning awkwardly against a tree. The parking lot hierarchy was still evident: lots of empty spaces up front marked in descending order by rank. "Warden" was closest to the front entrance, "lieutenant" farthest away. Other spots were taken up by gleaming F-series Ford pickups and Dodge Rams, all parked at angles to keep the battered Nissans and Saturns that belonged to the inmates' visitors from ruining their paint jobs.

I picked my way toward the building, shrugging a denim shirt over my tank top. The day had been blazing hot and though it was close to six in the evening, the temperature hadn't dropped below ninety degrees. The fabric felt like a horse blanket on my skin, but during orientation somebody had mentioned there was a dress code for visitors, and I didn't want to take the chance of inciting a prison riot with my bare shoulders (cue derisive laughter here).

Visiting hours were in session this time, and a cluster of people stood in front of the reception desk, waiting their turn to sign in. Others sat against the wall in gray molded plastic chairs. I squeezed through the crowd and up to the counter, feeling uneasily conspicuous and at the same time just a little bit worried that someone might mistake me for the kind of person who would know someone in prison. I attempted to catch the eye of the skinny gray-haired guard—the one who had shook his head and laughed at Jones's name the first time I was there. Finally, he looked up at me, a pencil poised over a log. "Who you here for?" He didn't recognize me.

"Um. She's a dog. Daisy?"

The guard grabbed a phone. "Canine Daisy to the brass's office," he said into it, gesturing behind him toward the red metal door. "Go right ahead, dear." I stepped past a younger guard whose clean-shaven head caught the reflection of the overhead light. He was watching a toddler struggling to pull the tiny pockets of her jeans inside out to show him they were empty. Her mother stood nearby with a bored expression on her face. I could feel her eyes on me and hated myself a tiny bit for feeling smug that I didn't have to empty my pockets or walk through the metal detector.

While I waited for the first door to buzz, signaling me to push it open, a clutch of visitors gathered behind me. They followed me through and we stared in silence at the handle of the second door, willing it to unlock. When it did, we stepped outside and walked toward the sliding metal gates. A sign warned "No Weapons Beyond This Point." An older woman was saying something in Portuguese to a young girl, her granddaughter, probably. The girl's eyes grew wide as her gaze climbed the towering chain-link fences that encircled us. The woman had lowered her voice to a whisper and the rest of us instinctively bent toward her to listen. Suddenly, the woman flung her arms and head back and jerked her body wildly as if she were being electrocuted. We all jumped except for the older woman, who grabbed her knees and laughed.

I knew the gates weren't electrified, but apparently the little girl didn't, because she clutched so tightly to her grandmother's hand that she nearly toppled the woman as the second gate shuddered open and we stepped through.

Our small group stepped into the building. While the others continued straight to the visitors' door, I broke off and walked past a soda machine toward shift command. The door slid open and I stepped in, peering through what looked like a bank teller's window, until I spotted the correctional officer inside. I lifted my hand to him and he waved back. We both watched the door slide shut. Just one more door between me and the puppy whose face I had memorized from the sixteen thousand times I'd opened the e-mail containing her picture.

THIS MUCH I knew about Daisy: She came from Guiding Eyes for the Blind, a New York nonprofit that breeds and trains dogs for seeing-eye work. She had been born three and a half months earlier, on May 18. When she was seven weeks old, a Guiding Eyes staff member plucked her and each of her siblings from their litter and introduced them one at a time to various distractions. Daisy was placed alone in a pen where she met an animated robot and saw a toy bat circling overhead. A can of paper clips was dropped beside her. She walked on paper that crinkled underfoot and was allowed to investigate a small animal cage containing anchovy paste. An adult dog was brought in to say hello to Daisy. And all the while an assessor took careful note of Daisy's breathing rate, the angle of her ears, the set of her mouth and position of her tail. The test was repeated with a human alongside Daisy, and finally, with a human using food as a lure to refocus and guide her through the series of distractions.

I'm not sure how Daisy's littermates rated, but she was deemed too reliant on the human for seeing-eye work and was passed over by the Guiding Eyes program.

Guiding Eyes dogs must be obedient but capable of making decisions on behalf of their humans. A Guiding Eyes dog will stop his owner from stepping off the curb in front of an oncoming bus. The ideal NEADS dog, on the other hand, would happily accompany his owner under the bus if he thought that was what his owner wanted. In other words, Guiding Eyes looks for dogs who are leaders; NEADS wants loyal followers.

NEADS loves Guiding Eyes rejects because they're expertly bred for confidence and submissive traits. Some seventy to eighty percent of Guiding Eyes–bred dogs who enter the NEADS program graduate as service dogs and are placed with clients, as compared to the thirteen to twenty percent success rate for dogs from other breeders. Daisy was eight weeks old when she arrived at NEADS's Early Learning Center and met Cindy Lopez and Cindy Ryan. The Cindys oversee the puppies and with their cadre of volunteers take them on trips into town, on visits to nursing homes and schools, and sometimes to stores. Some eighty puppies go through the puppy house each year, yet both Cindys recall Daisy was special, and not just because she bolted out the door when they were leading the puppies to the play yard one day and headed for the busy road nearby. Fortunately, she paused to investigate the pavement under a van parked in the drive and Cindy Ryan was able to scoop her out and carry her to safety. After that, NEADS installed a double gate system, much like the one in the prison, only manual. Despite nearly giving the Cindys a heart attack, Daisy had a sweetness to her that was obvious even when she was a tiny puppy.

The new arrivals spend their first forty-eight hours in the "nursery," a small room where they're quarantined from the other pups until it's certain that they're healthy. Then they are moved into the main room, where they're exposed to everyday life—the sound of traffic on the road outside, people coming in and out, phones ringing. Aural non sequiturs float from the speakers of a CD player: a cow mooing followed by a blender, followed by a car horn, followed by a vacuum cleaner, then five minutes of a whistling teakettle, and then a lawn mower. To survive in the place as a human, you have to learn how to tune out the sounds. Though getting to hang out with adorable, playful puppies all day long is a pretty good distraction.

The puppies get used to wearing the blue puppy-in-training vest, and they go outdoors in the play yard, a fenced-in area outfitted like the playground at a day care, with toddler-size plastic slides and climbing structures where the puppies practice walking up and down stairs and ramps, and get to view the world from different heights. There are also pinwheels and dangling whirligigs and wind chimes. There's a half-pipe that, depending on how it's positioned, can be a tunnel or a wobbly walking surface, and the ground is covered with rubber matting, metal grates, and other textures. Everything in the play area is there to help inure the pups to unusual sounds, movements, sights, and surfaces. Not every prop or piece of equipment works out, however. NEADS was forced to get rid of the fake, feathered chickens it placed outside the play yard after finding them chewed up, presumably by a very disappointed fox.

After about four weeks in the puppy house, the pups are sent to prison. Which was what had happened to Daisy about two weeks earlier.

I couldn't wait for the final door to slide open all the way, so I squeezed through sideways and followed the cinder-block walls past Captain Lefebvre's office, where he was talking on the phone, on to the cramped vestibule that led to the prison yard. And then I stopped short. There she was, as exquisite in her simplicity as the flower she was named for. Daisy sat next to her inmate, the top of her head barely reaching to his knee. Her plush butterscotch fur blended with the tan of his suede work boots and khakis. A little squeal escaped me and I clapped my hand over my mouth like a game-show contestant who'd won the grand prize. Daisy rose slightly on her haunches, her tail stirring the grit on the floor. "Sit." The inmate holding her leash drew out the word in a steady, coaxing tone. I tore my eyes from Daisy. The inmate was about six feet tall, hard and lean in his buzz cut and prison uniform, a stark contrast to Daisy's softly rounded lines. He looked dangerous, like he belonged here.

"It's like she knows you." Captain Lefebvre had appeared beside me. He must have been working a double shift to be there so late on a Friday.

"Yeah. You sure you two haven't met already?" The inmate's voice was low, rough, but leavened slightly with humor. He glanced at me, then ducked his head and looked down at the puppy.

My mind jumped around for something clever to say. I came up with nothing.

Captain Lefebvre spoke again: "Sharron, this is Keith, Daisy's handler." He waited while we mumbled hello to each other like two shy schoolkids meeting on the playground. Daisy was standing now, sniffing the floor, creeping closer to me. Keith guided her gently back to his side and she plunked her bottom down hard, into a sitting position.

"She's so obedient," I said to him.

He shifted his weight and stood up a little straighter. "Yeah, she's really smart. Picks up on commands real quick."

I looked back down at Daisy. Her tongue was hanging out in an openmouthed puppy smile.

Keith began telling me how often to feed her and some other things I didn't hear, so captivated was I by the gorgeous puppy in front of me—the velvety muzzle, the floppy ears—she could have been assembled in a toy factory, she was that perfect. Then Keith lifted his voice a few octaves, catching both my and Daisy's attention. "Are you ready, girl?"

"Yes!" I nearly blurted. Daisy tilted her head toward him, waiting for the next signal. Keith said, "Let's go!" and walked her toward me, offering me the leash. I knelt on the floor and let Daisy scramble onto my lap and lick my face. Maybe I shouldn't have done that; probably I should have acted in a more dignified manner, but the instant I accepted the leash, everything but Daisy melted away. I was in prison, but I was in heaven.

Once my face was sufficiently kissed, I stood up. Keith's expression was hard to read, but Captain Lefebvre was smiling. He turned to Keith to ask whether there was anything I needed to know before I left with Daisy.

"Nope. Just enjoy her. She's a great dog." His accent was thick Rhode Island.

Keith had portioned out Daisy's meals for the weekend into six clear plastic bags, each rolled into a tight cylinder and tucked neatly into a seventh bag. He handed the dog food to me along with a bright yellow folder containing a report to fill out and return on Sunday. He gave Daisy a quick scratch behind the ears and turned to leave. "Thank you, Captain," he said, somewhat formally. Then he turned back to me as he reached for the door to the prison yard. "Have a good weekend." He said it as naturally as if I were a coworker leaving the office on a Friday afternoon.

"You . . ." I called over my shoulder before I realized what I was saying. I had no choice but to finish the sentiment. "Too."

One of the officers on duty glanced up from behind his desk and raised his eyebrows at me.

Daisy raced ahead at the end of her leash, vacuuming the tile floor with her nose while I struggled to balance the paperwork with the package of food and alternated between chastising myself for wishing Keith a good weekend and trying to placate myself with possible scenarios in which it was an entirely appropriate sentiment. Maybe the prison served a special breakfast on Sunday morning. Perhaps his girlfriend would visit him . . .

I wondered what was going through Keith's mind as he walked back to his cell. When an inmate gets a new puppy, they have two weeks of unbroken togetherness in order to form the close bond that will be the foundation of the dog's training. Only when that period is up does the puppy go out for the weekend. Was Keith grateful for the break? Envious of Daisy, who got to leave prison while he was stuck there? Thinking about the idiot puppy raiser who wished him a good weekend? Worried that I'd mess up her training? If so, truth be told, he wasn't the only one.

It was unnerving how willingly Daisy left Keith to go with me. I kind of wished she'd shown the tiniest bit of reluctance, made me prove to her that I was trustworthy. But all I needed to do to win her complete and utter faith was take possession of her leash. She had more confidence in me than I did in myself.

At the final door back to the reception area I arranged my face into a blank expression and stepped past the crowd as though every day, I walk the world's cutest puppy out of prison and into my car. The officer behind the desk was hunched over his computer keyboard, signing in visitors, but the bigger, bald one turned to watch us walk by. "Puppy coming through!"

he called out, and the line of visitors broke apart to allow us passage.

Out in the parking lot, I was digging my car keys out of my pocket when a sturdy-looking woman with a blunt haircut and glasses spotted us from a few rows away and called out, "Is this a new one?" She trudged over and introduced herself as Bonnie, a fellow weekend puppy raiser. She asked permission to say hello to Daisy. Asking before greeting a dog is like a sailor asking permission to come aboard—a sign of respect. I was pleased with myself for remembering the command and told Daisy to "Say hello," even though she was already slamming her body against Bonnie's legs and jumping at her face. Bonnie's voice was stern as she told Daisy to sit. The puppy obeyed, but her body quivered in anticipation of another kiss and her tail swept an arc of blacktop clean beneath her.

Bonnie leaned down to pet Daisy, but her hand on Daisy's head was like a lit match to gasoline, igniting another explosive frenzy of licking and jumping. Bonnie sighed and stood up, pointedly ignoring the dog. She gave me the abridged version of her history as a puppy raiser. She was on her sixth dog, but most of them had flunked out. She ended up with the tough cases— mostly smooth-coated collies. I asked Bonnie whether she had a dog of her own. Some of the weekend puppy raisers do, and I was curious about how that worked out.

"No. I'd love a dog but we can't have one. My husband's allergic." Bonnie grimaced.

"What do you do on weekends?" I wanted to know.

Bonnie smiled slightly. "Oh. He sleeps downstairs on weekends."

"The dog?" I asked.

"No, my husband." She stood up and looked at my Outback wagon, then down at Daisy, who was sniffing the ground intensely. "Where are you going to put her?"

I swiveled to stare at my car and briefly considered the front seat before quickly abandoning the idea, sure Bonnie wouldn't approve. "Umm. The backseat, I guess."

My memory flashed to the image of leaving Jones in the backseat of my car while I ran into the house. When I returned, he was behind the wheel, looking so confident that had I slid into the passenger seat and said "Let's go," I wouldn't have been surprised if he'd turned the key and shifted into gear.

Bonnie looked doubtful. "Puppies are known to get carsick," she said. "You don't have a crate?"

"In the car? No." I was beginning to feel ill-equipped for this adventure.

"Well, she's too little to climb over into the backseat so she should be safe in the back-back. Here, let me help." She took the leash and dog food from my hand and waited.

"Oh. Thanks." I opened the back hatch. An empty two-liter soda bottle rolled out and bounced on the ground. "Sorry," I blurted, diving for the bottle just as Daisy leapt for it. I tossed the empty through the hatch and we watched it sail over the backseat and onto the floor. But when I reached for the leash, Bonnie nodded toward a plastic bag bursting with more bottles. "You better get those, too. You don't want the puppy chewing on them." There was also a snow brush. And a yellow plastic beach shovel. Together, they presented damning evidence that at least three seasons had passed since I'd cleaned my car. The problem with my car is that the only time I think of cleaning it is when it embarrasses me. And then it's too late.

When the back was clear, I lifted Daisy in. Bonnie and I watched her walk around, head down, ears flopped forward, tracing a path on the plastic mat with her nose. I lured her away from the hatch with a treat before shutting it tight. Daisy stared out at us as Bonnie and I said our good-byes.

My eyes were focused straight ahead as I pulled out of the parking lot, but my attention was behind me. If I were a cat, my ears would have been pointing backward, listening for a bark, a whine, the sound of a puppy throwing up. But Daisy didn't make a peep as we drove past the decrepit buildings, onto the main road, and up the ramp to the highway. Speeding down Interstate 295, I felt like I'd just pulled off a successful prison break. My emotions veered from elation at having this adorable puppy for an entire weekend to dread that I'd screw it up. I stole a glance in the rearview mirror. Daisy's back was to me. She was sitting perfectly still, staring out the back window, mesmerized by the highway unrolling behind us.

3

Wait

THE FRONT DOOR flew open the instant my tires reached
the driveway, and my eleven-year-old, Josh, skidded down
the sloping lawn to meet us. Before I'd yanked up the parking brake he was at the back window, peering in at Daisy. She
thumped her tail against the plastic mat and pressed her nose
against the glass, leaving heart-shaped smudges, desperate to
break the barrier between herself and this new little person who
obviously couldn't wait to meet her. My first concern (after the
danger of running over my youngest had passed) was to keep
Josh and the rest of my family from screwing up Daisy's training. I was seized with the need to be in complete control.

I flung my door open and got out of the car. "Okay, move
it, let me do this," I said, lifting the back hatch and chasing
the metal ring on Daisy's collar with the leash clip while she
attacked Josh's face with her tongue and he tilted his head back

and tried to speak without opening his mouth. I lifted Daisy out of the car and led her to the grass while Josh followed behind, exclaiming over her.

NEADS uses the command "Better go now," to encourage a dog to eliminate. It's a useful tool, one I could have used on those subfreezing nights when Tucker felt it necessary to personally inspect every scent molecule on the front lawn before selecting which one to pee on. For NEADS dogs, "Better go now" is like the canine equivalent of making sure the kids have visited the bathroom before a long car trip, but even more important. It ensures the dog gets everything out of its system before accompanying its owner onto, say, an airplane, where stepping outside to use the facilities is not an option. With Josh watching, I urged Daisy to "Better go now," and when she did squat, I praised her lavishly, to reinforce the connection between the words and the act.

"Well, hello there, cutie pie!" Marty appeared and picked up Daisy, who squirmed to better reach Marty's face with her tongue. I could actually feel the groove between my eyebrows getting deeper. "We're not supposed to pick her up," I said, not sure in fact whether that was true, but needing to establish my role as Daisy's handler. Unlike Jones, Daisy was irresistible. Marty placed Daisy back on her feet and, crouching, scratched between her ears while Josh swooped in and pressed his face against her so that Daisy was covered nearly head to tail with human affection. My first instinct was to seek out an unoccupied patch of Daisy and join them, but then the weight of my responsibility as a puppy raiser settled back in. Excitement over our first weekend with Daisy was quickly being replaced by annoyance with my family and the growing realization that I was going to have to spend as much time training them as I was working with the dog.

There's a big difference between training a service dog and raising a pet. When you bring home a pet puppy, you want to spend the first few days establishing a routine and forming a bond with the dog. You also want to set some basic rules of behavior, but most people tend to be pretty lax about consistency. As a NEADS puppy raiser, I—and my family—not only had to be consistent, we had to follow the organization's rules. There were a lot of them, and not just the ones you'd expect, like keeping the dog off the furniture. The dogs are trained to love their own names, so we were to use it sparingly to preserve its magical ability to capture the dog's attention. We had to resist the urge to blather incessantly to our puppy so the dog wouldn't learn to tune us out. We were to vigilantly maintain our role as "keeper of all things good," meaning we couldn't allow our puppy to help itself to anything it liked. Our puppy had to ask for, and earn, toys, treats, even permission to sniff the ground.

We also had to work the flipside as "protector from all things bad." During orientation, Kerry had pulled up a slide that read, "No experience is better than a bad experience!" After a moment of internal confusion resulting from me silently setting the phrase to the tune of "There's No Business Like Show Business," I understood that Kerry's all-important point was that we shouldn't expose our dog to something new if the experience might frighten the dog. So, if we're not sure our dog is ready for a trip to the train station, for example, we should stay away. When we do try something new and possibly scary, we're supposed to expose the dog in degrees. First from fifty feet away.

Next time, twenty-five feet away, and so on until the day when we're actually, say, boarding the train with our dog.

It can take months of painstaking reconditioning to desensitize a dog to something that once frightened it. Sometimes a dog will never get over that initial trauma. Best-case scenario, one bad scare could set a dog's training back months. Worst case, it could end its career before it begins.

So, yeah, I was a little bit tense that first weekend.

"Sorry, but we can't treat her like a pet. Remember, she's going to be a service dog," I told Marty and Josh. The three of us looked down at Daisy. Her eyes were squeezed shut and she was supplementing Marty's caresses by using her own back leg to scratch her head. At that moment, the notion that this buttery little puppy would assist a disabled person seemed adorably far-fetched, like watching a ten-month-old baby palming Cheerios into her mouth and discussing her most recent decision as a Supreme Court Justice.

I led Daisy through the garage and into the basement, where I tried to coax her up the stairs. She placed a tentative paw on the first one, looked into the dark, musty void between the steps, and withdrew it. I pulled a piece of biscuit out of my pocket and held it in front of her nose, urging her in a singsongy voice to follow it up the stairs. She thrust her head forward to take the biscuit, but sat back down when I pulled it just out of reach. Marty wasn't anywhere in sight, so I scooped Daisy into my arms and carried her up the stairs, where I placed her on the kitchen tile.

"So, what do you think? This is your weekend home!" I looked around the kitchen, imagining it from the perspective of a four-month-old puppy who had spent the last two weeks—

one-eighth of her life—locked up in prison. I felt proud and magnanimous, like a wealthy landowner opening his grounds to the factory workers for the annual picnic. I wanted Daisy to be impressed, to prefer the comparatively vast expanse of my house to a prison cell, and to associate these surroundings with me.

She lowered her tail and sniffed the floor around the trash can while I filled Tucker's old water dish, which I'd kept for sentimental reasons (and because I'm cheap), and placed it next to her on the tile floor. Daisy dipped her muzzle in, then trotted away mid-drink, streaming water from her mouth like a hippopotamus in a watering hole. Aviva came downstairs from her room and stopped short. "Is this Daisy? Oh my God, she's so cu— Ewwww!" Aviva jumped back, lifting her foot out of the puddles. "Did she pee?"

"It's water. Isn't she cute?" I ran off to get a towel and returned to find Aviva sitting cross-legged on the floor, cradling Daisy in her lap. She grabbed a handful of Daisy's skin and pulled to show me the excess. "Look at her puppy fat! You could fit a whole other puppy in there." I dropped to my knees and we took turns stretching and kneading Daisy's skin, marveling at how much room there was for Daisy to grow, while she groaned with pleasure at her Swedish massage.

Aviva and I have a long history of conflicts, so long that they predate Aviva herself by two weeks. That's when I reached my due date without so much as a sign or signal from her. Fifteen days, one application of a prostaglandin to induce labor, and six hours of pushing later, she finally appeared, red-faced and stubbornly gripping the umbilical cord in her tiny fist, refusing to concede that she had lost this fight. The obstetrician actually had to pry her fingers loose, and the battle of wills has raged between us since.

I always suspected that if I were a different kind of mother—a patient, more confident one—I would have brokered a détente early on and my children would be growing up in a peaceful home. But as hard as I try to be a diplomat, there are too many times when I step over the cliff of reason and go down in a screaming ball of fury.

Marty handles family conflict better than I, thank goodness. When Aviva was little and would threaten to find herself a new set of parents, ones who wouldn't make her pick up her toys, Marty would reach for the phone in the kitchen, surreptitiously press the hang-up button, and dial "Mr. Travers." Aviva would stand in the doorway, watching. "Hello! Is this Mr. Travers of Travers Adoption Services?" Marty would say, his voice full of good cheer. "I have great news. Our daughter, Aviva, has informed us that she would like to join another family. Oh? You have a placement, do you? It's a farm, you say? Called Sledgehammer Acres? What a unique name, it sounds marvelous! And the children break rocks all day long? Why, that sounds absolutely invigorating! Such healthy exercise for the little tykes. And, what is that you say? On Christmas all of the children get a gift? A brand-new . . . *sledgehammer?*" And on and on he would go until Aviva, in spite of herself, would burst into helpless giggles and pry the phone out of her father's hand.

Marty's humor lost some of its power when Aviva hit adolescence and became the human equivalent of a porcupine—cute to look at, but prickly. And dangerous, if you got too close. Around that time, she began a steady and sustained retreat into her bedroom and now spent most of her time at home shut away in there. I knew she came out to eat because I could hear her foraging in the kitchen, and stacks of dinnerware were visible when she left her bedroom door open a crack. The arrangement nagged at me, but only because it seemed to work out so well for everyone. It felt like we had given up on each other.

Now, sitting on the floor with Daisy acting as a buffer, a four-legged no-fire zone, we were able to set aside our differences and just simply be together, marveling at this dog who was so new to the world and had so much growing ahead of her. At one point Aviva, overcome by affection for Daisy, cried out, "Mom! I want to keep her!" She buried her face in Daisy's fur and I did the same so that we were both snuggling the puppy, our faces inches apart.

"I know," I said, my voice partially muffled by Daisy's fur. "I want to keep her, too." It would be the only time I would admit that out loud.

Later, after Aviva had disappeared back into her room, Josh and I spent the rest of the night playing with Daisy like she was a new toy, watching her as if she were onstage, testing her like she was preparing for midterms. Even Aviva quit her self-imposed isolation a few more times to check in on Daisy. We let her explore the house, following behind as she wandered through each room, sucking information in through her nose. She'd find Marty in the office reading and he'd put aside the newspaper to drop to the floor for a quick wrestling session, like he used to do with Tucker. He'd roll Daisy onto her back and she'd whip her head back and forth, play-biting at Marty's hands while he, on all fours himself, butted his head gently into her side. Then she'd continue her travels around the house, becoming acquainted with the jade plant in the foyer, the CD collection, the laundry hamper. During the course of the evening, I'd find myself smiling at our good fortune to be entrusted with this puppy. Already, I was falling hard for her.

Whenever I called Daisy, she'd wheel around and trot back to me, sure that something wonderful must be in store. In prison, the dog handlers use only positive reinforcement, and Daisy had already learned that training sessions meant lots of treats and plenty of praise. She practically trembled with eagerness while I took her through a series of commands, slamming herself to the ground when I told her "Down," swiping her paw in the air at "Shake," bouncing to her feet and settling on her bottom when I asked her to sit. The markings above Daisy's eyes gave her a permanently worried expression, making it look as if she was concentrating extra hard so as not to miss a command.

I'd put her in a stay and turn my back to walk away, willing myself not to sneak a glance while I strode to the other side of the room. Once or twice Daisy followed me, and I'd return her to the exact spot on the rug from where she'd strayed, hold out my hand like a traffic cop, and in a stern voice remind her to stay. Then I'd speed-walk to the other side of the room, turn and lift my voice into a joyful "Daisy! Come!" and she'd bound toward me, tail wagging, eyes intent on the hand holding the treat. She'd take it from me with a soft mouth, her velvety lips brushing my fingers. Then I'd praise Daisy, seizing the excuse to lean in for a cuddle. Daisy was a sensory delight. Her fur was soft like a bunny's and she smelled like freshly dried laundry— soap and warmth—but mingled with the slightly sour milk note common to puppies. It was intoxicating. As I breathed in her scent, my brain registered this olfactory information and tucked it into a scent-memory bank where it took its permanent place beside other pleasant memories—pressing my nose to the top of my babies' heads and inhaling deeply; my own mother's impossibly soft skin when, as a child, I'd rub my cheek against her arm and breathe in her rose-scented lotion.

At one point during the evening, Daisy got up and wandered into the kitchen, probably to see whether there were any new smells near the trash can. She was walking past the dining table when she stopped, holding her tail straight out behind her, stiff and unmoving. I followed her gaze to the sliding glass doors and, without getting up from the floor, stretched closer to get a look at what she was staring at. By now it was dark outside. There was nothing I could see. "What is it, girl?" I asked. Daisy glanced at me, then just as quickly turned back toward the slider, her tail wagging slightly. I pulled myself to my feet while Daisy, aware of my approach, ran up to the glass and stopped short. She was staring at her own reflection—at the strangely silent yellow Lab puppy who looked just as confused as she felt, and she didn't quite know what to do. It was probably the first time she had ever seen herself. Of course, they wouldn't have full-length mirrors in prison, or plate-glass windows or doors. "Look, it's you," I told her, sliding next to her on the floor. "And that's me." Daisy's reflection looked at me and wagged its tail. The movement distracted her and she shifted her gaze back to herself. Her tail went still again. It's possible we still would be sitting there staring at our reflections if Josh hadn't broken the spell with a tennis ball. Daisy whirled to chase it and I let the two of them play while I started in on the dishes. The pile had been growing since Marty cooked pancakes that morning. He has a habit of letting dishes stack up for twenty-four hours or more, as if they need to cure before he feels they're ready to be washed.

A few minutes later Josh skidded up to me. "Daisy peed."

"What? Where?" I ran into the living room and spotted a spreading puddle on the wood floor. I grabbed Daisy's collar and ran her to the front door, passing Marty in the hallway. "Daisy peed!" I struggled to keep the panic from my voice. Sound carries in our house and Aviva occasionally weighs in on matters from behind her closed door. As she did at that moment. "Eeeew! That's disgu—" I rushed Daisy into the night air before I could hear the rest of Aviva's comment. Daisy was ecstatic to be outside and got right to work investigating each blade of grass with her nose while I watched. I doubted there was anything left in her, judging by the lake she'd left on the floor, but I told her "Better go now" for a few minutes until it was clear that it was too late, I'd missed the opportunity.

Thirty minutes later, I was staring blankly at the television while Daisy gnawed at a stuffed lamb that I had bought at a pet store to keep her company in the crate. I kept replaying the events that led up to the accident. Daisy saw her reflection in the glass, she played ball with Josh, she peed. At no point did she stand in front of the door like Tucker used to do. She didn't whine or bark. How was I supposed to know when she needed to be let out? Earlier in the prison, I had asked Keith whether she was housebroken, and he was noncommittal, saying he takes her out so often that she doesn't really have a chance to have accidents inside.

A movement caught my eye. I glanced over at Daisy, but my eyes were drawn instead to a small heap of dog poop on the wood floor, barely grazing the edge of the rug.

I stared at it for a second, mystified by its sudden appearance before snapping to my senses. For the second time that night, I grabbed Daisy's collar and ran her to the front door and led her outside, hoping that too much time hadn't passed for her to associate the act with the outdoors. When we came back inside, Josh was in his room, Marty was cleaning up the mess with stoic reserve, and Aviva was yelling from behind her closed door, "I'm not coming out until that poop is gone!"

I didn't know what I was doing wrong. How was I supposed to know when she had to go out if she didn't tell me? I needed to talk to Keith about this. I actually headed toward my computer to e-mail him before I realized that wasn't an option. I couldn't pick up the phone and call him, either. He was locked in a six-by-nine cell. There was no way for me to get in touch with him. This was an entirely foreign feeling. I took instant access for granted. If the kids were having a problem in school, I e-mailed the teacher. When we were out of milk, I'd grab the phone and ask Marty to pick up a gallon on his way home from work. When an assignment gave me trouble, I'd walk over to the boss's desk. Keith might as well have been on the moon, that's how cut off I felt from him. On second thought, if he were on the moon, I'd probably be able to communicate with him. Prison was even farther away.

I suppose I could have called NEADS, but I didn't want to bother anyone there after hours. I also didn't want them to think I was incompetent, even if I felt that way myself. It was one thing to ask Kerry for a hand with a child-mauling poodle, but quite another to admit I'd let the puppy in my care have her way with my floor twice in the first four hours. I was beginning to wonder whether I was up to the task of raising a service dog.

I'd raised exactly one puppy in my life, and that was seventeen years ago. Maybe I'd lost the knack.

Finally, it was time for bed. I was exhausted. I left Marty to make sure Josh brushed his teeth, brought Daisy outside one final time, and nearly broke down and wept with gratitude when she peed on the grass.

———————

ONE OF OUR first mistakes when Tucker was a puppy was indulging her to the point where she grew to think of herself as the head of the household. It started the night we took her home. She yipped and whined when we shut her into her crate for the night. I steeled myself against her cries, but Marty is a much nicer person than I am. He got out of bed and climbed into the crate next to Tucker, singing "Sweet Baby James" softly into her oversize German shepherd puppy ears while she burrowed in closer for his warmth. Eventually she fell asleep and Marty was able to join me in bed. But the same thing happened the next night, and the next, at which point we realized that given a dog's natural life span of ten to fifteen years, Marty had between 3,650 and 5,475 nights more of crawling into the crate and singing James Taylor songs to the dog. The first night we left her to fall asleep alone was like listening to a junkie in detox.

Nobody would be singing Daisy to sleep. I lined the bottom of her crate with a soft quilt and eyeballed the narrow space between the bed and my bureau. It would fit, and if she had trouble falling asleep or woke up during the night, I could reach over to reassure her that she wasn't alone. I grabbed the crate and pulled. The wire door swung open and Daisy stepped through and rode inside while I dragged the crate into place.

Before I slipped into bed, I leaned into the crate for a final kiss. Daisy flipped onto her back and wiggled a bit before settling on a pose. Her back legs were splayed and her front paws curled delicately on her chest. The fur around each of her legs was sparse, exposing purplish skin. In a few months, the color would even out, but right now the mottled skin made her look so young and vulnerable; defenseless. I felt a tingle of dread. Both Kerry and Captain Lefebvre said they're strict about the kind of inmate who gets a dog—they rule out anyone with a history of animal abuse, for example. But still, they're criminals. My thoughts bounced around. People who end up in prison aren't known for impulse control; what's to keep Keith from losing his temper with Daisy? Puppies are adorable, sure, but they can be maddeningly frustrating. I wanted very much to strangle Tucker on those mornings in the backyard before work when she would draft me into an impromptu game of tag by placing a tree between us when I tried to grab her collar to go back inside. Keith spent hours locked up with Daisy in a cell no bigger than some people's walk-in closets. What would he do if she chewed up his only pair of sneakers? In spite of myself, I let one disturbing scenario after another play through my mind before calming myself with the only evidence available to me: Daisy herself. At only fourteen weeks old, she's already able to understand what her human is asking of her, to override her natural instincts to run and play and sniff everything in sight in order to catch the next command. She's trusting, she's clean, she's smart, attentive. Clearly, Daisy is loved.

Which had me wondering how Keith felt being separated from Daisy for the first time in two weeks. It was late. He would be locked back up in his cell for the night. Maybe he was thinking of Daisy right now, worrying, hoping I would treat her with kindness. He didn't know me any better than I knew him. He had to take it on faith that I could be trusted with Daisy, too.

I climbed into bed and slid beneath the sheet, replaying the day and wondering what was ahead of me. I was terrified I'd fail, that I'd be exposed as incompetent, that the people at NEADS would slap their foreheads at their stupidity for accepting me as a puppy raiser. That Keith would bitch about me to the other inmates. This was a familiar feeling to me. I felt the same self-doubt with just about everything I did—jobs, social situations, parenthood. When Aviva was born, I kept waiting for someone with a clipboard to knock on the door and tell me that a terrible mistake had been made, that in fact Marty and I were not fit to raise a child and please, hand her over right away.

Obviously, no clipboard-toting official has knocked on our door to claim our children (although there have been times when I fervently wished for it to happen and would have called to make sure they had the correct address). The frightening thing with Daisy, however, was that there really were people tracking her progress.

The fans in the windows did little to cut the sweltering heat in the bedroom and I had trouble falling asleep. My thoughts drifted to the day we brought Aviva home from the hospital. It was just as hot. Our car didn't have air-conditioning and sweat dampened our clothes because we wouldn't open the windows more than a crack for fear a gust of wind would pull our newborn from the straps of her car seat and suck her out into traffic. I blame my irrational thinking on postpartum hormones. Don't ask me what Marty's excuse was.

We weren't home five minutes when we made our first irrevocable mistake, and it involved our dog. Marty was unpacking the car while I settled the baby into her home. At least, I thought he was unpacking the car. In reality, he was tying two helium-filled Mylar balloons from the hospital to Tucker's collar with the plan to march the dog by the window where I sat. Except Tucker, being a two-year-old dog, didn't see the humor in the plan. All she knew was that two shiny orbs had materialized in the airspace three feet above her head and they were angrily crashing into each other. Tucker took off in a panic, trying to escape these threatening objects, which of course followed close behind no matter how fast she ran.

Marty came into the house, looking agitated, and broke the news that our dog had run away. I stared at him in shock while he grabbed his car keys and told me he was going to drive around looking for her. I stared down at our tiny, six-pound baby, swimming in the flowery pink jumpsuit my mother picked out for her coming-home outfit. And I thought about how I'd forever associate this day with losing our dog. I don't know how long I sat there crying. Eventually I pulled it together enough to call the police department and those in surrounding towns to report a missing German shepherd wearing a blue collar with balloons tied to it. Marty came home to check whether Tucker had returned, which set me on a fresh bout of sobbing, then took off in his car again to search some more. Hours had passed when a movement out the back window caught my eye. It was Tucker. She was slinking out of the woods and across our yard toward the house, trailing two scraps of Mylar behind her.

For the rest of her life, Tucker ran from the room whenever she saw a balloon. No experience is better than a bad experience.

———

SOMETIME DURING THE night, Daisy whined. I stuck my hand between the bars of her crate and felt around for her fur, smiling in the dark first at the shock of her cold nose, then at the warmth of her tongue on my fingers. The whining didn't stop, though, so I pulled myself out of bed and opened the door to the crate. Daisy rushed out, bunny-hopped down the stairs, and raced ahead of me into the living room, where she pooped in the exact same spot as before.

Fortunately, Daisy was accident free for the rest of the weekend. She woke me up again at five o'clock Saturday morning and I, not knowing the prison schedule, got up with her, figuring that was the hour the corrections officers roused the inmates. This time I had her leash handy. Silently and quickly, so as not to wake Marty, I pulled on a pair of shorts, opened the crate, and clipped the leash to Daisy's collar. I hustled her downstairs, thrust my feet into a pair of laced sneakers, then shuffled out the door with her. When we were back inside, I made a mental note to keep a towel by the door to wipe the dew off her feet, but for now I let her leave a trail of moist paw prints into the kitchen.

I emptied one of Keith's servings of dog food into a metal dish and placed it on the floor. Daisy sat in front of it and looked up at me expectantly. It took me a minute to understand that she was waiting for permission to eat. "Okay." I smiled, and she plunged her face into the bowl, whipping her tail back and forth with delight. I marveled at her self-control in the face of her most favorite thing in the world: food.

A NEADS dog has to be perfect in just about every way.

She can't be aggressive or territorial. One way to raise a gracious dog is to let her know that she doesn't "own" anything, including the bowl of food she's enjoying at the moment. Even though I wasn't fully awake, I whipped the bowl out from under Daisy's nose and held it out of reach. She sat back down and looked at me with that concerned expression. I placed it back on the floor and waited a moment until she pulled her gaze from the dish back to my face. "Okay," I told her, and she dove in to finish her breakfast. I stuck my hands in the bowl and sifted through the kibble. She carefully avoided my fingers, eating all around them. If anyone ever needed proof of Daisy's unfailingly gentle nature, they need only look at my hands, intact and scar free.

Later, after running Daisy through some sits, downs, and stays, a wave of fatigue rippled through my entire body, completely washing away the adrenaline surge that got me out of bed at five o'clock. In addition to the smaller crate upstairs, friends had lent us a large one, which we kept in the living room. I opened the door and blinked heavily while Daisy stepped delicately over the threshold, turned around, and flopped onto her side. I clicked the latch into place, collapsed on the couch, and slept. I don't know how much later it was when children's voices and the unmistakable sound of a tail thumping against metal roused me out of sleep. Josh's best friends, sisters Sarah and Catherine, who live next door and bookend Josh in age, were squatting in front of the crate, exclaiming over Daisy.

"Hey!" I said.

"Oh, good, you're awake. Can we take her out?" Josh already had his hand on the latch.

"Yeah . . . *No!* Wait." I jumped to my feet, remembering

the housebreaking accidents, and ran into the hallway to find Daisy's leash.

Josh and the girls followed us outside. Sarah and Catherine took turns with the leash, walking Daisy around the yard while Josh ran off to find his bicycle.

Kerry had written in my weekend instructions that I was to stick close to home so that Daisy and I could get to know each other and start forming a bond. And that's what we did.

I introduced her around the immediate neighborhood, where she met the two babies on our street, watched Josh ride bikes with Sarah and Catherine, and saw kids on skateboards and scooters. Later, I checked those off Daisy's "life experiences" list. Aviva even joined me on one of the walks, where we both were careful to stay safely within our newly demarcated conversational no-weapons zone by avoiding topics that didn't relate directly to Daisy.

"I wish I could go into the prison with you. I want to see what it's like," Aviva said after we had exhausted the topic of Daisy's cuteness. I glanced at my daughter in her size 00 short-shorts, her cheerleader ponytail swinging high from her head, and weighed possible responses. If I told her prison was no place for a teenage girl, she would get all bristly and offended. If I told her I wished she could, too, I'd be lying. If I didn't say anything—as I was doing at that moment—she would accuse me of ignoring her. Our every interaction is like a chess game; I have to think three or four moves ahead. Problem is, I'm a lousy chess player. No matter what I do, I lose. This time, I was saved from coming up with just the right response when the jingling of Daisy's tags set off a chorus of barking and howling from a neighbor's fenced-in yard. Five dogs lived in that house, including a couple of cairn terriers who looked like stuffed toys and an overfed golden retriever the size of a love seat. Daisy froze and stared at the house while Aviva and I laughed and picked up our pace, with me giving Daisy little tugs on the leash each time she stopped to stare in the direction of the howling. Once again, Daisy defused the land mines that Aviva and I somehow kept placing in each other's paths.

———

THROUGHOUT THE WEEKEND, Daisy and I explored the yard and played endless games of fetch. I encouraged her to "Better go now" on the pavement, on the gravel walkway behind the house, and on the grass, so she would get used to using whatever surface was available to her. In the house, we practiced "Through," which is the command for her to go first when entering a doorway. One of the most endearing commands is "Touch," which, to a NEADS dog, means "gently push your nose against your trainer's palm." "Touch" is a precursor to advanced commands to push elevator buttons, nudge light switches, and push doors closed.

Throughout the weekend, Kerry's "no experience is better than a bad experience" played through my head as I tried my hardest to control every moment of Daisy's visit. Sunday morning, she woke me at five o'clock again. By Sunday night, there were dark circles under my eyes. I was a little relieved when it was time for her to go. The family took turns saying good-bye to Daisy. Even Aviva came out of her room, holding her shimmery blue-painted fingernails out for a final "Touch."

On the road back to the prison, my gaze kept drifting to the rearview mirror for a glimpse of Daisy. I worried that she'd feel rejected, that somehow she'd failed the test and we were giving her back. But when we arrived at the prison and I lifted her out of the back of the car to place her gently on the pavement, she perked up at the familiar sights and scents of the parking lot. On the way through the courtyard, I thought about telling Keith about the housebreaking accidents, imagined him shaking his head in disgust at my failings, and decided to skip over that part of the weekend. But the second I saw him waiting just inside the prison yard door, it flew out of me almost against my will, like a dark secret I had to unburden myself of. I scanned his reaction for derision or disappointment, but he just seemed surprised. He jerked his head to the side in a questioning manner and spoke to Daisy: "Did you do that, girl?" I looked at Daisy, half expecting her to respond. Keith grew thoughtful and asked me a series of questions, like a technician trying to root out the source of an equipment malfunction. His response was exactly what I had hoped for Friday night when I reached for my e-mail and realized with a start that I had no one to turn to. I answered Keith's questions dutifully, telling him that on the first night only a couple of hours had passed since she had been outside and when she peed in the house. That I left the water dish out in case she was thirsty. That no, she didn't exhibit any signs that she needed to go outside.

He was silent for a moment. Later I realized he was probably thinking through his response so it would come across as a suggestion rather than an order. The inmates aren't supposed to tell the puppy raisers how to do their jobs. When he spoke, his tone was helpful. "This is what we do in here: We take the puppies out every hour, even if we don't think they have to go to the bathroom. That way we're giving them plenty of opportunity to use the outside. Also, I take Daisy out after she eats and when she wakes up. And try taking her water bowl away at six o'clock. Just until she's completely housebroken. That should cut down on accidents at night."

I wanted to pull up a chair and start taking notes. But we were in a prison, so I stood awkwardly instead and listened, nodding my head and gradually relaxing, feeling a little less alone in this endeavor. The concerns I had about Keith that first night with Daisy, when she seemed so vulnerable in her crate, all dried up and blew away, displaced by Keith's reassuring tone. He could have been anyone, anywhere, who takes his job seriously and wants to resolve a problem. If not for the correctional officers listening to our conversation, I might have forgotten I was speaking with an inmate.

Before I left, I repeated Keith's instructions and told him that next weekend I would try everything he suggested. "Seriously, I didn't know *what* I was doing wrong. I feel so much better now." I looked directly at him when I thanked him for the final time before turning to leave. Keith dropped his eyes to Daisy and mumbled something about hoping that would work for me. He seemed slightly embarrassed and I realized that he was probably unaccustomed to thanks or praise.

On the drive home, I replayed the weekend in my head. Caring for Daisy was harder than I thought it would be (though not as hard as being with Jones), but with Keith's advice, I felt ready for the next weekend. In fact, I already couldn't wait to see her again. There was something about that puppy that had completely captured my heart. I was halfway home when I realized that I'd been humming *Daisy, Daisy, give me your answer, do. I'm half crazy all for my love of you* . . . It seems I already was.

4

Are You Ready?

THE NEXT FRIDAY, I was faced with another one of those trick questions: Given the choice, would you leave your child at home alone, or would you lock him in the car in the parking lot of a medium-security prison?

I chose the latter.

For the past year, I'd been leaving Josh home alone when I ran errands. It was a relief when he was finally old enough that I no longer had to wrestle him into the car while I ferried his sister around and he was much happier staying behind to play outside or hang out with his friends. Except this time when he realized I'd be getting Daisy, he wanted to come along. I had just returned from dropping Aviva at gymnastics practice and was darting about the house, filling my pocket with dog treats, trying to remember where I left my keys, when the front door banged open.

"Can I come with you?" Josh asked. His shoes were caked with dirt from the back woods, where he was building a network of trails. He was naming the paths after dogs, so there was Tucker Trail and Jones Junction. His latest addition would be Daisy Drive.

"Take your shoes off, please." I watched while he used the toe of one sneaker to pull the other one off. "You can't come into the prison, Josh. You'd have to wait in the car and I don't know that I'm comfortable with that idea."

"I don't mind. Please?"

Now, sneakerless, he ran toward me with his hands folded into a begging gesture, beaming an enormous pleading smile.

I stared at him for a moment, then sighed. "Let's go. But I'm pretty sure that this officially makes me the worst mother in the world."

Josh, who started jumping up and down when I gave in, stopped and looked up at me, dismayed. "No! You're a good mom!"

I picked up his shoes and stepped outside to clap off the dried mud.

"Thank you. And you're a good kid." I gave him a quick back scratch while he sat on the front steps to pull on his sneakers, which were still laced.

Sometimes I suspect Josh sees his role in the family as protector of my feelings. I don't think this is necessarily a good thing, so I try not to appear vulnerable around him. But it is heartachingly sweet. One afternoon, when Josh was very young, maybe three or four years old, I was crouched on the floor wiping up a spill. Apparently, the waistband of my jeans had ridden down a little low because Josh appeared next to me and said in a small, grave voice, "Mommy, your blue underwear is showing. But don't worry," he reassured me, "I won't laugh."

The ride to pick up Daisy went by quickly with Josh to keep me company. The school year had just started and we talked a little about fifth grade and his new teacher. Before I knew it, we were turning into the road that leads to the prison. Unlike J. J. Moran, where the only glimpses of civilization from the prison yard are the bellies of the planes that roar overhead out of nearby T. F. Green Airport, the minimum-security prison is so close to the road that the inmates can practically stick their thumbs through the chain link and hitch a ride out of there.

When Josh and I drove past, the prisoners were out in the yard—really just a sad patch of dirt surrounded by chain link and littered here and there with cast-off athletic equipment. There were a few older men but most were in their twenties and thirties. They looked rumpled in their loose-fitting tan prison scrubs, like they had just got out of bed and were still wearing their pajamas. One of the guys stared at the sky from a weight bench while hoisting a barbell above his chest. Others half-heartedly punched a volleyball back and forth over a net that sagged dangerously low over a mud puddle, while still others walked in twos and threes around the perimeter of the yard, their heads bent in conversation. I was thinking about how the scene reminded me of one of those busy American folklore paintings, except drained of color and with inmates playing the role of the villagers, when I accidentally made eye contact with a dark-eyed inmate with a buzz cut. That set him and his two buddies hooting and shaking the fence like primates rattling their cages. I snapped back to face front but Josh twisted in his seat as we drove by. "What are they yelling at?"

I was silent a moment while I tried to think of the best way to frame it. Finally I decided on the truth: "It's their way of flirting," I said. "But remember, they're criminals. Nice men don't holler at women when they drive by."

Josh laughed with a hard edge of knowing that unnerved me and I realized somebody must have been talking with him about sex. Aviva was around his age when her best friend gave her the grade school version of how babies are made, which I'm pretty sure included visual aids courtesy of Bratz dolls in slutty outfits. When I tried to correct the record, Aviva curled into the fetal position and pressed her hands against her ears while I blathered on about love and self-respect and the dangers of STDs and unwanted pregnancies, all the while hating myself for torturing my child but powerless to stop. Later, exhausted and never wanting to repeat the experience, I asked Marty to have a preemptive talk with Josh. He agreed, but Marty doesn't like to rush things. He sat down with Josh to describe pollination and called it a day. His plan was to work his way up the food chain over the course of several months—or years—until he finally got to human sexuality. They got as far as the life cycle of mayflies but then too much time lapsed and everyone forgot about the plan, leaving poor Josh defenseless against his friends' interpretations of sex. And now here we were, my eleven-year-old son chortling like a frat boy.

I absentmindedly stroked my arm on the steering wheel while flexing my wrist. The muscles used to ripple impressively beneath my skin from years of hoisting children out of car seats, carrying them up stairs, flying them in the air above my head . . . now they yielded easily to pressure. My arms hadn't felt the heft of a small child in a long time.

With four years between my children, I sometimes catch myself thinking of Josh as my "backup kid," the one who's still there for Disney movies and snuggles long after Aviva outgrew those things. At night, I prop myself up with pillows in Josh's bed while he sits next to me so I can scratch his back while reading out loud from *Harry Potter*. He's perfectly capable of reading to himself, but that's not the point. He gets a back scratch and I get to be near my boy.

When I glanced sideways at Josh I saw that he was still smiling. His front teeth were too large for his mouth and stuck out awkwardly. Soon he would be getting braces, another ritual milestone on the way toward adulthood. Already I can see the end. In a year or two his voice will deepen and his limbs will thicken. He'll be able to see the top of my head. Cuddling with his mom will just be awkward.

I'd always looked forward to the days of not being tied down by kids, so it was a shock to discover that without them around, I was lonely and, quite frankly, pathetic. A few years earlier, Josh was in Connecticut visiting my brother and my sister-in-law, and Aviva got an unexpected invitation to spend a couple of nights with a friend's family on Cape Cod. I made sure Aviva packed her toothbrush, gave her some spending money, and, when her friend's mother pulled into the driveway to pick her up, watched while she buckled herself into the backseat. After they disappeared around the corner I stood in the driveway feeling unmoored, and for the next two days until she and Josh returned, I knocked about the house, not knowing what to do with myself. It was the first time since before we became parents that Marty and I were childless at home. And I was completely ill prepared for the gaping void they left.

How would I ever let them go for good?

I knew ahead of time that becoming a mother would lead to this. That's why I'd resisted having children for as long as I did. My sense of self is shaky enough, and I'd worked too hard forging an identity to risk letting a little baby swallow it whole. After Aviva was born I tried to hang on to myself, but in the end was powerless against the all-consuming demands of caring for her. My old self was swept away, replaced by this new identity, this mom who scrubbed the salt from her speech and swapped R.E.M. at full volume for Disney songs. Although, looking back, I realize I was a goner the day I cradled my pregnant belly between my palms and grieved the fact that once my baby was born, I'd never again be able to protect her as fully. I've devoted so much mental energy to my children in the years since, I wouldn't be surprised if an MRI revealed likenesses of Aviva and Josh embossed onto my brain. Who will I be when they're grown up and on their own? What will I do with myself? Not only do my children dominate my thoughts, but taking care of them gives structure to my days. Aviva was a toddler when I gave up being a newspaper reporter, with its long and irregular hours, and patched together a living wage by picking up free-lance work and part-time writing and editing jobs, the latest of which had turned into full-time employment. Marty and I saved on child-care costs when the kids were little by taking a tag-team approach to parenting. We arranged our schedules so one of us was home while the other was at work. My mother volunteered for a midweek gap in coverage. Yet even though Marty is as involved in the kids' lives as I am, I'm the primary parent for school and activities. I built my social scaffolding around my kids. I volunteered, went to PTO meetings; the people I talked with most were the parents of their friends and classmates. Work was practically the only thing in my life not wholly dependent on them and it never came close to being as important. Now all of those rungs and supports were being dismantled and I was clinging precariously to what little remained. With Aviva in high school and Josh in middle school, the volunteer opportunities had mostly dried up, the social interactions faded. Soccer, Little League, dance—those were as much for the parents as for the kids, with the moms and dads clustered on the sidelines or sitting together in the studio waiting room, catching up with one another and sharing intelligence about the schools and town. But those were either gone or transformed into drop-off activities.

Now it wasn't unusual for days to pass without me talking to a single adult outside of my family or job. And because I worked primarily from home, most interactions with colleagues were through e-mail. In striving to give my children enriching, fulfilling lives, I had neglected my own.

I wished I had tried harder to keep some of those friends I'd made through the kids. The give-and-take that requires has never been my strength, but being a natural introvert, it never really bothered me. But now, with the kids growing up at last and this phase of my life winding down, I couldn't help but feel that by letting so many people slip away, I'd squandered something valuable.

The future looked awfully lonely.

Which brings me to my secondary motivation for signing up to be a weekend puppy raiser. Aside from the simple pleasure of getting to spend time with a dog, having Daisy would return some purpose to my life and hopefully bring new people into my world. I don't know why it didn't occur to me that I was also setting myself up for another loss.

THE PRISON PARKING lot was patrolled by a uniformed officer in a gray van. Every so often, he'd shift it into drive and move to a different spot as if checking out the view before committing long term. I found a space several rows away from him and locked Josh in the car, cracking the windows slightly, warning him not to open it for anybody, then hurried to the entrance, casting glances at the other cars for potential kidnappers—or witnesses to my lax parenting. Maybe that's what started Keith and Lance on their lives of crime.

When I was first caring for Jones, Kerry had mentioned that Lance was due to be released soon. I wondered whether he was still incarcerated or was out in the world now. One Sunday when I returned the poodle, Lance bent to kiss the top of Jones's head, briefly flattening his curly Afro, and confided to me in a hushed voice, "When I get out of here, I'm gonna get a dog just like him."

Keith hadn't arrived in shift command yet and Captain Lefebvre's office was empty, so I stood just outside the doorway and looked around, jumpy from a mix of excitement at seeing Daisy again and dread that an outlaw would break into my car and hold Josh hostage in exchange for the release of prisoners. Or call Child Protective Services on me.

Captain Lefebvre's office was devoid of personal artifacts— no framed photographs of a wife or children, no desk ornaments. Not even a plant to break up the palette of gray metal and pale yellow cinder block.

In addition to Lefebvre's full-time duties as commander of the largest shift at medium-security, he works with NEADS to recruit, interview, and hire the inmate handlers; oversee and arrange the puppies' transportation to and from vet appointments; and motivate the dog trainers—be patient with them when they behave like children, discipline them when they act like criminals. But if that sounds like a lot of work, the hassle of overseeing the prison-pup partnership is worth it to Lefebvre. In fact, he says it's the best thing to happen during his twenty-year career with the corrections department. He runs the program like a startup company, poaching talent from other prison work areas, bending the rules when following them would undermine the mission of the program. NEADS shies away from using inmates who have been convicted of violent crimes, but murderers serve the longest sentences, making them the best hedge against high turnover. Lefebvre will consider anyone who's smart and keeps out of trouble, as long as he isn't a sex offender and doesn't have a history of harming animals. He solicits references from prison guards and every once in awhile he'll get a stack of applications six inches high. By the time he finishes weeding through them, "the pile is down to about here," he once told me, his palm scraping the top of his desk. Lefebvre and one or two of the folks from NEADS interview those applicants. For many of the inmates, it's their first job interview ever, and they're too terrified to speak. Others doom themselves by telling their interviewers they don't know anything about the program, but they sure like dogs. That just pisses Lefebvre off. He expects a lot from his dog handlers, the first being that they prepare for their job interview by finding out from the other handlers what it's all about.

Out of a thousand inmates under his watch, Lefebvre considers himself lucky to find a dozen solid dog trainers. He'll bring on an equal number to serve in apprentice roles. The backup job is another chance to cull the field, leaving the program with only the cream of the crop. His exacting standards may be why J. J. Moran has the highest graduation rate of all of the prisons NEADS works with.

On the wall above a pair of facing desks in the captain's office was a dry-erase calendar grid of the puppies' veterinarian schedule. I was scanning it for Daisy's name when a voice called out. "Which dog you here for?" I whipped around to see a couple of officers in the room across the narrow hallway. A chair squeaked as one stood up and came out from behind his desk. I spoke a little faster than necessary.

"Oh! Um, Daisy. She's new here and much better behaved than the last dog I had, Jones. He was a poodle." Sometimes when I'm trying to prove I'm not nervous, words fly out of my mouth, then hang awkwardly in the air like a cloud of gnats.

The officer drew back his head and considered me for a moment. "Ahhh! You're the one!" He waved his colleague over and roared. "Hey, hey! Look! It's her! The one we were watching with the poodle." He turned back to me. "We thought that poodle was going to drag you across the parking lot!" He must have noticed my puzzlement because he gestured toward the wall facing his desk. "We were watching you on the security cam."

"What? What do you mean?" I stuck my head through his doorway. A bank of four monitors hung from the wall opposite his desk, each tuned to a different location inside the prison buildings and on the grounds, including one trained on the very spot where Jones had sprung after the flock of birds on our first day together. I felt oddly exposed by the knowledge that I was being watched during my walks in and out of the prison. One of the monitors showed two bulky inmates facing each other over a game of checkers at a metal picnic bench. Where else did they point their security cameras? I imagined a microscopic one tucked behind Daisy's ear, beaming video into shift command of me undressing for bed.

The prison yard door buzzed, saving me from further mortification. I turned in time to watch Keith hold the door open for Daisy, who stepped delicately over the threshold before locking onto me. She whipped her tail back and forth and my heart gave a leap when she attempted to bound over. Keith tightened the leash and her expression changed from eager anticipation to surprise as she found herself drawn up short. "Side," Keith said, pulsing the leash. Daisy whirled and circled around until she was by his right leg, facing forward, her tongue hanging out in a goofy grin. Keith asked Daisy to sit. She complied, slowly, without taking her eyes off me.

"It looks like she remembers you," Keith said, his words igniting tiny embers of happiness inside me.

"You think?" I asked, enthusiastically agreeing on the inside. Daisy popped to her feet at the sound of my voice, beating her tail against Keith's leg and flattening the crease in his pants. Lance and many of the other inmates wore loose-fitting scrubs, but Keith seemed to prefer a button-down shirt and khakis. The shirt was well-worn, with a rectangle of gray adhesive over the left breast pocket where a name tag or number might once have been. Instead, a plastic "Offender" ID badge dangled from a metal clip. I learned later that the prison had retired the khakis and button-down shirts a few years earlier, but the inmates who still had them held on to them for special occasions, like visits or meetings with their attorneys.

Keith admonished Daisy for breaking her "Sit" with a quick "Eh-eh," a correction I remembered from the NEADS manual, and guided her back down to his side. I tore my gaze from Daisy's and watched Keith's face as he stared down at her and said her name. Lines were beginning to form around his mouth, the kind that would deepen with age, like mine. Daisy looked away from me and met his eye. "Good girl." His voice was low and grumbly, a mother bear whispering to her cub. He slipped her a piece of kibble from the black nylon pouch he wore around his waist.

Once Keith was assured Daisy wasn't going to spring back to her feet, he told her, "Let's go," and walked her toward me. I took the leash from Keith and bent down to give Daisy a quick pat. What I really wanted to do was roll around on the ground with her, but I restrained my emotions as Keith had restrained Daisy with the leash. I guided her to my side as Keith just demonstrated, then looked up for his reaction, hoping for approval. Instead, he handed me the plastic bag containing Daisy's meals for the weekend and took a few steps backward to maintain the distance between us. He gestured loosely toward Daisy. "About the housebreaking accidents, I checked with Christy and she pretty much said the same thing that I told you about taking her outside every hour and also to take away her water dish at six." Christy was the NEADS trainer who came to the prison on Tuesday mornings to work with the inmates. Keith looked at a spot above my head. "Hello, Lieutenant." I turned to see one of the officers standing behind me. He nodded his chin toward Daisy.

"Now this one is more your size!"

"Yeah. And much calmer, too. This one I can handle. I hope."

Keith looked confused and my inner hostess came bustling out, making sure everyone was in on the joke so no one would feel left out.

"We're talking about Jones the poodle and how big he was. I had Jones before he flunked out—thank God." I muttered this last part under my breath.

Keith smiled and nodded to indicate he understood. "Oh, right. Jones was a piece of work. Daisy will be great for you. Just remember, take the water away after six and bring her outside every hour."

"I will." I hoped he'd note the conviction in my tone and be assured that Daisy was in good hands.

This time when Keith wished me a good weekend, I didn't return the sentiment but instead simply thanked him. I hurried out with Daisy, my attention shifting from the puppy at the end of my leash to my child, alone in the car. I imagined returning to find the passenger door wide open, Josh missing, maybe a ransom note under the windshield wiper. The gates were infuriatingly slow, the way they kept sliding open long after I'd stepped through, then inched their way slowly back into a locked position only after reaching the end of their track. You could practically bake a cake in the time it took the pair of them to open and close. When I finally burst out of the building with Daisy, I caught sight of the top of Josh's head bent low in the passenger seat, and I was filled with such gratitude and love for this beautiful, patient son who was not only safe but still young enough that he wanted to be with his mother, even if it meant waiting in a prison parking lot. "Let's go find Josh!" The words came out in a rush of emotion to Daisy, who sped up to a trot to match my pace across the parking lot.

"Look who I have!" I sang out when we got within hearing distance. Josh flung aside his Nintendo and jumped out for a joyful reunion with Daisy. She was already beginning to feel like our dog.

WHEN WE ARRIVED at the house, Marty was home from work and eating buffalo chicken wings at the kitchen table while staring into his laptop. Daisy rushed over and put her paws on his lap and gave his face a quick lick before turning her head and sniffing in the direction of his plate. "Yuck. Down," he said, gently pushing her away. Marty was in reentry mode, a transition at the end of a workday that requires food and quiet time to catch up on his e-mail and his favorite news sites. I usually leave him alone until reentry is complete, but I could tell he felt badly for sniping at Daisy, because he reached down to scratch behind her ears.

I kissed his bald spot. "Next time tell her 'Off,' otherwise she'll get confused."

"How did the pickup go?" he asked me. I looked down at Daisy, who was sniffing under the kitchen table.

"Fine. Daisy's prisoner . . . inmate . . . whatever you call him, he thought she remembered me from last week."

"What's he like? Do you know what he's in for?"

I sat down on the floor and patted my knee. Daisy came within grabbing distance and I pulled her onto my lap for some puppy-handling exercises.

"They don't tell us. But my guess is he's either been there for a while or he's been in and out of prison over the years." I pressed the pads beneath each of Daisy's toes while I spoke.

"He's probably only in his early thirties, but he has that hardened prison look about him, like he's done a lot of time. He looks kind of scary, like, you wouldn't want to meet up with him in a dark alley. The last guy—Jones's guy—I couldn't figure out why he was in prison because he seemed so normal. He's the guy you'd find on the next bar stool telling stories and buying everyone a round of drinks. I think someone must have tricked him into driving the getaway car. But Daisy's guy—"

Marty broke in, "He's the one who said, 'Hey, do you mind pulling into this bank for a second? And leave the engine running.'"

I laughed. This was familiar territory for both of us. I met Marty when he was an editor and hired me to cover the police and courts for a daily newspaper in a decaying former factory town outside of Boston. (Our first double byline appeared over a story about a man who stabbed his wife forty-seven times on Valentine's Day.) Marty's father was a newspaperman, too, and would bring his work home—sometimes literally, as with "Uncle" Leon, a mobster and confidential source who would drop in on the Luttrell home for dinner every now and then. So, when friends asked whether Marty was worried about me going into a prison every week, I'd just shake my head and tell them no, he didn't see anything unusual about it.

Daisy was scrambling to get away, so I released my hold and grabbed the folder with the weekend communication sheet. I was really curious to know why Keith was in prison, but I'd be breaching protocol if I came right out and asked. We're not supposed to veer from puppy-related topics. I supposed I could try to sneak it into our twice-weekly conversation ("Daisy's in for a lot of fun this weekend . . . what are you in for?"), but that didn't seem realistic. If I knew his last name, I could try an Internet search, but the type on his ID badge was too small for me to make out. I looked down at the weekend report. It listed Daisy's name, but not Keith's. I studied his handwriting on the sheet, searching for clues to his character, his personality, his feelings about Daisy. Under "Special Concerns," Keith wrote in small, cramped letters, "Requires constant attention. Likes rocks, things on ground." There weren't any misspellings, which surprised me. And the language seemed sophisticated. "Requires constant attention." I don't know, but if you'd asked me, I'd say a common criminal would choose different wording, like "Keep an eye on her," or "Don't let her get away with nothing." Had he been a good student at one time? Did he enjoy school? I pictured Keith as I remembered Josh first learning to form letters, his face set in concentration as he dragged the pencil across the paper. I wondered what Keith's favorite subject had been, and whether he'd made it through high school.

I turned back to the paper in hand, and while I was examining Keith's advice to give Daisy constant attention, Daisy wandered into my office and pooped. The irony did not escape me.

———

OVER THE NEXT few weekends Daisy burrowed deeper into my heart. On Monday mornings while driving into the office for my work team's weekly meeting, I'd imagine her in prison and wonder what she was doing at that exact moment. First thing after punching the code into the keypad on the office door and unpacking my laptop, I'd pull up pictures of Daisy and show them around. When I learned that the freelance sound engineer who was helping me with a project had a dog, I e-mailed him a photo of Daisy. I did the same for my dog-loving primary care physician. Like with a first crush, I wanted everyone to know about my new love. All week I'd catch myself looking at the phone, wishing I could pick it up to call Keith, just to talk about Daisy.

On Fridays, I'd spend the drive to the prison imagining our reunion. My pulse would quicken when I pulled off the highway toward the prison to pick her up. I'd pull into the lot, check my eye makeup in the rearview mirror, as if Daisy would notice, then race toward the building, patting my pocket to make sure it was stuffed with treats. If Daisy and Keith weren't waiting for me when I turned the corner past the shift command office, I'd stand on tiptoes, scanning the prison yard through the barred window for a glimpse of Daisy's familiar, rolling trot alongside Keith's hurried steps. Inmates would pass through my field of vision, walking by alone or in pairs, all identically dressed in tan scrubs or gray sweats. Every now and then the verticality of the movement would be disrupted when someone would drop to palms and toes to do push-ups; or one would roll past in a wheelchair, a second bent forward and pushing from behind. Sometimes a dog would appear next to its handler, forming a horizontal line from its nose to its outstretched tail. If it was night, the yard lights would cast a yellowish glow on the scene, and the figures would emerge from the darkness like ghostly apparitions.

Eventually Keith and Daisy would come into view: Keith, colorless in his prison uniform, loping toward the command building; and Daisy, ears bouncing as she sped up or slowed down to match Keith's pace. When Keith pushed the door open and they stepped over the threshold, Daisy's eyes would lock on me and she'd fold her ears tight over her head like a bathing cap. She'd wag her tail and grin, and if I'd had a tail, it would be wagging, too. Instead, I'd grin back at her like an idiot, practically hopping from foot to foot while Keith had Daisy sit and meet his gaze before walking her over to me and giving her permission to "say hello."

At that point, a tsunami-size wave of dopamine would crash over my brain as I knelt on the floor to rub her muzzle and kiss the top of her head, inhaling the scent of her fur. "How's my girl?" I'd ask.

My girl. It was inevitable. I was already thinking of her as *my* dog.

As a kid reared on Lassie and Old Yeller, I grew up believing that every dog has its human soul mate—a partnership etched in the stars and fulfilled on earth. Sometimes it would take a while for human and canine to find each other, but eventually they would, and they'd live a mutually blissful life broken only by intermittent moments of chaos. The house would catch fire or a rabid fox would tear out of the woods, foaming and snarling. But then the music would swell and the dog would rescue its human, offering more proof that the dog was indeed sent from heaven. That's the way it worked, and I just couldn't wait for *my* dog. Except there was a problem. Well, two of them: parents who valued a house free of pet hair over their child's physical well-being and emotional completeness.

Petless, I consoled myself by imagining there was a dog somewhere out there searching for me, and I convinced myself that each stray that found its way into our yard was guided there by that invisible force whose purpose was to lead it to me. (Though the bowls of raw hamburger I left outside for them may have helped.) None of the dogs stayed for very long, and eventually I grew out of my conviction that human-animal matches are preordained. But there's still a part of me that believes an unseen force is at work when pets and people come into each other's lives. We start off as separate individuals living in the same home, but grow ever closer until we reach the point where we simply can't imagine life without the other. If you think about it, this isn't surprising. Dogs and humans have been working out the kinks in their relationship for thirty thousand years. We're way past the getting-to-know-you phase.

Some anthropologists theorize that we came into each other's lives when wolves bred themselves into dogs to take advantage of the free food humans offered. Others say humans had a heavier hand in the evolutionary process, domesticating wolves through selective breeding. I say that however it was that some wolves became dogs, it only explains half the story of the dog-human relationship. The other half is that during the last thirty millennia, humans evolved to love dogs, too—that somehow an affinity for canines became encoded in our DNA. How else to explain a baby's fascination with them? When my kids were small I could be playing the trombone, juggling teaspoons, and riding a unicycle back and forth in front of their high chairs, but if a dog appeared in their peripheral vision, they'd scream for the dog and I'd become as interesting as a blank wall. Josh learned to crawl by lurching across the floor toward Tucker so that he could throw himself at her. Then he'd sit back down on his diapered bottom, gleefully clutching clumps of fur in each tiny fist. When the kids were older and I posed them with the dog for our annual holiday card, they fought over who could hug Tucker closest.

So, while those tens of thousands of years of evolutionary entanglement ultimately brought Daisy and me into each other's lives, it was our forty-eight hours of unbroken togetherness each weekend and the work we were learning to do together that turned us into partners.

After our Friday-night reunions in shift command, Daisy and I would push past the throngs waiting to visit their inmates, ignoring their stares, step outside, and weave through the cars and trucks in the prison parking lot. When we'd reach my car, I'd open the door, meet her gaze, and tell her, "Jump!" She'd turn from me to look up at her target, rear back, wiggle her hindquarters, and spring forward. Then she'd turn around, tail wagging, to accept the treat she knew would be waiting for her. I'd pull out onto the highway, sneaking glances at her in the rearview mirror, and my heart would fill with what can only be described as infinite love.

When we'd pull into my neighborhood, Daisy would perk up. She'd poke her nose out the window crack, spilling drool onto the glass. "Where are we?!" I'd call out in a happy voice, and Daisy would turn toward me, her muzzle open and her tongue hanging out in a canine version of a smile, then just as quickly snap her jaws shut and turn away, distracted by some new sight out the window—a bird taking flight, a glimpse of the neighbor's black Lab.

Once in the house, she'd race from room to room, tail high, nose to the floor, reacquainting herself with the scents of my home. Her home. That our arrangement was only temporary was something I chose not to think about. It was just so pleasant to fantasize that she was my dog.

5

Heel

ONE OF THE things I missed most about Tucker was our daily walks. They were like a deep-tissue massage for my mind, working the knotty problems loose until my thoughts flowed freely again. I couldn't wait to continue the tradition with Daisy. Except it turned out that walks with her were nothing like that. In fact, they pretty much sucked. Any meandering thoughts in my head were zapped into oblivion until all that was left was a single laser point focused on one goal: to get Daisy to walk calmly by my side. She was focused and obedient during our training sessions in the living room. But on walks her nose took over. She'd strain at her collar in pursuit of a scent, intent on snorting each particulate into her finely sculpted muzzle. I was reduced to nothing more than a vaguely irritating sensation at the end of the leash, easy to ignore.

I had to become a tree.

"Being a tree" is a training technique to get your dog to walk on a loose leash without pulling or lagging behind. When the puppy forges ahead, you're supposed to stop dead in your tracks and stand stock still, like you've suddenly grown roots. The puppy will turn around to see what the holdup is, at which point you call her back to your side and resume walking.

Our walks would start out well enough. I'd hook Daisy's nylon leash to her collar and have her sit while I opened the front door. She would look up and meet my eye, waiting for my next command, and I would give her permission to go through the door. We would make it all of four steps before she would pull on the leash and I would turn into a tree. Just as the manual described, Daisy would trot back toward me with a questioning look. I'd reposition her by my side, then tell her, "Let's go." Daisy would peel out like a NASCAR driver. I'd stop. She'd return to my side. I'd say "Let's go," and she'd rev forward.

And that's how our walks went every weekend for the next few months. Lurching forward and stopping all around the neighborhood. I incorporated other techniques into my repertoire, hoping (but doubting) one of them would work. I'd feed her treats to lure her into position, but she'd be back at the end of the leash before she'd swallowed. So I'd hold on to the treat and she would follow along, her nose pressed into my hand, like it was magnetically attached. But then I'd start to feel sadistic and eventually let her eat the treat . . . at which point she'd gallop to the end of the leash. I'd abruptly switch direction as if I'd suddenly realized I left something back home. I'd stagger and drift across the sidewalk as if I'd just thrown back a couple of martinis. The intent of all that stopping, turning, swerving, and treating was to redirect Daisy's attention from her doggy-centered mission and onto me, the human holding her leash. I even tried threading the leash behind her front legs and up through her collar like we learned at orientation. At first she moved clumsily, lifting her paws high like a cat shaking water off its feet. But Labs are adaptable creatures and it wasn't long before she got used to the feeling of being hindered and was right back to straining at the now much shorter leash.

I was up against the canine nose. As humans, we can't even imagine the tide of information that flows into our dogs' brains. It's carried along air currents through their nostrils and is absorbed directly into the moist surface at the tips of their muzzles. To process all of that data, dogs have two to three hundred million sensory receptors in their nasal cavities. By comparison, humans have just six million.

During our walks, Daisy was reading, through her nose, the complete and continuously updated history of my neighborhood and all of its inhabitants, human and nonhuman alike. Apparently it was a pretty compelling story, because it made her forget all about me. *Me* being the operative word, because of all the service dogs I had encountered, not a single one of them strained at the leash with its nose pressed into the ground, as Daisy did. With me. Not Keith.

Sure, sometimes Keith would have to stop during their walks across the prison yard and direct Daisy back to position, but with him, she seemed to understand that the "Heel" command didn't automatically expire after three seconds; she would stay at his side when they resumed walking. Daisy was disciplined with Keith.

Since that first Sunday back at prison when Keith was so eager to help me with the housebreaking problem, I had come to look forward to our brief chats in shift command. He didn't make me nervous anymore; the officers did, the way they'd stand with their arms folded across their chests, listening to our conversation or sitting in their office, watching us in the round security mirror bolted to the wall above my head. I was terrified I'd do something wrong and be escorted from the prison, told never to return. But even so, that didn't stop me from testing the boundaries. We were allowed to talk about the puppy, but not any more than necessary. To me, it was necessary to talk about the puppy a lot. It was the same near-physical compulsion that I had when the kids were little and an endless source of fascination to me. Having been bored into a coma by other people's chatter about their children, I knew enough not to inflict my stories on just anyone. I'd save them up for the only people whose enthusiasm for the subject matched mine: Marty and the kids' grandmothers. With Daisy, Keith was the one person on earth who cared as much about Daisy as I did. I'd save everything up for him, and on Friday and Sunday nights it would all come pouring out in a rush of chatter.

"How do you do it?" I asked Keith on my fourth weekend with Daisy. "She won't heel or 'side' when I take her on walks. She starts off okay, but right away she's at the end of her leash."

"Yeah, she definitely has her own mind." Keith bent down and flipped one of Daisy's ears up and peered inside, checking that it was clean. He repeated it with the other one, massaged both at once to make up for the intrusion, then stood back up straight and looked me in the eye. From where I stood, Keith's eyes seemed to be the same tan as his prison uniform, which was similar in color to his closely cropped hair, which was about the same shade as Daisy. The effect was strangely soothing and

seemed intentional, as if he engineered the color scheme to blend quietly into his environment. "We're starting to train her with the Gentle Leader. That will help a lot."

I was familiar with the Gentle Leader from Jones. It's a strap that goes around the dog's nose like a horse's halter so you can lead the dog around by the head, instead of by the neck as with a traditional collar. The Gentle Leader is a particularly valuable tool for people with limited strength, as is the case with many NEADS clients, because with it the dog is less likely to pull. When I picked up Jones that first weekend, Lance gave me a quick lesson on how to use the Gentle Leader, but when I slipped the nylon loop over Jones's muzzle back home, the buckles and metal rings didn't seem to line up right. I pulled the buckles together with more force than seemed reasonable until they met and clicked into place. When I stepped back to examine the results, the fur on Jones's face was bunched so tight that his eyes were nearly squeezed shut and the metal ring for the leash stuck straight up from the top of his snout like a flower. Jones stared at me miserably. I eventually figured out how to use the Gentle Leader (with the help of an instructional video on YouTube). As bad as Jones was on leash, he was a thousand times worse without the Gentle Leader.

Most dogs don't take to the Gentle Leader right away (even when it's fitted so as *not* to cut off circulation to the face), so NEADS makes sure the inmates introduce it gradually, over time, and with plenty of treats and praise.

"She'll be a different dog when she has it on. You'll see; you'll love it. But that's still a few months away. For now, I don't know. She's definitely a sniffer," Keith commiserated. He turned and looked through the barred window out at the yard, where

a basketball game was in progress. "She knows every square inch of this place already. When she's out with you, there are all these new things for her to smell and see. Here, every day it's the same thing." He stated it as fact, without a note of envy or bitterness in his voice.

I was suddenly embarrassed for him, as if I had forced him to admit that he was incarcerated. "Oh, that's okay, I'll figure it out!" I said a little too cheerfully before turning to leave.

From that first day when I led Daisy out of the prison and wondered whether it bothered Keith to be left behind, I've felt twinges of guilt for being the one who swept in every weekend to fill Daisy with new experiences while Keith was left to molder within the locked gates and razor wire. If Daisy had sniffed up every scent in the prison after only six weeks, how did it feel to Keith, who I knew had been there at least a couple of years, given his history with the puppy program? Then again, he'd done something bad enough to land himself in prison. I turned my focus to Daisy and the multitude of distractions outside the prison gates. Prison doesn't have cats or woods or a Jack Russell terrier running back and forth on his front lawn behind an invisible fence. There isn't even a single tree for Daisy to investigate. What I needed were other puppy raisers to talk to, people who were going through the same thing I was, whom I could learn from and compare myself against. Like I used to do with other mothers.

When Aviva and Josh were little, I met monthly with friends for an evening away from the kids . . . during which time we'd talk almost exclusively about our kids. Oh, sure, we'd start off with good intentions, discussing current events or books. But invariably, one of us would follow a comment about, say, the

pursuit of profit over ethics with "I'm kind of afraid Aviva is heading in that direction. I found out she's been *leasing* her board games to Josh." (Okay, I was the one who said that.) Then someone would bring up the corporate CFO who was sent to prison, and another mother would reveal that she stepped outside to clear her head after sending her seven-year-old son to his room, turned around, and found her little boy *lowering himself from his second-story window!*

At that point, we'd drop all pretense of being more interested in the world around us than the messy, perplexing worlds in our own homes. We'd order another round of drinks, prop our elbows on the table, and talk about our children for *hours*. You could practically see the stress leave our bodies.

So, yeah. With Daisy using our floors as her personal toilet and forcing me to act like a tree during every walk, and my co-parent locked away behind bars, I yearned for other weekend puppy raisers. I craved their tips and tricks, but I also wanted to talk with them about how frustrating it was to work with a partner who was incarcerated. And I wanted to hear about their problems: the puppies who yipped in their crate all night or chewed the stuffing out of the backseat of the car. I needed to hear about the puppy equivalent of the second-story dangler, whose mom hauled ass upstairs, grabbed him by the arms, and lifted him inside to safety. Because maybe those stories didn't solve my own problems, but they sure made me feel less alone.

I hadn't seen another puppy raiser since meeting Bonnie in the prison parking lot on my first day with Daisy. I supposed I could loiter by my car during puppy pickup and drop-off times and hope to spot her, but that seemed weird and desperate. Instead, I pinned my hopes on the monthly training class that

NEADS requires puppy raisers to attend. My first class was scheduled at a doggy day care, exactly one month after Daisy's first weekend with me.

The morning before class, I brought Daisy into the backyard for a play session to burn off some energy. Daisy's a natural-born fetcher, unlike Tucker, who'd retrieve a tennis ball well enough, but wouldn't let go of it for anything except a second ball—and even then she'd sometimes try to fit both into her mouth at once. I whipped the tennis ball away from the house where the yard sloped slightly. Daisy tore after it full throttle, overshooting it, then banking back around to scoop it into her mouth. I turned to peer into the rabbit hutch before Daisy made her way back to me. Just as I suspected, both the food bowl and the water bottle were empty. In an instant, I was furious.

Aviva had begged us for a bunny when she was ten, so when a friend's rabbit produced a litter, we let her pick out a pair. They were adorable, with their twitchy pink noses and egg-shaped bodies that could fit in the palm of your hand. And I've been threatening to give them away ever since. Through no fault of their own, they've become an endless source of friction between my daughter and me. Aviva forgets to feed them, I remind her, and she responds as though I've burst past the government agents guarding the top-secret laser beam she's feverishly programming to deflect the meteor that's careening toward earth to demand she put down the controls *this instant* and go fill the bunnies' food dish.

I pulled the water bottle out of its holder and poked my head through the kitchen door. Aviva was at the table eating pancakes. "Their food dish is empty, too," I yelled, slamming the bottle on the counter.

"*O-kay!*" she growled through a mouthful of food. "I'll do it when I'm not *busy!*"

"And clean their hutch, too, or else you're not going out tonight!" This last order, I'm not proud to say, I added for spite. I slammed the door behind me before she could answer and forced myself to take deep breaths—a trick I first learned in childbirth class. Our instructor wisely told us it would come in handy again when our babies reached adolescence.

Daisy was amusing herself with the tennis ball by dropping it on the ground, pouncing on it, and picking it up again. "Wanna play?" I forced my voice to sound cheerful even though I was seething inside. I held out my hand and Daisy, her jaws propped wide open by the ball, waved her head back and forth and kicked her legs unnecessarily high in a joyful dance toward me to deposit the slightly soggy ball in my outstretched hand. I raised my arm and took a few steps back. Every hair on Daisy's body vibrated with anticipation. I released the ball and watched her wheel around to gallop after the throw. Soon, I wasn't thinking of the bunnies or my daughter. It was a relief.

I threw the ball until my arm hurt, gave Daisy a good, long drink, and opened the back of the car for her to get in. We were barely out of my neighborhood before she disappeared behind the backseat and I knew she was asleep. I congratulated myself for tiring out the dog and hoped her fatigue would pass for obedience in class.

No such luck. Daisy sprung to life as soon as we pulled into the parking lot of Happy Tails doggy day care. There was no easing into wakefulness for Daisy. Oh, no. Dog scent was in the air and it shot through her system as powerfully as if she'd lapped up a double espresso. Daisy thumped her tail against the plastic mat while watching another dog leap out of a car and walk with its owner up a deep set of cement steps into the one-story brick building.

A moment later, Daisy was pulling me up those steps. Inside the building she stopped short to sniff a yellow plastic toddler's slide hard enough to suck the color out of it, then led me into the training room, where she spotted her friend Perry from prison, and expressed her delight at this surprise by play-bowing and nipping at his sides. Perry's puppy raiser, a blond woman who introduced herself as Andrea, discreetly led her dog to another part of the room.

There were seven or eight other dog-human pairs in the room. Most of the dogs wore blue NEADS capes. Daisy hadn't received hers yet but she, like the others, had a red disc dangling from her collar stamped "Service Dog" on one side, and "NEADS" on the other. The effect was unsettling because it reminded me that all of the dogs were, in effect, on loan and that each person in that room, me included, would eventually have to give up their dog for good.

The class was led by Christy Bassett, the NEADS trainer who works with the inmates at J. J. Moran. With her long, wavy ponytail and a face that has barely outgrown its childhood freckles, Christy looks like she stepped out of the pages of a children's book about nineteenth-century farm life. She's quiet and calm, with a wholesome quality. The last place you'd imagine her is in a roomful of convicts. But that's where she is every Tuesday morning. In prison, the inmate dog handlers and their backups gather for class in the visiting room, a large space that could be mistaken for a cafeteria, filled as it is with rows of tables with attached, molded plastic seats—except the tables are bolted to the floor so they can't be used as projectiles and a correctional officer sits behind a desk on a raised platform overlooking the room. But there's been an effort to brighten the place with framed pictures of bunnies and seascapes, all painted by inmates. And at the front of the room, near two closet-size rooms where inmates meet in private with their attorneys, is a wooden sign incorporating the NEADS logo with the blue shield of the state of Rhode Island. Captain Lefebvre put in a special request for it from the carpentry shop, where an inmate designed and constructed it under the supervision of correctional officers and instructors.

You could tell the dogs recognized Christy from prison. They all wagged their tails and lifted their faces to her when she walked near them. In prison, Christy might open a training session with an interactive discussion on negative and positive reinforcement, and end it by clipping each dog's toenails. In between, she'll work on bonding or teach the inmates a new command. During one class, she had the inmates find a spot on the tile floor and arrange themselves in a circle with their puppies. Christy had the men flip the puppies on their backs and cradle them between their legs. The puppies accepted the treatment; they lay passively, legs splayed, heads turned to the side, while the scarred, tattooed convicts leaned over them, flopping their ears and playing with their paws, all while talking in high voices and affectionate growls. The backup handlers watched enviously. Then, on her signal, Christy had each inmate pass his puppy to the man on his left so the pups would learn to accept handling from others.

Christy keeps tabs on each puppy's progress while they're in prison, so by the time they're ready to return to NEADS for advanced training, she knows their strengths and weaknesses and has a pretty good idea which ones will make it through the rest of the training, and which clients waiting for a service dog she might match them with.

My first lesson in Christy's weekend puppy-raiser class was partly devoted to crate etiquette. Christy had us take turns luring the dogs into a hard plastic crate at the command "Kennel," then exit calmly when we gave them permission to leave. A dog's natural tendency is to fly out of the crate the instant the door opens, but these dogs would be going to disabled people who might easily be knocked off balance, so it's extra important that they learn to leave their crates with grace and care.

Christy reminded us that the dogs should know this from their inmates, but because dogs are not very good at generalizing—that is, applying lessons learned in one context to all areas of their lives—we would have to enforce the rule on weekends.

The first part of the exercise was easy; Daisy rocked the crate in her eagerness to jump in and investigate the smells the other dogs left behind. Christy had me lure Daisy into a down, which I did using a dog treat. But when I opened the door to let her out, Daisy popped to her feet and pushed her head through the crack, impatient to rejoin the other dogs.

Christy instructed me to gently shut the door on her until she backed away. We did this four or five times, with my pressing the door slowly into her muzzle until she'd duck back into a down, blinking up at me, then spring forward again when I'd start to pull open the door. I pictured Keith going through the same exercise in his prison cell. At least he wouldn't have had twenty sets of canine and human eyes on him.

When Daisy finally stopped trying to squeeze out of the

crate and lay passively inside, I opened the door slowly, willing her not to stand up, and when she stayed in position, I said a neutral "Let's go" and beamed with pride when she stepped calmly out the door.

We returned to our spot to watch the other puppies take their turns with the crate. The woman next to me had a blond dog with a wild coat of curls—a labradoodle, I learned later. I started to ask her about the dog, but Daisy, exploiting my straying attention, pounced on the curly-haired puppy. This was pretty much how the rest of the class went: with me trying to engage the other puppy raisers in conversation; Daisy trying to engage the other puppies in play; me and the other puppy raisers untangling our dogs' leashes; the other puppy raisers moving away from us.

At one point just after Daisy pulled me off balance in her eagerness to become best friends with a placid black Lab across the room, I looked around at the other dogs sitting peacefully at their handlers' feet, and realized that Daisy was the worst behaved in the class, which is to say I was the student least in control of my dog. It was humiliating, but a small part of me felt kind of proud of Daisy's fearless socializing. It's what I'd always wished for my children, who, when they were small and I brought them to preschool, would cling to me like baby monkeys until a teacher's aide peeled them off and led them to the blocks or a bucket of crayons. My kids inherited the shy gene from me. As a child, my view of new situations was limited to what I could see from behind my mother's leg. Even Tucker was shy. When we boarded her, the kennel people put her with the small breeds because the larger dogs made her nervous. When we'd pick her up after a trip, we'd find our seventy-pound German shepherd standing stiffly in the play yard, warily eyeing the Chihuahuas and pugs while the big dogs raced around joyfully in a separate fenced-in area. How different our lives would be if we had learned early on to approach new situations with Daisy's friendly optimism.

Before class ended, Christy asked whether I planned to bring Daisy to observe the graduation ceremony for NEADS dogs and their partners the following weekend. I stared at her, exhausted from the one-hour class. "Do you think she's ready for that?" I asked, disbelieving. Christy thought for a moment, then said, "Probably not. But she'll definitely be ready by the spring graduation." That was five months away and frankly, I couldn't imagine the day Daisy would ever be calm enough for me to take her into a public place. I was beginning to think that the only way she was going to make a good service dog was if she never left the house.

6

Watch Me

THERE ARE DOCUMENTED health benefits to living with a dog. Petting a dog lowers your blood pressure; walking a dog tones your muscles and pumps oxygen into your brain; and socializing a dog forces you into a state of mindfulness, which supposedly reduces stress. But *training* a dog—at least for me—created stress.

When you have a dog by your side waiting to respond to your every direction, you have to be present and aware. When that dog is learning to be a service dog, a moment's lapse can sabotage months of training. Being mindful isn't a natural state for me. I don't think it is for most people. Generally we walk around preoccupied, startling back to the present in brief jolts before tumbling back into the well of our own thoughts. Daisy forced me out of my own head—but I didn't come quietly. It's comfortable inside my head. I can have private conversations and indulge in elaborate fantasies that bear no resemblance to my actual life. I can tell people off. I can be witty and charming and well dressed. Who wouldn't want to spend most of her time in a place like that? Someone with a puppy, that's who. Because if you don't give that dog what it wants, meaning a clue as to what *you* want, it will find some other way to amuse itself. And puppies are not known for making good choices. I discovered this a couple of weeks after Christy's training class.

It was our sixth weekend with Daisy, a crisp Sunday in October, the kind of day that reminded Josh that Halloween was approaching and we still didn't have pumpkins for our front step. I was pleased when Aviva asked to come along with us to a local farm. She took the front passenger seat. Since the ride would be short, I let Daisy sit next to Josh, instead of in the back-back, which, judging from the kisses and tail wags, made them both ecstatically happy.

"Hey! Say hello to me, too!" Aviva leaned between the seats to claim some Daisy attention for herself.

"No, me!" Josh threw himself on Daisy like he was protecting her from a hand grenade. Aviva tried to strong-arm Josh away from the dog. We hadn't even left the driveway yet and already they were fighting. I wanted to slam their heads together.

"Stop it or we're staying home!" I yelled. It was frightening, the way a single altercation between the two of them could instantly bring me from relative calm to homicidal rage.

Fortunately, Daisy settled the argument by turning her back on Aviva and Josh to hang her head out the window.

I put the car into gear and blasted past Marty, annoyed that he preferred to stay home to cut the grass with his ancient push mower than pick out pumpkins with his family.

At the farm, Aviva and Josh wandered among the pumpkins, passing over the ones that were misshapen or too small while I let Daisy sniff at the stems. The owner's daughter, Mary Anne, greeted us and we stood on the gravel walkway, chatting in the afternoon sun about her day job as a high school math teacher. I was dimly aware of tension on the leash but ignored it while Mary Anne described the school's plans for covering her upcoming maternity leave. After a few minutes, she looked down at Daisy. "Should she be eating the rocks?" Daisy's nose was in the gravel; crunching sounds came from her mouth.

My first thought was, *Wow! Keith was right when he wrote that in the report! She really does like rocks!* My second was, *Oh, shit. Rocks.*

"Drop it!" I commanded. Daisy knitted her eyebrows in concern and looked up at me. We stared at each other for a moment. Then she dipped her head down and worked the pebble toward the front of her mouth with her tongue. Mary Anne and I watched silently as Daisy thrust her muzzle forward and, with a few more movements of her mouth, spit the pebble out. It arced through the air and landed with a wet *click* onto the gravel.

"It worked!" I wanted to give Mary Anne a high five but restrained myself. We used the "Drop it" command with Tucker, too, but she interpreted it as "Swallow what you have because I'm about to reach in with my fingers and pull it out of your mouth." My respect for both dog and trainer grew. I even allowed myself to feel proud for delivering the command and getting results. I couldn't wait to tell Keith about it when I brought Daisy back.

When we got home, Aviva deposited her pumpkin on the

front step and vanished into her room. Josh carried the others up, collecting grass clippings on his shoes, and was busy ordering them by size while I searched the house for Marty. I found him lying on his back on the living room floor with his eyes closed, trying to nap.

"You're not going to believe this. Daisy had a pebble in her mouth and I told her to drop it and she did."

Marty opened his eyes. "Really?" He sounded impressed. "How did you teach her to do that?"

"It wasn't me; it was Keith."

Marty closed his eyes again. "We should have had Tucker incarcerated."

A few hours later at the prison Keith seemed both pleased and proud when I told him that Daisy had executed a perfect "Drop it" earlier that day.

"How did you teach her that?" I asked.

"I'll show you." Keith stuffed one hand into the waist pouch where he kept kibble and scanned the vestibule where we stood. His gaze fell on a paper clip lying on a rickety wooden table with a Formica top, but he didn't reach for it. Maybe it was too small and flat for Daisy to grab between her teeth, or maybe he thought better of swiping a metal object from, of all places, shift command.

"Well, I'll just tell you." He described how when Daisy grabbed a forbidden object, like a shoe, he'd hold out a treat and tell her to drop it. "When she goes for the cookie, she releases whatever she's got in her mouth and then I praise her. After a bunch of times of hearing 'Drop it' and getting a treat, she'll automatically drop whatever she has in her mouth when she hears the command because she's like, 'Okay. Where's my cookie?'"

"I wish I'd known that with my dog Tucker," I told Keith. "I spent nearly fifteen years pulling stuff out of her mouth. Or trying to, anyway. She'd usually swallow it first."

Keith's expression changed from mild amusement to concern as my remark sunk in. "So what did Daisy have in her mouth?"

"Oh, um. You know, just something she found on the ground." I shoved my hands in my coat pockets and turned to leave. "Okay, so, I'll see you Friday." I didn't want Keith to know I'd been inattentive to a confirmed pebble eater on a gravel walkway. That's as bad as turning your back on a crackhead in the drug evidence room. But apparently Keith found out for himself, because a few days after our conversation, I got an e-mail from Christy: "Daisy has been pooping out rocks in prison. She may have been eating them when you weren't aware . . ."

I guess I didn't catch her soon enough.

———

PRISON OFFERS INMATES a number of rehabilitative services. There are vocational programs, addiction counseling, psychiatric services, educational programs, worship for every known religion—and quite a few lesser known ones (what is Viking paganism, anyway?)—but most everyone agrees that it's the puppy program that engages the inmates most fully. To be successful, dog handlers have to be mentors, parents, caretakers, and teachers to their four-legged charges. Their days, nights, everything revolves around their dogs. So, while the fact that Keith noticed the content of Daisy's (ahem) output surprised and embarrassed me, it also confirmed what I suspected was true: Keith loved this puppy with the same fierce devotion as I, but he was by far the more conscientious parent. I'm the type who leaves her son in the prison parking lot. Keith, I imagined, would have been on the phone with his address book in his lap, making alternative arrangements for his child.

Keith's dedication to Daisy seemed remarkable, all the more so because he was a convict. Years of raising children and my time with Daisy taught me that there's nothing harder than being responsible for another being, human or otherwise. To do it right, you have to put your own needs aside. You have to control your worst impulses. You need to be patient, to project a positive attitude. Those are not the characteristics that come to mind when I think of someone who's landed himself in prison. I wondered whether Keith had a dog as a child. Maybe by pouring himself into Daisy, he was escaping into the past, to a time when he still had a future.

Keith never did have a dog growing up. He was allergic to dogs as a boy. That's what he told Captain Lefebvre when Lefebvre asked him to apply to be a dog handler. But that wasn't the only thing. Keith didn't see the point of training a dog. He already had a job working in the prison gym. And he took advantage of other opportunities the system threw his way: he earned his GED, then took enough college courses to earn his associate's degree through a program offered by the local community college. When we met, he was taking correspondence courses and was halfway toward a bachelor's degree in sociology. Keith also participated in an outreach program in which he and other inmates would tell middle and high school students about life in prison and the consequences of bad choices. He had enough on his plate. Besides, he told Captain Lefebvre, what did he know about dogs?

But Moran was having such success with its puppy program that NEADS wanted to expand. Lefebvre needed more handlers and he recognized a quality in Keith—a focus and an even keel—that he felt would suit Keith to the work and, quite frankly, would probably do Keith some good by showing him what it's like to be responsible for another being. It wasn't as if he'd get that chance otherwise, being locked up in prison. Captain Lefebvre kept after him, calling out encouragement in the prison yard, recruiting the other dog handlers to talk up the program to him. Eventually they wore Keith down. He agreed to an interview and was admitted into the program as a backup handler. He inherited a couple of dogs partway through their training, but both flunked out shortly thereafter: one had that cursed prey drive and the other suffered low confidence. Daisy would be his first puppy from beginning to end.

Given Keith's initial reluctance to be in the program and his less than stellar experiences with the first two dogs, it didn't surprise me when one of the other inmates told me he thought that Keith was one of those dog handlers who are only in it for the single cell and the three-dollars-per-day salary. There are a few like that in the program, but Captain Lefebvre accepts that not all of his dog trainers' motivations will be pure. And what did it matter, anyway, as long as they did their jobs and graduated service dogs in the end?

So this other inmate, Mike, thought Keith was one of those guys . . . until the day Christy led Daisy into the visiting room. Mike was on his fourth dog by then and knew how it felt to get your first puppy—that excitement that just floods you, like you're a little kid again and it's Christmas morning and you just looked under the tree and spotted the shiny new bike that you've been dreaming about, and dangling from the handlebars is a tag with your name on it.

All of the dog handlers were there, waiting for Christy to arrive to teach their class. There was a laid-back energy to the room, with some of the guys sitting together at tables and talking quietly in small groups, dogs at their feet. Others milled about the room, running their dogs through last-minute training exercises, as if warming up before a game.

Finally, the door slid open. Christy stepped through, smiling. At her side, taking in the scene that had just opened up before her, was Daisy, who Keith later recalled as the most precious little puppy he had ever seen. He could barely move, so stunned he was by his good fortune.

Mike watched Keith's face as Christy walked Daisy over to him, saw the hard set of Keith's features soften, and an entirely new expression wash over him, as if something lying dormant in Keith finally woke up. And Mike started to rethink his assumptions about his fellow inmate.

I knew what he meant; I had the same change of heart about Keith after watching him with Daisy.

WHEN KEITH BROUGHT Daisy back to his cell that first day, he began the process of reinventing himself from convict to puppy dad. The crate was already set up from the previous dogs, but Daisy was still so small that Keith had to use a divider to halve the cage so she wouldn't turn the extra space into an en suite bathroom. He had a soft, blue blanket that he planned to use to line the bottom of the crate, but NEADS doesn't allow bedding until the puppies are housebroken and can be trusted not to chew, so for now he left it on his cot. The crate looked uncomfortable, and Keith worried that Daisy wouldn't sleep well. At 10:30 p.m., Keith flicked on his cell light to signal to the officer on duty that Daisy needed a last-chance potty break. In the mild August night air, he watched this miraculous little puppy sniffing in the grass and gently urged her, "Better go now." When she did, he praised her and fed her bits of kibble. Back in the cell, he lured Daisy into the crate, telling her "Kennel," followed by more kibble when she stepped through the door. He watched as she turned around a few times, sniffing the plastic tray, then plopped onto her side with a little sigh. Only then did he lay down himself on his own thin mattress. Throughout the night, he kept waking up to check on his new puppy, and each time he peered through the darkness into the crate, Daisy's eyes were closed and she was breathing deeply. At least one of them slept soundly that night.

For two weeks, Daisy never left Keith's side. He taught her to love her name, calling it out, then rewarding her with kibble when she responded. He'd sit with her on the floor of his cell, rubbing her ears, kneading her toe pads, talking to her, all while feeding her kibble, as if Daisy needed any more reason to learn to love human affection. They worked on proper positioning, so important to service dogs, who must not wander in front of someone unsteady on their feet or step in the way of a moving wheelchair.

While the prison environment seems ill suited to raising a puppy, in many ways and with the right kind of inmate, it's the perfect place to create good dog trainers. Full-time puppy training in my house simply couldn't happen given the demands of work, kids, errands, and chores. I'm sure I'd start off well intentioned, but then one of the kids would need help with homework, then the cartridge in the printer would need to be changed, which would lead to a quick check of my e-mail, which would turn into aimless browsing on the computer. Eventually I'd remember the puppy, but only when it trotted past carrying the last of the jade plant in its mouth. Keith not only had little else vying for his time and attention, he had developed a hyperawareness of his surroundings and learned to stay out of trouble by regulating his own behavior. He had to be present and aware; it was a matter of survival. All that was left for him to be a successful puppy trainer was to learn how to nurture. Fortunately, Daisy made that easy. From the very beginning, Daisy managed to crack Keith's hard coating just enough to reveal the best within him. During those fourteen days together, Keith learned to read Daisy. Whereas I'd look at Daisy and see a dog (the most beautiful, sweetest, most loving dog who walked the earth), Keith would look at her and see into her head. He could tell whether she was nervous or confident by the set of her ears, the angle of her tail, how taut or slack the skin was around her mouth and eyes. As a result, and in the same way that a parent knows subconsciously how to nurture his baby, he'd use that information to give Daisy exactly what she needed at that moment: a murmur of encouragement or a burst of enthusiasm; a firm correction or a session of snuggles and belly rubs.

I had to be more like Keith. After Christy's e-mail to me about Daisy pooping out rocks, I grew a temporary double chin from peering down at her. It's a miracle I didn't trip over a curb and break my neck. I was afraid if I turned away, she'd suck in a pound or two of gravel while I wasn't paying attention, and return to Keith like a living Beanie Baby. My family's nerves were forever being rattled by my sudden, sharp "Eh-ehs!" whenever I caught Daisy about to misbehave.

As the weeks passed and Daisy lengthened and grew taller, she became more adept at the commands we practiced together. And I was training my own mind not to wander but to focus on Daisy. Keith would track each command Daisy had mastered by checking them off on the weekend report. One of my favorites was "My lap." I'd sit on the couch or a kitchen chair, give her the command, and she'd put her front paws up on my lap while I leaned in to kiss her face, slip her a reward, then tell her "Off," and she would spring back so all four feet were on the ground. People who use wheelchairs or have limited mobility use the command to gain easy access to their service dogs. "My lap" is useful for checking your dog's ears or brushing his teeth. But I suspect people use it just as often to coax a snuggle and a kiss from their dogs.

If Daisy were my dog, I'd skip the "Off" part of "My lap" and let her stay there as long as she wanted.

Working together deepened our connection, as if with every request Daisy answered, our souls touched. And always, I was conscious of Keith's influence; she absorbed the best he had to give and radiated it back out to everyone around her.

Through her, I was getting to know him, slowly and in degrees—and with each passing weekend and every exchange we had about Daisy, it was harder to remember what had made him seem so scary to me on that first day. Daisy was so firmly embedded in mine and Keith's hearts that it was as if each Friday, he entrusted me with a piece of his soul and on Sunday, I returned it with a piece of mine. He had poured so much of himself into Daisy that it was impossible for me to look at her without feeling his presence. When Daisy poked my leg with her nose to remind me she was still there, I'd imagine her doing the same with the other person in her life. When I brought Daisy outside and hollered "Free time!" and stood watching while she tucked her tail and barreled around the yard, I'd wonder whether Keith did the same in the puppy play yard—and whether he put himself in her body and soared along with her, as I did. We were each other's Brigadoon, existing only for a thin slice of time in a single spot on the planet each week.

There were a few times when Keith sent his backup handler to deliver Daisy on Friday night or pick her up Sunday evening. I'd leave prison feeling cheated, as if the curtain had just opened on a Broadway play to reveal the understudy in the lead role. And to be honest, I was also miffed at Keith. If I were him, stuck in prison with only two opportunities each week to speak to his dog's other parent, I'd do everything in my power to get down to shift command. Missing his appointment meant the door slammed and I'd have to hold in all of my questions and news about Daisy until the next time.

Worse than not seeing Keith, though, was missing a weekend with Daisy. There were a couple of times during our first months together when, after double-checking the treat supply and setting out Daisy's food and water dishes for the weekend, I'd get an e-mail from Christy that Daisy wouldn't be going out—that she had been diagnosed with parasites and therefore couldn't leave the prison. I'd feel like a small child whose most treasured possession had been snatched away. Our weekend pattern had etched itself so deeply into my subconscious that when she remained in the prison, I would wake up Saturday morning, listen for Daisy stirring, and be swept away by disappointment when I rose on one elbow and saw her empty crate. To make it worse, I'd have my own kids' disappointment to deal with, Josh's especially. Usually Marty and I would try to make it up to them by going out to a restaurant, something we ordinarily couldn't do on weekends since Daisy came into our lives.

Still, Daisy and I were together for most weekends in those early months, and one of the great pleasures was filling out her weekend report, because it allowed me to relive our experiences together: the visits to parks, the car rides, the games of fetch. I felt like a divorced parent who makes up for not being there every day by swooping in on weekends and whisking the kids off to Six Flags and letting them stay up past midnight, watching movies and eating Twizzlers. I was the fun parent. Keith was the one who made her eat her vegetables and do her homework. I think that got to him at times, particularly when Daisy, tired out from her weekend, would plod back to him in shift command as if she would just as soon not be there. "What's the matter, girl? You don't love me anymore? You want to stay with Sharron?" He'd try to make a joke of it, but the twinge in his voice betrayed real hurt. I'd reassure him that Daisy had a busy day and would be fine in the morning after she had a good night's sleep. And truthfully, most Sundays Daisy was as excited to see Keith after the weekend as she was to be with me on Fridays. In the prison parking lot I'd dawdle at the car, taking too long to hook the leash to her collar, stroking her ears and kissing the top of her head while she'd practically prance with joy at the prospect of being with Keith again.

Back in shift command, he would break into a shy grin when he'd spot us. I'd have Daisy sit and meet my gaze with the "Watch me" command while Keith stood with his weight evenly distributed and his hands clasped behind his back, a posture I figured he learned during head counts. Like this, he reminded me of a small boy, waiting patiently for a wonderful treat that he'd been promised. I don't know why, maybe it was the way his toes pointed slightly inward and the hem of his pants bunched up in folds over his work boots, or maybe it was the way his affection for Daisy softened his expression, and seemed to erase the lines around his eyes and mouth.

Then I'd walk Daisy over and hand Keith the leash and the yellow folder with the weekend paperwork. He would bend to ruffle the fur around her ears before coaxing her into position beside his right leg. I always expected him to plant a kiss on top of Daisy's head, like Lance used to do with Jones. But then again, Keith was more reserved. While Daisy settled back against his side, I'd return to my spot at the threshold of the hallway and the vestibule and recount the weekend, trying to paint a vivid enough picture that he could put himself into the scene with us. And he'd stand transfixed, hanging on to every word, stopping me every now and then to ask questions, until a movement in the round security mirror above my head would catch his eye. Then he'd wait for me to pause for breath and he'd turn to leave with a "See you Friday?" The officers would get agitated when we talked too long. When Keith and Daisy walked away, her tail would be high and swaying slightly and they would appear locked in conversation, heads tilted toward each other. I imagined Keith was asking Daisy about her weekend.

ONE SUNDAY IN late fall, my friend Deb and I took Daisy and Deb's golden retriever for a walk at a wooded conservation area about a mile from my house. Daisy and Tanner were overjoyed to see each other, so much so that Deb and I had difficulty carrying on a conversation while they tugged at their leashes. We followed the trail down a short hill. At the bottom I led Daisy through a thicket of bare blueberry bushes to avoid a mud puddle.

"I don't want to bring her back to prison all muddy. I think her prisoner . . . dog handler guy bathes her before she goes out with me." I still didn't know how to refer to Keith.

Later, Keith would confirm that for me. He'd dampen a towel, squirt it with a small amount of shampoo, and rub it through Daisy's fur to remove any dirt she'd accumulated during the week. Then he'd rinse her with the same towel and brush her coat. Her cape, collar, and leash he would soak in the tiny stainless-steel sink in his cell, then buckle them through the chain-link fence outside to dry. On rainy or snowy days, Keith would switch on the small plastic fan in his cell and hang the wet equipment in front of it. He also brushed her teeth three times a week. It was a point of pride that he send his dog out clean and pretty for her weekends away.

"What's he like? Do you see him?" Deb asked.

"Just for a few minutes on Friday and Sunday nights." I wasn't sure how to explain what he was like. Since the beginning, I'd been trying to fit together scraps of information to form a more complete picture of Keith.

"He seems nice enough," I began. "You know, for a criminal." We both laughed at that. "I don't know. He's probably in his early thirties. I think he likes sports." Sometimes when I returned Daisy he'd be wearing sweats and bouncing slightly in his white prison-issued sneakers like he couldn't wait to get back to the basketball court. "Um, what else? It's so hard to say because I don't know anything about him, only what I can pick up during those few minutes when we talk, and even then we're not allowed to say anything not related to Daisy. He takes exceptional care of her, that's for sure."

"Yeah, I can see that." Deb was watching Daisy sniff at a fallen tree. "Do you know whether he has family nearby?"

I shook my head. "You know, I don't think he does." Once Keith told me about being allowed to bring Daisy into the visiting room so he could see how she reacted to children. He laughed softly when he described Daisy with the kids, how she ran right up to them wanting to play, and how gentle she was with the little ones. It was clear this was an event for both of them; if Keith had people in his life who came to see him, bringing Daisy into the visiting room would be routine.

We walked on, the only sound the leaves and sticks crunching beneath our feet. The forest spread before us in every direction. We kept to the path, but there was nothing to stop us from wandering through the trees if we wanted. A heaviness settled over me as I thought about Keith in prison. I bet he was the kind of kid who loved the woods, like Josh. Despite the fact that Keith's hair was receding a little above the temples, there was something adolescent about him, as though he was pulled off the track to adulthood before he was grown, and there remained a piece of him frozen in boyhood. Sometimes his word choice was juvenile. More than once he told me Daisy acted "scary" when he meant skittish, as in "Daisy was a little scary when I put the Gentle Leader on her." Other times he would surprise me by being well spoken, talking about reward theory and persistence. He never misspelled a word on his weekend paperwork.

My voice broke our silence. "I think he's spent a lot of time in the system, probably he's been in and out a lot over the years. He has a sort of hardness to his features, like he's been living around convicts for a long time." This came close to being confirmed for me one Friday. I hadn't quite rounded the corner into shift command when I heard Keith talking with an officer. He was reintroducing himself, reminding the officer that they first met in the early 1990s, when Keith was in "juvie." That meant either he'd been in prison an awfully long time, or this was at least the second time he'd been incarcerated.

"Do you know why he's in prison?" Deb asked.

"No, but my guess is that he's one of those punks who kept getting caught for petty crimes like breaking and entering." I described the arraignments I used to sit through when I covered court. Kids, eighteen or twenty years old, would be facing a breaking and entering charge, and already have a record bursting with juvenile offenses. The judge would sentence them to six months or a year. They'd serve their time, be back on the street, and end up in court again for something else. After a few rounds of this, the judge would get tired of seeing their faces and give them a longer sentence. Keith, I theorized, was one of those kids who just couldn't stay out of trouble.

"He probably started out shoplifting candy bars and worked his way up to stealing cars."

"Well, he couldn't be that bad if they trust him with a puppy, right?" I could tell Deb was trying to figure out how to feel about him. Like me.

"Right," I said. "He can't be that bad."

7

Let's Get Dressed

AS LABS GO, Daisy is on the sensitive side, acutely aware of what's happening around her and keenly attuned to the humans in her life. These are good qualities for a service dog, but they cause her to be wary of new sensations—the weight of the woven nylon puppy-in-training cape on her back, for instance. Keith had been working on desensitizing her to the cape for weeks before she was ready to go out for the weekend wearing it. One Friday when Daisy and I had been together for more than two months, I leaned against the cinder-block wall in the vestibule of shift command, waiting for Keith to show up with Daisy. The space doubled as a sort of way station, with a water fountain attached to one wall and a microwave and a four-slice toaster atop a high table. I was reading the wrapper on a loaf of store-brand white bread someone had left near the toaster when I caught sight of Keith and Daisy through the narrow barred window, making their way across the prison yard. A patch of blue popped through the pair's usual palette of beige and tan. I couldn't believe it; Daisy was wearing the cape! My smile was so wide I could feel it pulling at my face when Daisy stepped through the door into shift command, sporting the spiffy vest with its NEADS patch. She was no longer simply an adorable yellow Lab puppy; she was adorable *and* professional.

Keith grinned when he saw my expression. "You like it? She's official now." He looked down at Daisy, whose obliviousness to her appearance made her seem that much more endearing.

"She looks good in blue!" I said.

"Yep. She does." Keith laughed politely, then described Daisy's gradual introduction to the cape. "It took a while to get her to this point where she wouldn't back away when I tried to put it on her. At first I'd put it on her for a few minutes, give her a few treats, then take it off. Then we'd do it for longer periods of time. This past week she wore it everywhere, out in the yard, to chow. So she should be fine with you." We both gazed proudly at Daisy sitting calmly by his side in her NEADS cape.

Daisy in her blue training cape was what I had been envisioning since that day in the supermarket when we met the man with the NEADS puppy. I felt like I'd graduated to the next step, where I could bring Daisy into public places without having to explain why. I was eager to get started on this stage of my weekend puppy-raising work, to expose Daisy to life's full array of experiences and distractions. And I suspected that Keith was eager to have his training tested in the real world. I never spoke with him about it, but if I were he, working under controlled conditions, I'd want to know how well my "Heel" held up in a shopping mall, for instance.

Unfortunately, he had me as Daisy's puppy raiser. The cape may have transformed Daisy into an official service dog trainee, but it didn't solve the problem of her (my) dismal leash-walking skills. I just didn't have the nerve to bring her into a restaurant or a supermarket. Daisy was obedient in all other ways, but I couldn't shake the vision of me waterskiing behind her en route to the meat counter. So instead I focused on "safe" field trips, like the pet store, where dogs are allowed, and quick trips to the drugstore or Home Depot, with its pet-friendly concrete floors. Once I mustered the nerve to bring Daisy into a fabric store because we needed material for one of Aviva's projects. I poked my head in the door first and asked the cashier permission, explaining that Daisy was in training to be a service dog. "Yes, service dogs are okay," she said with a cold authority. Even then, I kept expecting alarms to go off and a big net to drop down from the ceiling, that's how strange it felt to wander the aisles with a dog.

On Sunday mornings I'd drop Josh off at religious school and walk Daisy around the building. With Daisy's cape, I felt bolder, and began taking her inside the school. We started slowly. First, we'd stand in the vestibule like doormen, greeting people as they passed through. Eventually we ventured inside, where I let Daisy explore the lobby. It wasn't long before she developed a devout following among the kids (and most of the adults). At dismissal, a knot of children would form in the hallway around Daisy, growing larger as each class was let out. Daisy would flip onto her back while small hands stroked every square inch of her body. Sometimes she'd wash the midmorning snack off the preschoolers' faces. I'd hold the leash, watching for signs that things were getting out of control (or *more* out of control) while Josh stood to the side swinging his book bag, quietly proud to be the one who got to go home with this oh-so-desirable dog.

———————

I DID HAVE a chance to test-drive Daisy's new cape in a shopping mall, but within the safety of a training class. Kerry Lemerise left NEADS to take a position at Guiding Eyes for the Blind. Her replacement was longtime NEADS trainer Dave Hessel.

Dave scheduled his first puppy-raiser training with us on a Monday evening at a three-story shopping mall in downtown Providence. Daisy was diagnosed with another case of parasites the week before and we were forced to endure another weekend without her while she went through her course of medication. Daisy was always with me—even when she wasn't—running in my subconscious like a software program that I'd call up to power my daydreams. So actually getting to spend time with Daisy on a Monday night, particularly after missing a weekend together, was a treat and I was excited beyond reason to bring her to a mall. Around four o'clock, I logged off my work computer and called Marty to remind him I'd be out and that he should leave the newsroom in time to make dinner for the kids. "So if you see a bank robbery in progress on your way out the door, ignore it, okay?"

He made no promises. Asking Marty to ignore a breaking news story or to be on time for anything was like asking Daisy to stop sniffing the ground. In fact, because of his chronic lateness, we almost never met. I showed up (on time) for my job interview with him and stood in the rain outside the locked bureau office for close to half an hour, debating whether to wait or just go back to Maine, where I was living at the time. I was still arguing with myself when another reporter showed up for work and let me in. Marty strolled in later with that day's newspaper tucked under his arm, mumbling something about being up all night covering a breaking story.

Marty was late for Aviva's birth, too. He didn't miss it, but he was wrapping up at work and running errands while I was in the delivery room trying not to bite through my index finger during contractions. Without him there to coach me through the breathing exercises, I gasped and held my breath and thought how sad it was that this baby would be born to parents who were about to divorce. Then a nurse mentioned the possibility of an epidural. By the time Marty strolled into the delivery room, I was happily numb and only a tiny bit annoyed. "I stopped on the way because I thought you might like some reading material," he said, waving a supermarket tabloid with a photo of an exhausted woman lying in a bed surrounded by a field of newborns. The headline screamed, "MOM GIVES BIRTH TO 14 BABIES AT ONCE."

So, yeah. Before I left for the puppy-training class, I made sure the kids knew there was a pizza in the freezer. As often as I wanted to stomp on the brakes to slow their accelerating passage through childhood, it was times like this when I had something to look foward to that I was thankful that Aviva and Josh were becoming self-sufficient. A new adventure awaited, one that didn't involve my family or my work, and it consoled me that there may be life beyond raising kids, after all. And, though I wasn't ready to admit it, I was beginning to suspect that my job wouldn't be around forever, either.

1

Aviva and Josh pose with Daisy, seven months, for the Luttrell's annual holiday card.

Sharron, Josh, and Daisy take a break during a trip to Faneuil Hall Marketplace, Boston.

2

3

Aviva and fourteen-week-old Daisy get to know each other on Daisy's first weekend furlough from prison.

4

Daisy holds
Sharron's glove
before going out
into the cold for a walk.

Daisy enjoys the sunshine.

5

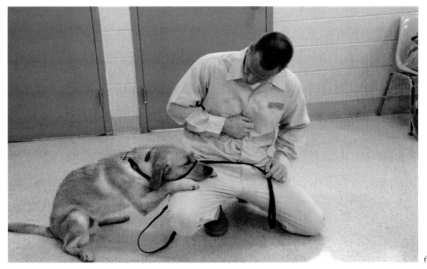

6

Daisy says her prayers with some help from her inmate trainer, Keith.

7

7

8

A NEADS puppy meets his trainer for the first time.

NEADS Puppy Trainer Cindy Lopez smiles while Captain Nelson Lefebvre receives a kiss from his namesake, Nellie, a puppy-in-training at the J. J. Moran Medium Security Facility in Cranston, Rhode Island.

Inmates at J. J. Moran Medium Correctional facility walk through the prison yard with NEADS trainer Jen Banks.

NEADS trainer Christy Bassett (standing) introduces a client to the dog trainers at J. J. Moran Medium Correctional facility.

12

A puppy in training mails a letter for the inmate who is training her.

13

A NEADS client and her new dog practice working together.

Daisy takes a break from apple picking.

14

Daisy, one year old, takes her first train ride.

16

17

18

19

20

Ty Billitti Photography

Daisy at ten months,
looking rather official in
her puppy-in-training vest.

A pack of NEADS dogs visit the Milford (Mass.) Senior Center. Daisy is the one in front.

David, nine, hugs Daisy shortly after they were matched.

ON THE WAY to pick up Daisy from prison I got caught up in the radio reports about the economic meltdown. The financial markets had crashed a few weeks earlier and now the news was dominated by explanations of default credit swaps and subprime loans. Economic analysts were predicting the recession would deepen. Marty and I had managed to hang on to our jobs through other recessions, but I had a bad feeling about this one. I worked for a corporate benefits provider, writing articles and producing audio recordings meant to help employees balance their personal lives with their careers. We had been on a tear since the month before, creating tip sheets and podcasts filled with advice for people facing job loss and home foreclosures. I tried not to dwell on what it meant that many of the corporate clients my coworkers and I depended on for our own livelihoods were reeling and on the edge of collapse. Yet how could I not? As hard as Marty worked, his salary wasn't enough to cover the household bills and the kids' activities. Without my income, we wouldn't be able to keep up. Adding to my concern was that we had just made a deposit for Aviva to travel to Costa Rica that summer on a service-learning trip. Marty and I wanted her to see some of the world outside her bedroom in a place where she could use Spanish, a language both she and Josh had been learning in a school immersion program since kindergarten. We also wanted her to know what it felt like to work hard to make someone else's life a little better. But now, listening to analysts predicting a global financial crisis, I was uncomfortably aware of how close we were to being the ones forced to accept help rather than give it.

My headlights swept over a line of parked cars as I turned into the prison and searched for a space in the lot. The building, bathed in an orange glow from the streetlights, looked almost tranquil. The radio went silent as I cut the engine. The latest economic indicators didn't mean anything to Daisy. Or to Keith, either, from where he sat.

———

IT FELT A little strange to see Keith on a Monday evening, as if I was intruding on his personal life, like when you realize the person at the next table ordering the salmon is your dentist. It must have felt even weirder for Daisy, who by this point had probably internalized the pattern of my visits and been surprised to find her weekday evening routine of light training with Keith interrupted by a walk to shift command and me, her weekend mom, waiting inside.

As usual, Keith had Daisy sit at his side. He bent down toward her. "Are you ready for school?" She opened her mouth and let her tongue hang out in a goofy smile and with that, the last scrap of worry about Marty getting home late, and the recession and money fluttered out of my consciousness. Keith walked her toward me and handed me the leash. "Do you need any treats?" He reached for the nylon pouch around his waist. I patted my pocket and told him I was all set. "We should be back around eight," I told him, feeling very much like the noncustodial parent after an amicable divorce.

Back in the car, I plugged the address of the mall into the GPS Marty had given to me for my birthday. Aviva and I had played with all of the voices before settling on an Australian-accented male. I named him Ian, and because we'd known each other for only a few weeks, I didn't quite trust him. So while I was willing to follow his voice prompts to the highway, I needed proof that the first right off the highway was indeed Francis Street, as he insisted. Problem was, I couldn't read the street sign until I was passing it. I grew flustered and Ian didn't help matters when he told me with barely contained annoyance that he was "recalculating." I missed the next three turns trying to read the street signs and Ian kept recalculating until eventually I ended up on a street that ran parallel to the mall. I spotted a metered parking space, threw the car into reverse, and backed into it at the precise moment the driver behind me pulled into it. He leaned on his horn and I slammed on my brakes, bathing Daisy's calm silhouette in red from the reflected glare of my brake lights.

Swearing, I shifted back into first gear and headed for the parking garage. I was fifteen minutes late when I hustled inside with Daisy. There was an escalator that led straight to the food court where the class was meeting, but NEADS has a rule against bringing service dogs on escalators. Too many things can go wrong; their toenails could get caught, they might get spooked and try to jump off. We trotted past the escalator for what felt like ten city blocks until we found a glass elevator. We took that to the upper level, where we doubled back in the direction we'd come from.

I was sweating by the time we found the class at the edge of the food court. It was easy to spot: A small group of men and women had pushed a couple of tables together near a kiosk selling cheap watches. Poking out from between chair legs were tails and paws and the occasional snout sniffing in the direction of a man bearing a tray with samples of General Tso's chicken.

I recognized Bonnie and dragged a chair over from a nearby table to sit across from her. A young guy with scruffy facial hair stopped talking and looked up at me. When I apologized for being late, he waved his hand dismissively, telling me they had just started and I didn't miss anything. It was Dave. I'd soon learn that he was reliably late to every single class, a quality that endeared him to me because it reminded me of my husband and, quite frankly, took the pressure off me to be punctual—which doesn't come naturally to me, either.

Dave was polling the group about problems they were having with their puppies. I positioned Daisy under the table and coaxed her into a down. The person sitting to my left, a perfumed young woman in a dress and heels who later introduced herself as Colleen, turned to me and whispered, "She's so cute, I just have to pet her. Sorry!" and leaned over to cup Daisy's face in her hands. Daisy squirmed and wiggled under her touch, inching her nose toward Colleen's dog, a black Lab named Lady. The two puppies rolled onto their backs and sides, nipping and pawing at each other while Colleen and I attempted to contain the situation. We ducked under the table and slid our dogs by the collars in opposite directions while Dave spoke with an older couple about their yellow Lab's high energy level. I had come heavily armed with treats, and I popped these in Daisy's mouth to regain her attention, while trying simultaneously to listen to Dave's advice. Out of the corner of my eye I noticed Daisy squirming toward Bonnie's smooth-coated collie. Before I could react, Bonnie planted her sneakered foot firmly along Daisy's side and nudged her back into place. I was both impressed and a little bit stung, as if she'd disciplined my child. I didn't dare look at Bonnie for fear she'd be looking back disapprovingly. A group of teenagers walked by with trays, trailing the scent of French fries and burgers. Daisy stopped biting at the spot on her side where Bonnie's foot had been to lift her snout in their direction. I was eyeing her warily when Dave stood up and clapped his hands together. "Okay. Let's see these dogs walk through the mall. Is everybody empty?" Dave noticed my confusion because he clarified, "Did the dogs go to the bathroom before you brought them inside?" I had no idea when Daisy last went and Dave must have sensed it, because he suggested we walk across the mall to one of the exits and practice going through doors while taking the dogs outside to relieve themselves.

Heads turned as we got up from the table, got our dogs into position, and set out across the mall. I kept Daisy Velcroed to my side by feeding her a steady stream of dog biscuit pieces. The walkway was carpeted. Just how humiliating would it be if Daisy squatted on it with all of these people watching? I quickened my pace, slowing only to lessen the distance between me and the rest of the group whenever it got too wide. A guy wearing a white ball cap and gold chains flattened himself to the railing when we passed by and said to no one in particular, "Whoa! Show dogs!"

Dave had us gather in front of the mall entrance and gave us some pointers on negotiating doorways with a dog. I never thought much about doors until Daisy came into my life. Doors are everywhere. Some you pull, some you push. There are automatic doors that swing open and ones that slide open. There are revolving doors. When you're training a service dog, you have to anticipate each door's heft and the direction in which it will swing because if it whacks the puppy on the way through or catches her tail, you're going to end up with a dog who doesn't want to go through doorways. And that's a big enough problem to flunk a dog.

Dave asked us to go through the heavy glass doors, one by one, while he watched. When it was my turn, I faced the door with Daisy sitting by my side. "Move her to your other side so she's less likely to get hit," he told me. I guided Daisy to my left so my body was between her and the door. I walked Daisy through stiffly, aware that Dave was watching. He gave me a thumbs-up and motioned for us to continue through the second set of doors that led outside. I opened the door to a chirping chorus of "Better go now"s from the other puppy raisers, who were following their dogs through mulched border gardens. Daisy and I joined them, but nobody was having much luck, what with the cigarette butts and gum wrappers and other interesting treasures in the bushes. We were all about to give up when Tasha, the high-energy Lab, squatted on the pavement. The rest of us looked on enviously.

We filtered back into the mall to rejoin Dave. He had noticed the glass elevator on the trip over from the food court and wanted to see how the dogs reacted to it.

As with the doors, we took turns riding on the elevator, two at a time, while the rest of us chatted. I found myself next to a young, tall guy whose yellow Lab was about the same age as Daisy but with a heftier build. With his plaid flannel shirt and wire-framed glasses, he looked like a mild, thoughtful version of a Seattle grunge rocker. I introduced myself and he told me his name, Justin. "And this is Nellie," he said, looking down at the floor where Daisy and Nellie had wasted no time starting a wrestling match and were using their teeth to pull at the fur on each other's faces. I recognized the name right away. During our first telephone conversation, Nelson Lefebvre had confessed shyly that NEADS named a puppy in his honor. "You're famous!" I said to Nellie, kneeling down to swipe Daisy away with my forearm. Daisy tried to leap over my arm to get back to her new friend while Justin told me that his wife wanted a puppy but they weren't sure they could manage it full-time. The puppy program seemed a good way to get a feel for what it would be like before taking the plunge with their own dog.

The elevator returned. Colleen and Bonnie stepped out with their puppies; Justin and I walked in with ours, joining Dave. Though truth be told, I didn't see the point in bringing Daisy, since she'd already ridden the elevator up to the second floor without a problem. The doors closed and the floor below loomed larger as the elevator descended. Daisy was quiet and still as I expected. "Treat her. She's nervous." I looked at Dave, who was watching Daisy stare at the floor. She looked fine to me, but I slipped her a piece of biscuit. She accepted it without bothering to turn and give me her full attention.

"What are you using for bait?" I showed Dave the dog biscuit pieces and he handed me a hunk of something brown. "Freeze-dried liver. She'll love it." I broke off a small piece but Daisy had already turned and was sitting at my feet, looking from me to the liver in my hand. I popped a piece into her mouth. "Good. Keep feeding it to her. You want to make her forget about the elevator," Dave said. I broke off another piece, and another, all the way down to the first floor and up to the third.

Freeze-dried liver, along with anything else particularly stinky, is what's called a high-value treat. These work on dogs like methadone on a junkie. High-value treats dissolve all worries and distractions—glass elevators, tempting kitty cats—so the only thing the dog cares about is getting his next fix.

I was beginning to understand that despite all those years with Tucker, I knew very little about dogs. I certainly never classified treats according to their tastiness. A biscuit was as good as a hunk of steak to me because to my inexperienced eye, Tucker would eat both with the same gusto. Had I looked closely, as I was learning to do with Daisy, I would have noticed that one results in a much stronger positive change in behavior and can be deployed for the most challenging situations.

On the way back to the prison to drop off Daisy that night, I thought about what Dave saw in the elevator that I had missed. Clearly I still had a lot to learn because when I had asked him about it, Dave described the way Daisy's ears were set slightly back. But to me, a Lab's ears always look the same—floppy. Tucker was much easier to read. Her oversized ears sprang from the top of her head like twin signal flags, twitching and rotating with her every mood. When a dog strayed into our yard, she'd flatten them to the sides like airplane wings. When she heard the grumblings of thunder in the distance, she folded them behind her and dropped her body to the ground. Tucker pretty much showed her feelings on her face. A Lab just looks like a Lab to me, so unless Daisy trembles or runs away with her tail tucked between her legs, I'm going to assume she's feeling pretty good, no matter what's happening at the moment. I didn't think I'd ever be able to catch the subtle clues into Daisy's state of mind.

———————

I SEARCHED THE rearview mirror for Daisy, but she was sleeping in the back of the car and out of sight. In my mind, she was the only dog in the class that evening. The others were just background scenery. It was unimaginable to me that any of the other puppy raisers were as crazy about their dogs as I was about Daisy.

Ian got me lost only twice on the way back to the prison, but still, I was the last of the puppy raisers to return, and it seemed more quiet than usual in shift command. Through the barred window, yellow lights cast an eerie glow over the prison yard and glinted weirdly off the metal chain-link fences. The prison blocks rose in the distance like flat mountains on an alien landscape. Keith came into view, his lithe figure moving steadily toward the door. His ID badge swung from his shirt pocket. It was so tantalizing. His last name was right there. Four or five years ago I would have been able to make out the tiny letters and looked up his crime. Now I can't read the headline of a newspaper without magnifiers. Even if I were to show up in shift command with my reading glasses, I'd have to lean toward Keith's chest and step forward and back until I located the precise distance where the letters came into focus. If I worried now about acting suspiciously in front of the officers, imagine what they'd think then. Not to mention what Keith would think, or how he'd feel. I'm pretty sure he'd catch on to what I was up to. I thought about asking Captain Lefebvre, but I was afraid to. While the NEADS manual doesn't explicitly forbid asking about the dog handlers' sentences, there's supposed to be just one topic of discussion between inmates and puppy raisers, and that's the dog. Plus, Captain Lefebvre projected authority so thoroughly that when he leveled a silent gaze at me, I'd turn all shifty-eyed and want to unzip the shallow pockets on Daisy's cape to prove I'm not using her as a drug mule. There was no way I'd risk that look by asking him for Keith's last name.

The day that Kerry came to my house to help with Jones, I took advantage of a lull in conversation to ask her why Lance was incarcerated. She told me she didn't ask why the inmates were there. "I don't want to know what they did. We're both better off that way," she said.

If only I had her self-control.

8

Stay

ON DECEMBER 27, nearly four months into my year with her, Daisy surprised me with a late Christmas present. We were going through our morning prewalk preparations: I slipped her vest over her head and reached under her belly to snap the buckle shut, sneaking a kiss onto the top of her head before reaching for my parka and hat. Daisy took up her position by the door and watched. My mittens were in the hall closet. I had dug one out of the wicker basket and was starting to pull it on when, realizing I still needed those fingers, I dropped it to the floor. I shrugged on my parka and was working the zipper into its notch when I felt a pressure against my thigh. Daisy had the mitten in her mouth and was pressing it into my leg. Could this be intentional? I took the mitten from her, said "Thank you," and let it drop back to the floor. Daisy grabbed it gently by the thumb and lifted her face toward me.

I think the only reason she didn't say "I believe this is yours?" was because her mouth was full.

I traded the mitten for a jackpot of treats, popping one piece of biscuit after another into her mouth while gushing praise. Marty and Aviva were still asleep, but Josh was in the living room, watching cartoons. Daisy raced me in. "Josh! Look what she can do!" I dropped the mitten on the floor. Daisy looked at it, then back at me. "Get it," I urged.

She did.

"Oh my gosh! Do it again!" Josh jumped off the couch. I dropped my mitten again and this time she didn't hesitate; she plucked it off the floor and held it out for me. Josh and I descended on Daisy with hugs and kisses. "Let's see if she can pick up something else," Josh suggested. I scanned the room, skipping over the collection of TV remotes, a stack of newspapers, a stray marker. My gaze settled on the "airport"—a queue of small metal airplanes on the floor by the fireplace, waiting for takeoff.

When Josh was about eighteen months old, I was coming down the stairs with a basket of dirty laundry when something unusual caught my eye and I stopped short. Lined up in a neat row against the bottom step was every small, wheeled toy that we owned. It was as if a tiny parking lot attendant had snuck into the house and offered half-price rates on game day. There were minivans and hot rods, an oil truck, a plastic scooter, and a chunky red car with Ernie at the wheel. I was trying to process the scene when Josh toddled into view, clutching a yellow bulldozer. He dropped to his knees and, furrowing his brow in concentration, guided it into place precisely alongside the others. Until that day, Josh played with his cars by tasting their wheels and throwing them across the room. Now, suddenly he was *parking* them. Overnight he went from being a baby to a full-fledged human being capable of planning and execution.

We've been sidestepping toy parking lots ever since, along with school-bus depots, towns, and, lately, airports. I grabbed a red plastic bin and showed it to Daisy. "Let's see if she can clean up the airport." I pointed at one tiny metal airplane after another until Daisy had picked up each one and deposited it into the container.

After that, every so often while washing the dishes or working on the computer, I'd feel a sharp, steady pressure in my thigh, look down, and find Daisy gazing up at me, a miniature airplane in her mouth.

Things changed between Daisy and me after that morning. Prior to that, I was the one doing things for her: feeding, walking, petting. She gave me affection and companionship in return, but still, the relationship tilted to one side. Now she was *reciprocating*, giving back literally and figuratively. Just as the outlines of Josh had sharpened for me on the morning he transformed from drooling baby boy to thinking child, Daisy and I had now shifted into a sort of mental alignment. And while I didn't think it was possible, I was falling even more deeply in love with her.

Our attachment grew stronger over the weeks and months, and my family and I developed little rituals that reinforced our bond with her. In the morning, when Daisy heard the hum of my hair dryer, she'd sit up from the bath mat and look at me, legs braced against the floor. I'd press the button that turned off the dryer's heat, ask "Are you ready?" and ruffle the fur on her face with the stream of cool air while she squinted her eyes shut. Keith told me that Daisy would do the same with the small plastic fan he had in his cell. He kept it on high speed most of the time to muffle the noise in the prison block. For Daisy, he'd set it on the floor and she would lie in front of it with her eyes closed, perhaps dreaming that she was in a car with her head out the window and Keith at the wheel.

Josh taught Daisy to play hide-and-seek. He'd grab a handful of biscuits and ask Daisy to sit and stay. She'd remain rooted to her spot, ears quivering to the sounds of Josh jogging through the house in search of a hiding place. Finally Josh would yell, "Okay!" and Daisy would take off, tearing through the house, tail straight out, searching from room to room until she found Josh standing in a closet with the door cracked open, or crouched behind the couch, or flattened against a wall. They'd greet each other as though they'd been separated for a lifetime and repeat the game over and over again until all the biscuit pieces in Josh's hand were gone. While Josh taught Daisy human games, Marty played with Daisy on her terms. Every once in a while he'd spontaneously drop to all fours and play-bow to Daisy. Daisy would return the gesture, her tail whipping back and forth, and Marty would respond by rearing up and slapping his hands on the floor. Daisy would do the same, leaping from side to side, and Marty would bulldoze forward to butt heads. The sessions usually culminated in a wrestling match and end with Daisy on her side, panting through a wide, tongue-dangling smile.

Even Aviva, with her prickly teenage-girl attitude, was enamored of Daisy. Every now and then, Aviva would sit cross-legged on the floor so she could pull Daisy onto her lap. Daisy would lie there on her back, eyes closed, and relax into the pose, her forelegs drifting to either side while Aviva stretched Daisy's fur like so much extra fabric to see whether Daisy had made any progress in filling it out. Often, I would drop to the floor beside her, as we did on Daisy's first day with us, to take advantage of the opportunity to spend a moment with my daughter on the neutral ground Daisy offered.

At Christmastime, I even included Daisy in our annual holiday card, posing her between Aviva and Josh for the picture and signing her name with a tiny daisy dotting the *i*. If my thoughts strayed to the next Christmas season, when she wouldn't be in the photograph, I swept them aside. They didn't fit my preferred version of reality.

However, there were communication challenges that forced me to acknowledge that Daisy wasn't my dog—that I was in fact coparenting a puppy with an incarcerated man with whom I had only a few minutes of rushed conversation each week. The worst was when something would come up at the last minute to prevent me from taking Daisy back, or out as scheduled. I'd call the prison, but could never be sure that whoever was on duty would pass along the message to Keith in time, or at all. I'd picture him packing up Daisy's food for the weekend and settling in with her to wait for me. And wait. And wait.

One Friday I packed my pocket full of treats, slipped behind the wheel of my car, turned the ignition, and nothing. Just a click followed by silence. Marty was still at work. I dialed the prison and explained the situation to the officer who answered the phone. "Will you let him know I'll be there in the morning?"

"Yeah, yeah, we'll let him know. Who is this for again?"

"Daisy. The guy who has her is Keith. I don't know his last name." I wanted to believe the officer would run right over to A-block and hand-deliver a pink "While You Were Out" note to Keith, but I suspected he hung up the phone and went straight back to whatever he was doing before it rang. All evening I tied myself up into knots, wondering at what point Keith and Daisy would realize I wasn't going to show up. Daisy's a Lab; they're resilient. It was Keith I worried about. He was stuck in that six-by-nine cell with nothing but Daisy and his thoughts—and sometimes just his thoughts. There was no way I could know what went on in Keith's head, but I suspected it could be a dark and lonely place, given his circumstances.

I took Marty's car to the prison the next morning. The officer on duty and I made small talk while I followed Keith's progress across the yard with Daisy. I couldn't tell by his expression or body language whether he was upset or angry. The door was still closing behind him when I asked whether he got my message about the car trouble.

"Yeah, I did. Are you okay? Your car didn't break down while you were driving here, I hope." He looked concerned.

"Oh, no. Nothing like that. I didn't even get out of my driveway. It's just a dead battery." I was touched and wanted to put his mind at ease. He had enough to worry about.

Another time I let him know a week ahead that I'd return Daisy a day late the following weekend. On that Monday, she was asleep in the backseat and I was nearly at the prison when a stream of cars passed us going in the opposite direction. They were still emptying out of the prison parking lot when I pulled in. Guards wearing riot gear were milling about outside the front entrance. I knew I should turn around and follow the line of traffic, but Keith was expecting Daisy. The prison guards stared at me from under their black helmets as I walked toward them, leading Daisy on her leash. I felt silly and conspicuous, like a little girl asking to play with the older boys. I might as well

have been wearing a frilly dress and carrying a lollipop. A tall, gray-haired officer had his face shield flipped up and was sucking down a cigarette. "You can't go in there!" he hollered, smoke the color of his beard pouring out of his mouth. "Bring the dog back tomorrow." I paused for a moment and weighed whether to ask him to tell Keith about this unexpected change of plans. I thought better of it and left.

I never did find out what happened that required riot gear, other than there was an "incident" at one of the other prisons in the complex. And Keith didn't say much when I described the scene to him the next day when I returned Daisy, other than to tell me that they were in lockdown all day, meaning the inmates were confined to their cells. He was probably glad that Daisy avoided that punishment and got an extra day of freedom.

As difficult as communication was, in some ways Keith made it worse. He was protective of his training with Daisy and wouldn't reveal what he was working on until she was solid with the new skill. I suppose he was afraid I'd try the commands at home and mess up the training. A weekend puppy raiser's job is to socialize the dog and reinforce what he already knows, not train him to do new things. But I speak from experience when I say that having a dog who can follow directions is just too tempting to ignore, and sooner or later during the weekend, you're bound to get bored with the usual commands and pry open the lid to try to coax some new ones out of your dog. Problem is, non–dog trainers often get it all wrong. We'll say "Paw" when the word is "Shake," then grab the puppy's leg and ratchet it up and down until the dog loses balance. Or we'll wander off to answer the phone in the middle of a down-stay and forget all about the dog until we stumble on him in another room, chew-

ing on a chair leg. So, it was understandable that Keith kept quiet about his work in progress, but what I didn't get was why he didn't tell me about the party tricks.

I'd first learned about party tricks when I had Jones for those few weekends. I was leading the poodle out of the prison through the reception area when a woman waiting to visit her boyfriend called out, "Is that one of those service dogs?" I brought Jones over, and she told me she'd heard all about the dogs from her boyfriend. "They're wicked smart. The guys teach them all sorts of tricks," she said. "They pretend they're shooting them with a gun and the dog falls over like it's been shot." I was turning that image over in my head when the woman sitting beside her said, "Yeah, and they teach them to say their prayers at night. It's so cute. The dog will put its head on its paws like it's praying."

When I got home I cocked my finger like a gun and pretended to shoot Jones. Nothing happened. I told him to pray. He didn't even look at me.

Not long after the weekend that Daisy surprised me with the mitten, we were practicing commands when I wondered what would happen if I pretended to shoot her. I pointed my index finger and made a noise like a gun going off. She hesitated a moment and looked like she might just drop to the floor. I did it again. She looked down at her feet, then up at me with that worried expression on her face, the one that said, "I think I know what you want, but I'm not positively sure, so I'll just stand here until I get further clarification." I pointed my finger again, but this time I said, "Bang!" Daisy threw herself down onto the carpet and lay on her side with her head up, twisted toward me to meet my gaze. I reeled off another bang and she

jerked her head flat to the ground and stared into the distance, blinking. "Good girl!" I laughed, and Daisy sprung to her feet, tail wagging, very much alive.

I learned of more tricks through the other puppy raisers and tried them on Daisy. She knew how to roll over, lift her paw for a high five, and, most endearing, would press her muzzle into my ear when I asked her to tell me a secret.

One Friday when I stepped into shift command Keith and Daisy were already waiting for me by the prison yard door. Captain Lefebvre was working late again and came out from behind his desk to oversee the exchange. I think he was making small talk when he asked Keith whether Daisy had learned anything new, but I saw an opening and I seized it.

"Daisy told me a secret," I said, smiling.

Keith snapped his head up at me. "You know about that?"

"Yup," I said, enjoying the moment. "That and roll over and bang."

Keith was quiet a moment. Then he smiled. "What about 'Say your prayers'? You know that one?"

Captain Lefebvre jumped in, "Oh yeah. You've got to see that one." He and Keith looked around the room. There was a refrigerator and the high table that held the microwave oven. "I'll get a chair. Will that work?" Lefebvre said, heading toward his office.

Keith dropped to one knee, the other leg bent at ninety degrees, like he was about to propose. "Nah, this is good. This'll work." I stared down at the top of Keith's head. He had a fresh buzz cut. I had a strong urge to reach out my hand and ruffle it. Josh has the same haircut and for the first few days after he comes back from Priscilla the barber, while it's still soft and downy, I find excuses to touch it. I'll catch him in a backward hug as he walks by so I can kiss his hair. I'll rub his head "for good luck" in the morning before he leaves for school. I was surprised to feel this almost maternal reaction toward Keith—but in a way, didn't Daisy make us family of sorts?

Keith called Daisy over and reached into his pouch for some kibble. Daisy sat down in front of his bent leg. "Daisy?" Keith said. "Say your prayers." Daisy placed her front paws on Keith's leg and settled her chin on them while Captain Lefebvre and I watched as if we were witnessing a miracle.

A few weeks later Keith smiled mischievously at me when I walked into shift command. "We have a surprise for you." There was a slight lilt to his voice.

"What? What do you mean?" His playful tone made me smile and I had a flash of what he must have been like as a boy, hiding a bouquet of wilted dandelions behind his back to surprise his mom or bringing home As on his report card.

"We have a new trick for you. Do you want to see?"

I laughed. "Of course I want to see!"

Keith produced a piece of kibble and showed it to Daisy. She turned to face him, tail wagging. "Daisy? Take a bow!" Daisy lunged forward onto her front paws, rump up in a deep bow, then popped back to her feet, tail wagging, to accept her treat. I clapped and made an all-around fuss over the new trick while Keith stood, beaming. It was like he had given me a gift and admitted me into the club all at the same time.

———

BY THE TIME the New Year rolled around, Daisy and I had become as in sync with each other as if connected by a cable. If

I were to stand up while Daisy slept beside me, she'd spring to her feet, ready to follow. If I glanced nearly imperceptibly at my right side, she'd immediately position herself against my flank, searching my face intently so as not to miss the next command.

It felt like Daisy had always been with us, so it was easy to delude myself into believing she'd never leave. However, occasionally my brain would let some indisputable evidence slip through to wreck the fantasy, and my thoughts would light on the future, to when Daisy wouldn't be with me or even with Keith. A hard little knot would form in my chest, so I'd force myself to think like a dog—in the present. Anything else seemed too painful, or too dangerous. Still, most every weekend Josh and Aviva would look up at me from their seats on the floor next to Daisy and whimper that they wanted to keep her. I'd respond with some variation of sure, we can keep her, if you're willing to give up the perks of being a fully able-bodied person. Sometimes that would quiet them down, but as often they'd fire back, "Not if she flunks out of the program."

About thirty to forty percent of NEADS puppies do not make it all the way through the training program. They called them "Fabulous Flunkies," and NEADS keeps a waiting list of several hundred people who have signed up to adopt one. Fabulous Flunkies make terrific pets. They're expertly trained and in most cases, their "flaw" is minor for a pet (or even valued, like alert barking) but unacceptable in a service dog.

There are any number of reasons a dog will be released from the NEADS program. A prey drive that won't quit, for instance, as was the case with Jones. Or there may be health concerns. Hip problems, so common in large breeds, will torpedo a service dog's career.

The majority of flunk-outs, however, developed habits, behaviors, or reactions that couldn't be trained out of them. Dogs have failed for being nervous around traffic, for lunging during walks, for quivering on glass elevators. One dog was released from the program after developing a deathly fear of hats, another because he barked at sweatshirts whenever he came across one hanging from a railing or draped over the back of a chair.

Flunkies are offered first to their breeders, then to their weekend puppy raisers, for a fee. Next in line are the correctional officers or other workers at the prison where the dog was trained. That's how Anthony Del Signore, or Del, as everyone calls him, ended up with Leo, a tricolored, smooth-coated collie that Bonnie had been puppy raising. One of the perks of Del's job as the visiting room officer was watching the weekly puppy-training class from his raised platform. Del was taken with Leo from the start—his alert expression peering out from a face mask of black and tan, and that needle nose, long and pointed like an anteater's. So when he learned that the collie was flunking out of the program for barking at shopping carts, Del called NEADS. He wanted to be one of the first in line to adopt Leo.

On Leo's last day in prison, Del stood to the side while the dog's inmate handler, a big blond guy named Chris, rubbed Leo's head one final time and bent to kiss the dog squarely between the ears. Del took the leash and walked out of the visitors' room—Leo and Chris holding their gaze until the door slid shut between them.

It wasn't long before things at Del's house got a little weird. He'd wake up from naps and find the lights on in the front hall. At first, Del figured his girlfriend left them on. Or wondered whether he himself had flicked the switch in his postwork exhaustion. Then one day, his neighbor was mowing his lawn when he spotted Del coming home from work. The neighbor turned off the motor and walked over to tell Del his porch and hall lights had been flickering on and off.

Leo greeted Del at the door, tail wagging, and the figurative light went on over Del's head. He'd seen some of the dogs practicing turning on and off switches during the training classes, but didn't know that Leo had learned that skill. Del couldn't remember the command, so he called to Leo, "Switch!" and pointed to the light switch. Leo stared back, uncomprehending.

Days later, after Del learned the correct command from Chris, he brought Leo to the hall light switch. "Leo!" he said. "Nudge." Without hesitation, Leo reached that long nose under the light switch and flipped it on. Mystery solved: Leo had been turning the lights on and off during the day while Del was at work, probably hoping a handful of kibble would appear to reward him, just like in prison.

———————

I DIDN'T ALLOW myself to think too hard about Daisy maybe becoming a Fabulous Flunky, but occasionally someone would ask me whether I would keep her if she didn't make it through the program. I'd laugh and say yes, I probably would. But as the weeks went on, it got harder to say good-bye to Daisy on Sunday nights. I'd spend the drive home searching the radio for music that expressed my longing, clichéd as that sounds. I felt hollow, like I'd left a part of myself behind the razor-wire fence. I wouldn't admit it to anybody, most especially not to my children, but I was starting to want Daisy to fail.

9

You Know Better

THIS MAY SOUND odd, but I came to enjoy prison. Despite the jokes friends and I swapped about Daisy plastering my valuables to the roof of her mouth and smuggling them out of the house, it was easy to forget she lived with convicted felons. The reception area was often jammed with visitors, and while some of them wore grim expressions and stared at their feet while waiting to sign in, most struck up friendly conversations with one another, joking and chatting with the sort of instant camaraderie that develops when strangers are thrown together and forced to wait.

Given that the one thing I knew about the visitors was that they consorted with known criminals, I was always slightly surprised when they helpfully rearranged themselves to form a path as I threaded my way through the crowd toward the reception desk. I'd expected they'd rise up as an angry mob and push me back to the end to wait my turn, but that never happened. There were so many rules regulating visits, they probably figured the officer at the reception desk would set me straight if I was trying to get away with anything. First there was the dress code, which, it turns out, had something to say for just about every part of your body. I had never actually read the dress code, which was why I didn't realize that I broke it every time I walked into the prison wearing sandals or clogs. Shoes can't reveal toes *or* heels. If you're a male, you're not allowed to wear tan khakis. If you don't understand why, just ask Justin, who was on his way to fetch Nellie when a correctional officer mistook him for an inmate and demanded to know just where exactly he thought he was going. If you're a woman, you can't get into the visiting room while wearing an underwire bra. This has more to do with triggering the metal detector than any fears that you'll somehow work the underwire loose during the visit and slip it to your boyfriend to fashion into a shiv. Once, I overheard the officer at the reception desk insisting to a weary-looking older woman that he couldn't, wouldn't, in no way let her in without her underwear and that next time, she should make sure to wear a different bra when she came to visit her son.

The same people who moved to let me pass would often still be waiting in line when I returned from shift command with Daisy. Our appearance always triggered a change in pitch in the conversational hum. We'd hear kissy noises and a few "Aww-aaas," rising in tone on the second syllable. Mothers and grandmothers would point out Daisy to their children. Some of the littlest ones were terrified of her and would bury their faces in their parents' legs, willing us to go away. But others would toddle over boldly, their hands stretched out to grab Daisy's nose or tail. The older kids would ask permission to pat Daisy while assuring me they knew all about dogs because their aunt (or neighbor or best friend) had one they get to visit now and then. Daisy was drawn to children, whom she thought of as fun-size humans. Every person she met was a potential friend, but every child was a potential playmate. Kids are exactly the right height for a dog, and they tend to move quickly, like puppies. They're also careless with food, waving it around in their fists, or leaving traces of meals on their faces. When Daisy spotted a child, she'd whip her tail back and forth and grin widely with an open mouth. When I'd give her the "Say hello" command, her tail would move faster and faster until the momentum reached the rest of her and her entire body would wiggle while she made it clear to the small human that she couldn't be more delighted to have made his acquaintance.

After a few months of my twice-weekly excursions into the prison, I started to recognize some of the people who worked there. I had a few favorites. The skinny gray-haired officer at the reception desk, Smitty, was one. Eventually Smitty learned who I was. I'd stand in front of his desk, willing him to look up, and when he finally did he'd stare intently, pointing his finger at me before declaring in triumph, "Daisy!" Another favorite was Lou, who sometimes worked the reception desk with Smitty. He would leave food out for the wild bunnies who visited the courtyard, usually apples, which he would cut in half so they wouldn't roll away when the bunnies bit into them.

There were also a few I was happy to avoid, like the lieutenant I walked in on once while he was hollering into the phone at someone who hadn't shown up for work. The veins in his neck were raised and pulsing. Now, I appreciate the value of a well-placed swear word, but this guy wasn't just sprinkling his sentences with swears, he was coating them. Dunking them in a roiling vat of viscous, dripping swear fluid, then flinging them, splattering, into the phone. The lieutenant never looked up when I walked into shift command, just kept screaming his dark, ugly, slimy, swear-coated sentences into the phone so loudly and for so long that my face burned with embarrassment as I stood awkwardly in the hallway outside his office. I wanted to clap my hands over Daisy's ears, and mine, too. I cringed at the thought of Keith or Daisy being on the receiving end of that temper.

I was staring hard at a crack in the tile floor, imagining myself disappearing right through it, when the prison yard door buzzed open and Keith appeared in the doorway. I was never happier to see him. Keith cocked his head and hesitated on the threshold for a moment, listening, before gingerly stepping in while holding the door so it would close softly behind him. He widened his eyes at me, the way you would when you know someone's in big trouble. I tried to break the tension by making light of the lieutenant's tirade. "I think he might be upset," I said in a low voice.

Keith grimaced. "You should see him when he's really mad."

A burst of nervous laughter escaped me. "I'm not sticking around for that."

While I certainly wouldn't call Keith and the nicer correctional officers my friends, I saw them more frequently than anyone else outside my immediate family, turning them into a sort of community for me. And when I worried about what the future might hold, those weekend excursions made me feel less alone.

ON A SATURDAY in late January, I checked "watch people sledding" off Daisy's list of life experiences. We were in a conservation area a short drive from our home and had climbed partway down from a dam to a spot where the land sloped gently toward a river. Below us were two children flinging their small, snow-suited bodies onto plastic toboggans while their mother stood guard before a clump of dead marsh grasses at the bottom of the hill. I asked Daisy to sit. She lowered her haunches into the snow without taking her eyes off the children.

Josh hadn't wanted to come along, and I felt a little conspicuous, standing on the top of the hill, watching somebody else's children play. So when they trudged back up the hill dragging their sleds by yellow ropes, I smiled at them and waved to their mother.

"My dog needs to see people sledding. Is it okay if we watch?" I called out to the mother, realizing before I was even done speaking how creepy that must've sounded. "She's in training to be a service dog!" I hollered.

One of the kids waddled closer in her puffy pink snowsuit and peered up at me from beneath her pom-pommed hat. "Why is he wearing that?" She pointed at Daisy's cape.

"Oh, that's her cape. It's so—"

"Oh. He's a girl?" the girl interrupted, then laughed. "I mean *she's* a girl."

"Yup. Her name is Daisy. The cape lets everyone know that she's learning to be a helper dog, and when she's all done with her training she'll help somebody who maybe is in a wheelchair or has trouble walking."

"How?" The boy had joined his sister and they were watching Daisy, who by now was rolling on her back in the snow. The mother approached. She looked cold and tired.

"I'll show you." I took off my right mitten and shook a piece of dog biscuit from it into my palm. I had taken to storing dog treats in my mittens on walks to save the step of digging into my pocket. I dangled the other mitten from my hand. "Daisy . . ." She paused midroll with all four legs in the air, looked at the mitten, then shifted her gaze to my other hand, where she knew there would be a treat. She bounced to her feet and I dropped the mitten in the snow. "Get it," I told her. She dove toward it with more force than was necessary, clamped the mitten between her teeth, thrust it into my outstretched left hand, then took the treat from the right.

"Can I try?" the girl asked, already pulling off one of her mittens. While she and her brother took turns having Daisy retrieve various pieces of outerwear, I gave their mother the background on Daisy.

"Won't it be hard to give her up?" she asked.

I gave her the same response I gave to everyone who asked. "I don't know. I haven't had to do it yet." But of course I knew it would be hard—so hard I couldn't talk about it.

"Well, if she doesn't make it as a service dog, you get to keep her, right? Maybe she'll fail."

The kids were on their knees now, feeding snowballs to Daisy. Their sleds lay in the snow, forgotten.

"She won't fail. But if she does, yeah, maybe I'd get to keep her."

———

THE SUN WAS low in the sky on the drive back to prison on Sunday, and the temperature had dipped back down to freezing after a warm day that left lacy patches of snow on the highway median strip. Daisy made little snoring noises from the backseat. If she did fail, she would slip so naturally into the family . . . She would be the kids' dog in a way that Tucker, who was already six years old when Josh was born, never was. Marty and I used to bring Tucker and the kids to the same park where Daisy and I watched the sledders. In winter, Marty would strap Aviva into a pack on his back and she would sing in his ear while we cross-country skied and Tucker raced around, dipping her snout in the snow. When Aviva was older, we'd pull her in a red plastic toboggan while Josh rode in the backpack. Before they were born, when it was just me and Marty and our dog walking the trails, we would put Tucker in a down-stay just below a rise, then sneak behind a cluster of pine trees. When we were sufficiently hidden, we'd call her name. We always heard her before we saw her, crashing up the trail, panting. She'd overshoot our hiding place, lose our scent, and stop cold. From behind the pine boughs, we'd watch her circle back and sniff the air. I'd try unsuccessfully to stifle a laugh and Tucker would pause to deploy every one of her senses in our direction. When she registered our presence, she'd rear back for maximum propulsion, and before we'd have time to cover our faces with our hands, she'd be upon us, seventy pounds of ecstatic dog.

God, I missed that so much. I wanted to do that with Daisy. I wanted the kids to have those memories, for all of us to start over again with Daisy as our dog—my dog, especially.

———

KEITH WAS WAITING for us inside the prison yard door, shoulders stooped under an invisible weight as he huddled into his canvas jacket. His head was bare, and the tops of his ears were bitten red from the cold. Always soft-spoken and reserved, he seemed quieter and more withdrawn than usual as we made our exchange. I had just said good-bye to Daisy and handed him the leash when he spoke.

"She tested positive again," he mumbled.

Daisy had been diagnosed with parasites four or five times since she arrived at the prison. Each time the veterinarian would prescribe an antiparasitic, Daisy would go through the entire course of treatment, and a few weeks later, she'd test positive again. The prison doesn't allow dogs to go out when they're on medication but eventually they made an exception for Daisy because the parasites had already cost her too much outside socialization time.

I didn't know much about dogs and parasites, but I wondered whether there was something about Daisy that made her particularly susceptible to them. I looked at Keith. He was wondering the same thing. "I'm thinking she might not make it—they might just kick her out of the program." He was looking down at Daisy, who had settled into a "side" position by his right work boot.

"Because of parasites?" I asked.

Keith met my eyes. "There's something wrong," he insisted, his voice low and tense. "She can't shake them and nobody knows why. If she's a carrier, she'll keep infecting other dogs, which means they'll flunk her." He shifted his gaze back to Daisy and slumped his shoulders. "I don't know. It's not good." Daisy raised her head to meet his eyes. Maybe it was my imagination, but she looked weary, too. "You ready, girl?" he asked. His voice was flat, without the usual upward inflection he used with Daisy. Daisy stood up and they turned to leave.

I wanted to ask more, but Keith's demeanor was unnerving. He seemed so fragile. And it was obvious he didn't want to talk about it anymore. "Okay," I said uncertainly. "I'll see you on Friday."

His response, if there was one, was drowned out by the mechanical buzz of the door being unlocked. I heard it clang shut when I stepped into the hallway and waited for my own door to open, and I pictured Daisy and Keith making their way through the chill air, heads down and defeated, back to their cell. I had expected a surge of joy at the prospect of Daisy flunking out of the program. Instead, I felt like I had swallowed sawdust.

This was a side of Keith I hadn't seen. It was as if he had just tallied up all of the hours, weeks, and months of time—all of the patience and skill he poured into Daisy—only to discover that it added up to nothing. The news that his dog might flunk had erased his last hope and left instead yet another failure in what was undoubtedly a long string of them. And for the first time I understood that for him, it wasn't about training a service dog, or even about Daisy. It was something much bigger than that.

Captain Lefebvre had once told me that the best trainers are those who consider their work a chance to redeem themselves, even if only a tiny bit. They know they can't make up for the damage they did, the hurt they caused to their victims and their families, but they can chip away at it. Every dog they train, every life made whole as a result, lets a chink of light into the dark wreckage they've wrought and that threatens to bury them.

That's what keeps them going through those difficult early days with the puppy, when they're cleaning up the latest housebreaking accident of the day or stuck in a tiny cell with a sick dog and eight hours to go before the doors unlock. The dogs allow them to salvage something good in themselves.

Suddenly, wanting Daisy for myself seemed almost unbearably selfish. If I got to keep her, that would mean Keith had failed. He would be devastated. Had I only taken a moment during these months to think of what Daisy's success must have meant to Keith, I could have become a truer partner to him in this shared mission of ours rather than let myself be pulled off track by fantasies of Daisy becoming my dog. It wouldn't have taken much—all I'd have had to do was look at myself and what Daisy had done for me. She'd filled me with pride simply by retrieving a mitten or dropping a pebble on command. Unlike me, who had a family and a career and accomplishments to feel proud of, Keith had precisely one way to demonstrate his worth: Daisy. And now he faced losing that.

———

SMITTY'S CHAIR WAS empty when I hurried back through the reception area and out into the cold. On my drive out to the main road, I saw that the men at minimum security were in the yard, breathing out clouds of steam, hopping in place or jogging along the fence to get warm. The tans of their boots and uniforms blended seamlessly with the ground, giving the impression that the men had been pushed up from the frozen dirt. Topping each man's head, blazing through the gloom like a roadside flare, was a fluorescent orange knit cap. It was mesmerizing. In spite of myself, I slowed the car and gaped at the scene. Of course, a few of the guys pulled their hands out of their pockets and strutted toward me, gesturing and saying things I couldn't hear through my closed window. I tore my gaze away and pressed on the gas, but the image of the prisoners in their screaming-orange caps haunted me, like they had been corralled and kept there for my personal amusement. It made me feel ashamed.

As I headed north on the highway, Daisy's absence throbbed like a phantom limb as it did every Sunday evening, only this time I felt the presence of every person involved with her training: the breeders who set her on this course; the volunteers in the puppy house; Captain Lefebvre; Christy; and Keith, especially Keith. Daisy's failure would hurt each of them, but Keith, I now understood, had the most to lose.

———

FOR THE REST of the week, I could think of little else but Daisy being taken out of the program, and Keith left with nothing to show for it but another failure. I talked with Marty about it. Told my coworkers over lunch. I described all of the people who had some investment in Daisy. Whenever anyone would try to cheer me up by pointing out that if Daisy failed I might get to keep her, I'd feel queasy and ashamed. Adopting Daisy under those circumstances would be akin to looting—swooping in and plucking the shiny treasure from the ruins of Keith's failure and keeping it for myself.

And because in my mind everything that goes wrong is somehow my fault, I was convinced that Daisy picked up the parasites while with me. Everywhere I looked was a potential source of infection—the compost bin that Marty built in the backyard (even though there was no possible way Daisy could get into it without me knowing); the spills around the kitchen trash can; wads of dust under . . . everything. Finally, I couldn't stand it any longer. I called Christy and left a message on her voice mail, recounting my conversation with Keith and asking whether she thought there was something in my house or yard that was infecting Daisy. A few hours later, the phone rang. It was Christy. She sounded puzzled. "The parasites aren't something we would fail a dog for," she said. "I don't know where Keith got that idea."

"But she keeps testing positive for them," I argued.

Christy assured me that there was no reason for alarm. Sometimes it takes a few different medications before they find the one that will work for a particular dog. As for the source, it was most likely the prison.

I held on to the phone for a long while after we hung up, turning it end over end, testing its scant weight. I was relieved—so relieved that Daisy was secure in the program—but I was perplexed. I had assumed that Keith had it on good authority that Daisy would flunk out of the program because of the parasites. Now it appeared as though he jumped down that dark hole all by himself. Our respective roles were starting to rearrange themselves in my head. I had considered Keith the expert in all things Daisy, a natural assumption considering he spent every moment with her, nearly every day of the week. But apparently, he could get things wrong.

"Think of it, he's probably had a lifetime of everything going to hell. Why wouldn't he expect things with Daisy to turn out any differently?" Marty said later when I told him about Christy's phone call.

"Well, why wouldn't he just ask somebody if Daisy would fail for parasites?" I challenged him.

"Who's he going to ask? Some guard? Another inmate? That's probably where he got the idea in the first place."

I thought of the lieutenant's violent outburst in shift command; of the inmates in their orange caps and their predatory posturing when I drove past minimum security. From the very beginning at NEADS, we'd had it drummed into our heads, and I assume the dog handlers did, too, that no experience was better than a bad experience. For Keith and his fellow inmates, it was mostly bad experiences. They never knew what they would get when they stepped outside their cell doors. Would it be the calm, friendly Captain Lefebvre, or the cursing madman I'd heard on the phone that time in shift command? Would the other inmates leave them alone or would they threaten and intimidate? How could anyone who lives in prison possibly reintegrate into society after being trapped in that reality every single day until their sentence was served? And how long was that for Keith? I thought of him making his way with Daisy through the winter chill back to their cell and how, if he were tracked from space, the signal representing him would never leave the narrow borders of the same trodden speck of land.

I realized that I didn't know prison at all. What I saw each weekend was only a sliver, a brief bright flash in a relentlessly churning tide of monotony and despair. During the dog exchanges, the inmates are at their best, most polite, most professional. They're deferential both to the brass and to us, the puppy raisers. More than that, though, their spirits are lifted by the chance, even if it's only for five minutes or less, to talk to someone from the outside. And not just anybody, but the one person in the world who loves their dogs as much as they do. If it filled my heart to talk with Keith about Daisy, it did the same for him, and possibly more.

But the conversations would end, often with a warning look from the shift commander, and Keith would turn his back and wait for the guard to buzz him back into the ugly, sometimes brutal, often mind-numbingly boring reality that is prison. That he would so readily accept that a recurring case of parasites would doom his dog started to make sense when I let my sanitized, puppy-populated theme park version of prison harden into something closer to reality. Reliable information is scarce in there, leaving ideal conditions for rumor to spread and private fears to take hold and grow.

In prison, the dogs are a gift, rare beauty in an ugly place composed of hard, flat surfaces—all concrete and metal and muted colors with nothing to catch the eye. Time is segmented; each period has its own designation: meals, recreation, visiting hours. Inmates can go outside during one of two recreational periods. For the other, they're stuck inside the cell block, where they can play backgammon or cribbage or watch TV in their cells. And there are the lockdowns, which happen twice a day. The speakers squawk and everybody files back to their cells to be accounted for.

Daisy's backup handler, a slightly built, ruddy-faced man named Dennis, says prison is like the movie *Groundhog Day*. "I know what time it is every minute of the day," he said to me once, pointing at his bare wrist. "And I don't wear a watch."

That's the official structure of prison life. Operating within that is a testosterone-fueled culture of gang members, murderers, drug dealers, and the occasional upstanding citizen who got drunk and killed someone with his car. It's like living in a reality television show; nothing is as it seems; nobody can be trusted, not even the correctional officers. You don't have friends in prison, you have alliances. They're formed for power or protection, then broken over a dirty look or a stolen pair of prison-issued sneakers. Grudges fester like infected wounds.

The civilized world is very, very far away and many of the inmates had their membership revoked decades earlier. As easy as it was for me to forget that Keith lived in this world when we were grinning at each other over Daisy's latest accomplishment, all it took was a stray comment to remind me. The weekend before Daisy was spayed, I mentioned to him that I was going to miss being with her while she stayed in the prison to recuperate. He looked up at me, confused, then nodded his head. "Oh, right. She's getting cut."

I drew in my breath at the violence of the word—a reminder that I shared custody of a dog with a prison inmate whom I really knew nothing about.

Yet when I showed up the first weekend Daisy was allowed out after the spay, Keith's voice was tight with worry when he asked me to keep her quiet and away from other dogs. He guided her into a down on the cold, hard floor of shift command and had her roll onto her back so he could point out where the area around the stitches was slightly puffy and red so I'd have a baseline from which to judge the progress of her healing. I didn't know this at the time, but Keith had carefully swabbed her incision so it wouldn't get infected and carried her up and down the cell block stairs at least three times a day so she could relieve herself outside.

I suspected, but didn't know for sure, that before the puppy program, Keith had never cared for another being in his life.

Captain Lefebvre had described being moved by the tenderness with which the inmates cared for their puppies even though most had never thought of anyone other than themselves or, in many cases, experienced that kind of nurturing in their own lives. "The inmates are the people most protective of the dogs. They would probably throw themselves in harm's way if someone tried to hurt their dog," he told me.

From the outside, you'd think that having a dog in prison is a perk, but as with everything else in there, it isn't that simple or straightforward. Depending on who you talk to, the dog handlers are either the prison's "rock stars" or they're reviled by jealous inmates and a few correctional officers. There's some truth to both claims. There are inmates and staff who admire the handlers' skill and say the puppies have softened the edges on even the most hardened among them. But there are bullies everywhere, most especially in prison, who will latch on to any sign that a fellow inmate is vulnerable and go in for the kill. Inmates will woof at the dogs, drop food for them to eat, mockingly call the handlers the "dog walkers," and taunt them for picking up feces. Others are well meaning but clueless. They'll interrupt a training session by riling the dog up to play. Even just walking up and petting a dog during training is a setback when the handlers are working on a new task. It's frustrating and stressful, always having to be on the alert for the next jackass who'll screw things up. The handlers who are good enough to stay in the program have learned to treat these incidents as opportunities to train their dogs to ignore distractions. Some of them realize that it's also good practice for holding their own tempers because to strike back means risking a fight—and in prison, it doesn't matter who's at fault;

if you fight, you end up in segregation and you lose your dog.

The worst thing that can happen to a dog handler is to lose his dog. Being accepted into the NEADS program is to be handed a ladder and encouraged to climb higher than ever. The fall from up there hurts so much more. There's the emotional pain of having your dog ripped from you prematurely. Then there's the insult of seeing someone else, usually the backup handler, take over and give the commands all wrong. Or worse, do them perfectly. Losing your dog is to be cast out of the group, to see the other guys file out of Christy's training sessions smiling down at their dogs and maybe even one another, their humanity freshly renewed for another week.

The second-worst thing to happen to a dog handler is to have his dog flunk out of the program. And that's what Keith thought he was facing.

10

Closer

AFTER THE PARASITE incident, I became determined to see Daisy graduate. Now I understood how important it was to Keith. Daisy was his child in the same way that Aviva and Josh are mine, and all children are potential personified. As babies, they contain all of the promise we can dream up. They'll play first violin in the symphony. They'll get that elusive math gene and sail through their classes. They'll be president. We try to get them there by correcting our own mistakes through them. It's because of regrets about personal failures that Marty and I have raised children who do not give up easily. They push past their fears and they work hard in school. Their achievements are our own. Actually, they're better than our own. I have no doubt that Keith's pride in Daisy when she positions herself at his side in a textbook-perfect "Heel" is no less than mine when Aviva earns an A in biology or Josh holds the door open for his grandmother without being asked. Maybe it's even stronger for Keith. God knows he must have had his share of regrets. I didn't know how long he'd been in prison or what he'd done, but seeing him on the edge of depression when Daisy's failure loomed told me he needed her desperately. It was clear that Daisy was his promise for the future, his shot at finally making his life worth something.

To help Keith, I needed to accept his limitations and develop my own expertise to shore up those areas where imprisonment skewed his perception. I'd have to tear the filter off and let the unpleasant truths flow in. It felt kind of like when you recognize your own parents' flaws for the first time. Once you accept that they're human, you start the process of growing up yourself. This was no longer about me wanting a dog on weekends; it was about helping Keith do something good, maybe for the first time in his life.

That next Friday Keith met me in shift command and handed me Daisy's food and paperwork along with a folded envelope containing a new round of medication. I accepted Daisy's leash and settled her by my side.

"She won't flunk because of the parasites." My tone was gentle. Keith had so little, I didn't want to take away his standing as the expert on Daisy.

"Yeah?" Keith straightened a little and searched my face.

"I called Christy and she told me that it's common for puppies to keep getting parasites and they just have to keep trying different medications before they find one that works."

Keith shifted his weight and looked down at Daisy. His hands were empty now and he didn't seem to know what to do with them.

"They said she might be a carrier or something. And that was grounds to flunk her." He rubbed his head and looked up at me again. "But you talked to Christy and she said she'll be okay? So, that's not true? She's okay?" His expression was so hopeful I wanted to cry.

"Yes, the parasites are no big deal." I got Daisy to her feet and turned to go.

Keith inhaled deeply and in a rush of air said, "Okay!" He smiled and lifted his chin. "That's good news. Real good news."

"She'll be fine." I smiled back. "She's going to make it through the program."

To keep that promise, I would need more help than Keith could give me from prison or that Dave offered in his once-a-month training session. I still hadn't figured out a way to connect outside of class with other puppy raisers, either, and I was starting to feel time pressing in on me. Daisy had her cape. She was at the point in her training where she needed to be exposed to restaurants and supermarkets—places where my deficiencies as a dog handler would stand out like a, well, like a dog in a restaurant or a supermarket. I had to move her up to the next level of training, past the sledding hills and the walks around the neighborhood to the more challenging ones that she would need to make it as a service dog.

When I brought this up to Dave, he told me about Christina Rossetti, a private dog trainer who had a contract with NEADS to work with the inmates and puppy raisers at two Massachusetts prisons. Christina operated a little differently than the other trainers at NEADS. She required her puppy raisers to bring their dogs to her Saturday-morning drop-in class every week, where they trained alongside her private clients and full-time puppy raisers from another nonprofit, Canine Companions for Independence. Unlike NEADS, CCI doesn't use prison inmates to train their puppies; they hand the dogs to full-time raisers, then call them back after about eighteen months for intensive service dog training. It was exactly what I needed: a class every week and a chance to get to know other puppy raisers.

Daisy was eight months old, and we'd been together four months, when we wound our way through an industrial park to the low brick building that houses Alpha Dog K9, Christina's dog training school. Just the weekend before, Daisy left the prison for the first time wearing the Gentle Leader. The transformation was stunning. Dressed in her cape and the Gentle Leader, Daisy was focused. Those teeth-grinding walks that ended with me wrung out and needing a nap (or a strong drink) actually became pleasant. Daisy's nose never dipped to the ground but pointed forward, eyes ahead. With the Gentle Leader, I could imagine her wearing the official red service dog vest, confidently helping her person navigate the world. That's not to say my throat didn't tighten when I thought of Daisy as someone else's dog. It did. But I had a mission now, and with the parasite scare behind us, nothing would stop us from fulfilling it.

Of course, we still had work to do, as I discovered the second I opened the car door and the canine-scented environment outside Christina's training school walloped Daisy full force in the nose. It was too powerful even for the Gentle Leader to tame and Daisy pulled me toward a narrow strip of grass abutting the brick building. A dog with a head the size of an anvil had its face pressed against the back window of an approaching car. "Let's go!" I tugged Daisy toward the building, hoping to get inside before the driver could witness the struggle between us. A sign posted above a small metal trash can by the entrance reminded patrons to "Please empty your dog before entering," so I wheeled back around to the grass. The trip proved fruitless, fuming though it was with evidence of dogs before. A stout woman with a bowlegged pit bull rounded the corner. Daisy's head shot up and her tail swung back and forth like a high-speed metronome. "Oh, no you don't." I blocked her with my body, pinning her between the building and my legs, but she pushed her face between my knees to watch the pair open the door and slip inside. After a moment, we followed them inside, where even my inferior human nose registered the change. The air was thick with a mixed bouquet of cleaning solution and canine. The place was teeming with dogs—some wearing blue NEADS capes, others wearing CCI yellow, and a whole lot of civilian dogs: German shepherds, a pair of matching fluffy white bichon frises, two Australian shepherds with abbreviated tails and startled expressions. Daisy bounced around at the end of the leash, all training forgotten, play-bowing to dogs on her right, her left, straight ahead—she was in heaven and I was in shock.

I recovered enough to locate a hook for my coat and pocketbook, then looked around for someone who might be in charge. The room was cavernous, with high, industrial ceilings, the floor covered with a black rubberized mat. Someone had taken pains to make the space feel less impersonal by painting the walls a soothing hunter green and cream, with inspirational quotes about dogs written in calligraphy. A mirror spanned the entire back wall, giving the illusion that there were twice as many people and dogs in there. And there were plenty already, believe me.

A tall, strapping woman in jeans and a thick sweatshirt embroidered over the left breast with the profile of a tiny German shepherd was in the center of a loose cluster of people and dogs. Both the humans and the canines seemed to be equally enamored of her. It was Christina. I steered Daisy toward her and introduced ourselves. "Excellent!" Christina said. "We're about to get started. Heel your dog around the room and I'll be right over." She pointed to the ring where others were walking their dogs in a wide circle. Daisy and I slipped into the stream. I couldn't believe it—she fell neatly into step beside me, once again acting the part of the professional service-dog-in-training, ignoring the other dogs and walking smartly at my side. Daisy must have been familiar with the drill of following a circle of dogs around a room from her prison classes. I knew that we had come to the right place. I couldn't wait to tell Keith.

CHRISTINA CARRIES HERSELF like a cop, which she was before she ended that career—and nearly her life—four years earlier when her cruiser met a telephone pole during a midnight to 8:00 a.m. shift. Christina had established her department's first K9 unit with a German shepherd named Merlin and discovered that she had a gift with dogs, so after her injuries forced her early retirement, becoming a dog trainer seemed a logical next step.

Christina is so natural with dogs that I suspect she has canine genes mixed into her DNA. I once saw her pry open a puppy's mouth, stick her nose inside, and inhale deeply. "I love puppy breath!" she said with a sigh. Christina says when she meets a new weekend puppy raiser, she can tell right away whether the person is a dog *lover* or a dog *trainer*. And after a couple of classes, I could see the difference, too. The dog trainers are the people whose attention never wavers. They're quick to notice a wayward nose and pull it back into position. They ask for their dogs' complete attention with a "Watch me!" before moving on to the next task.

And there was me. Clearly a dog lover. It wasn't easy for me to admit that, either. I had always prided myself on my clear-eyed view of the line between animal and human. I never blurred the two, never cooked for Tucker nor, with the exception of an occasional T-shirt and socks over the years, dressed her in cunning outfits. But after watching the no-nonsense puppy raisers interact with their dogs, I had to admit to myself that I didn't belong in their category. For one, I was way too concerned about crushing Daisy's spirit and stifling her natural curiosity with my demands. I loved her like a child, even while recognizing that she was an animal. And there was my own curiosity. It kept me from giving Daisy my undivided attention, which, it turns out, is critical to human-dog communication. While Christina patrolled the line of puppy raisers, tossing biscuits on the floor in front of each dog to test its response to "Leave it," I'd turn to the person next to me and ask about his dog, failing completely to notice Daisy worming her way toward the treat.

There was also—and this is going to sound weird—my discomfort with a dog's subservient role. It didn't seem fair to me that Daisy had to do everything I said. The problem with that attitude is that dogs can sense when their handlers are softies and easily taken advantage of. Over time, and by watching Christina and her puppy raisers, I understood that service dogs *want* to be told what to do. To them, work and play are one and the same. When I issue Daisy a command, I'm not being a cruel taskmaster, I'm being the game master. Ambiguity, wavering attention, long, involved explanations about, say, the effect of grass on a dog's digestive system when a sharp "No" is called for; these just lull the dog into tuning you out while continuing to rip mouthfuls of grass up by the roots. If Daisy were allowed to follow her own inner commands (*Daisy, eat rock! Daisy, sniff Bailey's ass*), she'd learn she could reward herself, meaning I'd lose my power as the holder of all things good. Not only that, she'd carry that behavior back into prison and Keith would know I'd been loafing on the job.

In time, I'd learn to apply the lessons of human-canine communication to other areas of my life. That's how I solved the issue of Marty leaving dirty dishes in the sink. Just as I'd do with Daisy, I framed my request to Marty in language he could relate to, telling him that leaving dishes in the sink attracted more dirty dishes. "It's like the broken windows theory, except instead of vandalism and neglect leading to higher rates of crime, in our house, dirty pots and pans tell the kids that it's okay not to clean up after themselves," I said. Either the notion appealed to Marty or he simply couldn't resist testing the theory. Either way, he stopped leaving dishes in the sink and so did the kids. All my dog-training practice was paying off.

AFTER A FEW trips around the room that first morning at Alpha Dog K9, Christina strode into the center of the circle and clapped her hands. "Okay. We're going to practice recalls!

Everyone sit your dog against the wall and put your dog in a stay." She told us to drop our leashes and walk across the room if we trusted our dog wouldn't follow us. A few people dared take only a few steps from their dogs, but I had confidence in Daisy's stay. She seemed to know what was expected of her in class. I found a spot between a golden retriever and a black Lab, looked Daisy in the eye, and told her to stay. When I reached the other side of the room and turned around, Daisy was leaning forward, watching me, determined not to miss my next command. She was smaller than the dogs on either side of her, slender and fine-boned. To me, she was the most beautiful dog in the room.

One by one, Christina instructed each of us to call our dogs. Every now and then, an extra dog would break away from the line and run happily over to the person who gave the command, and the actual handler would stride across the room to march the now embarrassed-looking dog back to its place.

While I waited for my turn, my eyes flicked between the dog being called and Daisy, watching for her reaction and willing her not to break her stay. I didn't have to worry. She remained rooted to her spot, and when she followed a dog's progress across the room, she would lock back onto me, as if reaffirming that she had made the right decision by staying put.

Christina seemed to know most of the dogs and their owners. She called them by name and laughed at their quirks. She accused the golden retriever next to Daisy of being conceited, then laughed uproariously when he proved it by admiring his reflection in the mirror while trotting toward his handler. Christina tossed her short brown hair to mimic the golden's long, flowing fur. "Look at me! I'm Sutton. I'm so handsome." She laughed.

I whipped my head around and stared at the golden, who was wearing a blue NEADS cape. I counted silently on my fingers. Eight months had passed since the orientation when I practiced puppy-handling exercises on the tiny ball of fluff. The math worked out. It was him! Sutton, almost all grown up. Later, I sought out his weekend puppy raiser, who told me that after the puppy house, Sutton was sent to a minimum-security prison in Massachusetts for training. She took him everywhere with her on weekends, even to New York City to see a Broadway musical.

When it was my turn, I called, "Daisy! Come!" She didn't barrel toward me like some of the other dogs, but loped with her head slightly tilted as if it were weighted down by the leash dragging behind her from the Gentle Leader. Her progress across the room was so slow, you could practically hear the clock on the wall ticking off the minutes until she reached me and settled into a position, front and facing me.

"Good job, Daisy. I'm glad you finally made it!" Christina said, before moving on to the next dog.

For the next exercise, Christina announced that we would be playing musical sits and downs, explaining that we would heel our dogs around the room while she turned up the volume on her stereo. When the music stopped, we were to tell our dogs to sit. The last dog to sit would be "out" and sent to the center of the circle with his owner. Christina slipped behind her desk in the corner of the room and fiddled with a boom box until the Marshall Tucker Band blared. We stepped off with our dogs and marched around in a loose circle. The music stopped midlyric and a chorus of voices said "Sit." Christina strode out from behind her desk and fixed a look on a broad-headed Lab. "Deacon, out!"

She made a dismissive motion with her hand. Deacon's handler, a young graduate student, shrugged her shoulders with a helpless little smile and led the ten-month-old Lab in the blue cape into the center of the room to sit out the rest of the game. The song picked up where it left off and the rest of us marched on.

Round by round, the cluster of humans and canines in the center of the room grew larger until the only dogs left in the game were Daisy and a jowly male Lab named Tobia from CCI. Tobia's puppy raiser was a pro who had been fostering dogs for CCI for more than fifteen years. She was the one Christina pointed to when she scolded the rest of us about our sloppy dog-handling skills. "Look at Robin. Her dog is exactly where he should be, nose lined up with her knee, *and* he's constantly checking in with her. That's what you should be doing with your dogs." I was no match for Robin, but maybe Tobia found his equal in Daisy because somehow here we were, facing off against each other in the final round of musical sits.

The music started up again and we pitched forward, falling into step in time to the music. I caught my reflection in the mirrored wall, striding ahead with a determined look on my face while Daisy bounced alongside. I felt slightly ridiculous, but intent on winning. The music stopped and Daisy plunked her rump down beside me even as I was telling her to sit. Tobia was also sitting, but I didn't see who made it to the floor first. Christina strode into the ring carrying a nubby orange barbell toy in her hand. She was smiling at . . . us! "Daisy is the winner!" she said, and held out the toy to Daisy, who accepted it graciously between her teeth. Christina might as well have handed her a gold medal, that's how proud I felt. In my mind, we were on the podium, hand (and paw) over our hearts, while the National

Anthem played and the crowd cheered. In reality, we got back into line for another round of play, only this time Christina substituted downs for sits and Daisy behaved like an arthritic camel lowering herself slowly to the ground. We were tagged out immediately. Okay, so we had some work to do, but oh, those sits! I couldn't wait to tell Keith how well our dog did against some pretty tough competition. Marty and the kids would be tickled by the news, but only Keith would match my pride.

Before class ended, Christina stood in the middle of the room, feet planted slightly apart, and gave us some general pointers, offering them casually, almost as asides, ringing them with anecdotes and sound effects that made them irresistible. I hung on every word as if they had been woven into a towline that, if I held on tight enough and long enough, would bring me and Daisy through safely to the end.

At the end of the hour, I thanked Christina and let her know I planned to be back the next Saturday. "Thank *you* for coming." She smiled. "And you, too, Daisy! You looked great!" Daisy scooted over to Christina and sat before her, craning her neck to meet Christina's eyes. Christina asked me whether there was anything in particular I was working on with Daisy. "How does she do walking alongside a shopping cart?" she asked. I sucked in my breath and confessed that I hadn't gathered the courage to bring her to a supermarket. Christina raised an eyebrow at me. "How old is she?" I told her eight months.

"Oh, sweetheart. Get over it."

THE NEXT DAY, when Josh and I returned home from religious school, I knocked on Aviva's door.

"Yeaaaaah?"

"I need you to play backup for me," I said through the crack.

"What do you mean?" She sounded annoyed.

"I'm taking Daisy to the grocery store. It's a big step for me and I need your moral support."

My daughter won't clean her room. She won't listen to me when I demand she be nice to her brother. She'll argue with me until we're both crying in frustration, but if there's one thing I can count on her to do, it's to be there for me if I tell her I need her. It's how I know that no matter what she puts me through now, she loves me and she's going to be okay. We'll be okay. I heard Aviva's bedsprings creak. "When are we leaving?"

IT SORT OF shocked me, the way Daisy went willingly wherever I led her. Which is a ridiculous way to feel. She is a dog, after all. What's she going to do? Stop in her tracks on the way into the grocery store and say, "Wait a minute. Won't we be violating a board of health regulation if I go in there?"

I picked a small supermarket, figuring the exit would always be within reach in case we had to make a quick getaway. The three of us walked through the automatic doors, Aviva lagging a few steps behind so anyone watching wouldn't immediately identify her as being with us. I had crammed several plastic shopping bags and a wad of paper towels in my pocketbook just in case Daisy had an accident. I prayed she wouldn't.

I wasn't ready for a shopping cart yet so I lifted a green plastic basket from a stack near the door. "Will you be in charge of this?" I handed it to Aviva without taking my eyes off Daisy, whose nose was tilted high in the air. The doors had deposited us into the produce department. I led Daisy toward the lettuce. Aviva studiously avoided eye contact with the other shoppers, who I noticed were watching us. I pulled a plastic bag from the dispenser and examined the heads of romaine when a movement to my right caught my eye. I looked down in time to see Daisy lift her face and gently pluck a wet lettuce leaf from a head of Boston bib. "Drop it!" I commanded firmly but quietly so the produce man stocking tomatoes nearby wouldn't hear. Daisy gazed at me with that worried expression, the lettuce leaf dangling from her mouth. I swiped it away while Aviva increased the distance between us.

At the deli counter I grabbed a ticket and waited for my number to be called. Daisy was inching toward the glass for a closer look at the meat inside when a woman standing next to me turned and said, "Oh! You dropped your ticket." I looked at her, then down at the floor where the pink slip of paper lay a few feet away from me.

"Thanks," I said, bending down, but she stopped me. "No, no! Let me get it," she said with that overly helpful tone people use when speaking with small children . . . or people with disabilities. I opened my mouth to explain that Daisy wasn't my service dog, but the woman was already handing the ticket to me. "Thank you," I said just as my number flashed on the sign. The hair-netted woman behind the counter leaned over to look at Daisy while I gave her my order. I thought she was going to ask Daisy whether she'd like a slice of American cheese, just as she used to do when Aviva and Josh were small enough to fit in the shopping cart.

The aisles were less tempting to Daisy than the perimeter

of the store, filled as they were with prepackaged and canned foods. Although she did manage to lick a wayward grain of rice on the floor before I could stop her. At the refrigerated meat cases at the back of the store, I kept my body between Daisy and the meat and used my leg to gently knock her back into position when she tried to cross over to get closer to the goods.

Throughout the store, people stopped to watch us and a few asked us about Daisy, just as I had done on that Mother's Day. Spotting a dog in a supermarket is amusing and unsettling at the same time. There's something vaguely human about a service dog trotting up an aisle or standing placidly in front of a display of canned soup as if trying to decide between chicken noodle and minestrone.

We made it through the bakery department and headed toward the checkout. Aviva unloaded the basket onto the belt while I kept Daisy from drooling on the rack of candy bars. I looked away from Daisy long enough to notice a package of Pepperidge Farm cookies slide by on the belt. Aviva glanced sideways at me. "Is it okay that I got those?" she asked.

"Honey," I answered while pulling Daisy's nose out of the backside of the cashier in the next aisle. "You deserve an entire case."

THAT EVENING I stood in my customary spot in shift command and watched Daisy settle into a down next to Keith's right leg. I had handed him the folder along with Daisy's leash. He asked me how things went over the weekend. "Daisy went to the supermarket today." Keith's features tightened; he looked at me with a mixture of hope and trepidation.

"How'd she do?" He held Daisy's leash at his sternum and began wrapping the end around his hand.

"She did great."

He dropped his hands to his side and smiled broadly.

"Yeah?"

"Yup. The meat department was a little bit of a challenge, but she fought her instincts and she won. She didn't dive into the meat case and rip apart the packages. She was a champ. I was very proud of her."

Keith laughed and I looked up at him, startled. It was the first time I'd heard a real laugh from him. I wanted to hear it again.

"I also took her to a training class with Christina." Keith nodded his head in recognition and I realized he thought I meant Christy. "Christina's also a NEADS trainer but she works with the inmates at a couple of prisons in Massachusetts." That last part I added haltingly, feeling awkward at mentioning prison to Keith, which is ridiculous if you think about it, seeing as we were standing in a prison. I launched into a description of musical sits, watching his face for flashes of his own memories of playing musical chairs at birthday parties. "And"—I paused for dramatic effect—"Daisy won! There were probably twenty other dogs there and she beat them all."

"Hey! All right! You won the game, girl? You won the game!" He bent down to scruff Daisy around the face and lowered his face for a kiss.

"She didn't do as well with musical downs, so we still have some work to do, but I've got to tell you, she has those sits down like a pro. The music would stop, I'd stop, and she'd plunk her rear down and look up at me for her treat while the other dogs were still standing or walking around trying to figure out what to do next."

Keith laughed again and I knew he was imagining the scene, watching his dog outperform the others. All that was missing were a pair of comfy chairs and all the time in the world so we could sit and talk until we ran out of words. There was so much to tell about Daisy and so much I wanted to know. How did Daisy spend a typical day, Monday through Friday? Where besides Christy did Keith get information about dogs and training? Were there any dog books in the prison library? If so, which ones? Did Daisy have a best friend in prison? At home we always stopped halfway through our walk around the block to play with Reese, a beagle mix. I wanted to tell Keith about hide-and-seek with Josh and to ask what games he played with her. But of course there were no comfy chairs and no more time to talk before the officer on duty, a tall, stocky guy, stepped out of his office to move me along. I stood about as high as his chest, so I craned my neck, looking up past the wall of blue uniform, and tilted my head toward Daisy. "Look at this dog," I told him. "She's going to change somebody's life."

She already had.

———

DAISY AND I made the thirty-minute drive to Alpha Dog K9 every Saturday after that first class. Over time, I got to know Christina and the flock of puppy raisers she nurtured with the same care she gave to her own dogs. A few of Christina's puppy raisers were true disciples, modeling themselves in tone and stance after their teacher. They approached their task with the same degree of seriousness, anticipating distractions and redirecting their dogs before they could get into mischief. Dogs learn a great deal by watching other dogs. Humans learn the same way. By watching the other puppy raisers and with Christina's reminders, I became more assured and consistent with Daisy. During one class, Daisy gave me a hard time with downs. Instead of dropping to her belly, she would stand there, looking around as if she were trying to remember where she had left her car keys. Eventually, she would lower herself into a long, slow, leisurely down, as if she had decided that maybe she would take a little rest after all. Christina stood with her hands on her hips and stared at me. "Listen to yourself. You're drawing out the word and you're asking her to down. You're saying 'Dowwwwn-nnn?' You're giving her the choice, and she's saying, 'Yeah, okay. When I get around to it.'" She took the leash and Daisy, who was smitten with Christina, sat at her feet, about as close as she could get without actually sitting *on* Christina's feet. "Down!" Christina commanded, and Daisy flattened to the ground, tail wagging at Christina. "Here, you try it," she said, handing the leash back to me before moving on. Daisy followed Christina with her gaze.

"Down!" I mimicked Christina as best I could and Daisy looked at me, expressionless, paused for a moment, then dropped.

I paid closer attention to Keith during the dog exchanges, too. Keith had the human-dog communication thing down, both spoken and unspoken. It was obvious in his economy of both words and movement with Daisy. They took up little space together. If Daisy strayed even halfway to the end of her leash, he would step backward, pulsing her toward him until she returned to position. When he issued a command, no rush of words came before or after. Just the command. And it was never repeated.

I became more deliberate, authoritative with Daisy. And, to my amazement, my interactions with my children became more thoughtful, less impulsive as well. In the same way that I was learning to read Daisy's body language, I found myself paying closer attention to Aviva and Josh—to their tones and nonverbal signals—and to my own. Christina and Daisy taught me that the way you say something is just as important as what you say. Actually, more important.

Back at home I deployed my newfound self-awareness when Josh met me at the door.

"Aviva was in my room and she lied about it."

"I didn't go in his room. He was in *my* room!" Aviva's voice preceded her into the hallway, where I was taking off my shoes. Daisy ran into the kitchen, and a moment later we heard her tag clanging against the metal dish and the sound of water being lapped up.

"Because you were in *my* room first! Mom! Tell her she can't go in my room."

"Oh my God, Josh. You're such a baby."

"Mom! Make her stop!" His voice was accusatory, like it was my fault. My muscles tightened and my face grew hot, familiar anger rising, but instead of letting it all out in one mad, screaming frenzy, I kept my voice steady:

"Please stay out of each other's room. Discussion closed."

Of course they ignored that last part and kept arguing back and forth, but my personal victory was in not jumping into the ring with them like I usually do. This time I stayed above it all and it felt pretty darn good . . . until their fighting got to me.

I sat on the floor and pulled my shoes back on. "Daisy needs a walk."

Aviva looked at Daisy, who, thirst quenched, was now on her side, eyes closed and breathing deeply.

"Oh, really?" She raised her eyebrows at me.

It didn't matter. Daisy was game. And by the time we got back, the house was quiet again.

11

No

SPRING ARRIVED IN name only. The air was a cold, damp mist that turned my knuckles red as I made my way through the prison parking lot to pick up Daisy. Still, the sky was softly illuminated behind the cloud cover, an encouraging sign that the days were lengthening and the worst of winter was over.

Smitty greeted me in his typical jokey manner and dialed the correctional officer in Cell Block A. The usual procedure is for the CO to pass the message along to the inmate, but apparently today Keith wasn't in the block, because while I was waiting to be buzzed into the courtyard, I heard Smitty's voice over the loudspeaker, summoning Keith to shift command by name. His full name.

It took a moment to register: I was hearing his last name. The missing piece. The word I could type into a Google search box or the corrections department database, which lists inmates' convictions and sentences. The answer to why he was in prison. If I got lucky, maybe I'd pick up a few scraps to stitch into a more complete picture of him—perhaps a parent's obituary would pop up, or I'd find his name buried in a list of 5K race times. I repeated his last name over in my head while walking into shift command; while waving to the officer on duty, who lifted a lazy hand in greeting; while watching Keith himself make his way with Daisy through the yard, his stride so familiar by now that I could pick him out in a crowd in prison or out. When he reached the door, he caught my eye through the barred window and smiled before pulling his eyes down to Daisy. I smiled back, even as I said his name again to myself, silently fixing the word with the face.

If I had second thoughts about finding out Keith's crime, they were too fleeting to give me pause, the pull to know more about him too strong. That he was a talented trainer and an exceptional caregiver to Daisy just wasn't enough for me. I was pages away from the end of a mystery. I needed to know the end.

I grabbed Daisy's leash and her food and turned to the door, impatient to leave. "Anything I need to know?" My voice was hurried and I noticed a flash of confusion in Keith's eyes. But it was gone quickly as he picked up on my cues and turned to his own door. "No. She should be good for you this weekend." Usually I take as much time as I'm allowed in shift command; I felt a twinge of guilt and hoped Keith would figure that I was simply in a rush to get somewhere.

Back in the car, I unclipped Daisy's leash and kissed her hello before closing the back door and sliding behind the wheel. I yanked my pocketbook out from under the seat and dug around for a pen and something to write on. I found an old ATM slip, which I pressed against the dashboard to smooth the wrinkles. Holding it taut, I scribbled on the back of the slip to coax the ink from a ballpoint and wrote Keith's last name. I folded the ATM slip neatly in half and tucked it into a zippered compartment of my purse. With his last name in writing, I was finally able to relax. On the drive home with the radio blasting, I played with the idea of just leaving the slip in my pocketbook, of not looking at it again. I do that with chocolate sometimes. Just knowing it's there in case of emergency is enough to keep me from wanting it. But I knew I'd give in to the temptation even as I hated myself for being so weak. It felt unseemly to want to know about Keith's past and I couldn't help but think that if I were a better person, I wouldn't need to pry.

AT HOME, AVIVA was at the kitchen table sipping a Dunkin' Donuts Coolatta and finishing off some sort of bagel sandwich. The front of her gymnastics leotard was smeared with white chalk from the uneven bars. She put the Coolatta down while I kissed the top of her head and Daisy investigated the floor beneath the table. "How was prison?" she asked, smiling at the notion that she could legitimately pose that question to her mother.

"Prison was good. How was gymnastics?"

"My coach is *insane!*" Daisy startled at the sudden outburst and bumped her head on the bottom of the kitchen table. "Oh, Daisy! Ouch! I'm sorry." Aviva rubbed the spot between Daisy's ears. "Yeah, so, during conditioning we had to climb up and down the ropes without touching the ground in between. You wouldn't believe how hard that is."

I stared at my daughter, in awe of her commitment, the way she powered through physical challenges, complicated piano recital pieces, schoolwork. I opened my mouth to say that at the precise moment Marty came into the room and challenged Aviva to show off her muscles.

"Come on! Let's see 'em, show us your arms of steel." He reached for her bicep, but she shook him off.

"Dad! Quit it! I just want to eat and take a shower, okay?"

I shot Marty a dirty look. If that were me, tired and hungry, I would have been tempted to unleash the power of one of those arms on him.

He turned to me. "And how was *your* day?" Daisy came out from under the table and was wiggling her body ecstatically against his legs. He reached down to ruffle her fur.

"Good." I told him about a project at work. I didn't tell him I had Keith's last name. For one, I didn't want to bring it up while Aviva was in the room. I'd learned long ago that the surest way to lose control over a situation is to talk about it in front of the kids. They seize any half-formed idea or thought balloon that comes out of my mouth and turn it into something I suddenly have to deal with. But also, it seemed premature to say anything. I didn't know what I would find out, if anything, so there didn't seem much point in bringing it up.

———

LATER THAT NIGHT, when the kids were in their rooms and Marty was practicing guitar upstairs, I settled in front of my computer, alone except for Daisy, who lay curled on the floor beside me. I didn't know whether I would find much, just figured I'd let Google take me where it would. My anticipation was high, though, and if Google didn't yield results, well, I was a journalist—I knew how to research. There was the Rhode Island Department of Corrections inmate database, newspaper archives, and online court documents. Mostly I wanted to know why Keith was in prison—what got him there in the first place. But at the same time, I hoped his crime was minor enough not to warrant much publicity. I *liked* Keith. He had earned my affection by being a thoughtful and talented partner in raising the most loving, sweet-tempered, extraordinary dog alive. I didn't want that to change.

Still, I forged ahead, typing his full name in the search box along with a few key words. The first few Google entries turned out not to be him. Then, about five results down the list, I found what was unmistakably a court document. I clicked on it and caught my breath when the full text of a Rhode Island Supreme Court appeal filled my screen.

It was filed by someone I'll call John Smith, who had been convicted of first-degree murder and a number of related charges. I skimmed over the first few paragraphs, searching for Keith's name, then stopped cold when it appeared toward the bottom of the page. I went back to the beginning and started reading again, more slowly.

It was all laid out right there in the dispassionate language of the courts, a description of a crime that happened seventeen years ago. Keith was sixteen, his friend John, seventeen. They were with friends, drinking at the home of an older boy. Apparently, the party lasted all week long. Police showed up a few times when neighbors complained about the noise, but the next night the kids would be back.

So far, it seemed like any one of the parties I went to as a teenager. Someone fresh out of high school and in his own apartment would invite a few friends to come over that weekend and before you knew it, the word would be out, spreading through the school like a cold virus. Carloads of kids with six-packs of Budweiser and screw-top bottles of Boone's Farm Strawberry Hill wine would descend on the home, everyone getting drunker and louder as the night wore on. The worst that would happen was a girl would twist her ankle stumbling across the yard on her three-inch platform sandals. Or maybe a couple of guys would start swinging at each other and their buddies would have to pull them apart.

This party, it was clear from the document in front of me, would not end well. The twenty-year-old host owned guns. Early in the night, he tucked a .22 revolver into his waistband and carried it with him as he mingled with guests.

This was where Keith's name first appeared. John and Keith lived in different towns but knew each other from playing pickup hockey. Looking for something to do that late-fall night, they found out about the party and showed up with a couple of other friends. At some point during a night of drinking, the party host threatened John with the gun and ordered him to get out of the house. John was humiliated. He grabbed Keith and the other friends who brought him there, and they left the party. They drove around for a few hours, nursing their injured pride and complaining that the party host needed to be put in his place. In my mind, John was beefy and half-wild and Keith, at sixteen, his slouchy sidekick. With Keith's encouragement, John vowed revenge.

My stomach was beginning to hurt and I thought maybe I should stop reading. But I kept going, my index finger on the mouse's tracking wheel, my gaze flying over the words, afraid to linger too long on any one of them. Something bad was going to happen and I wanted to get it over with.

Later that night, John and Keith had their friends drop them off back at the apartment. The police had been there once again about the noise, and the party host—once the police had left—had used his gun to order most of his guests to leave. When John and Keith knocked on the door, the host ushered them inside.

There were only a handful of people still partying by then. One of them convinced their host to leave the gun in the bedroom so nobody would accidentally get hurt. At some point during the night, Keith and John snuck into the bedroom where John found the .22-caliber handgun and Keith helped himself to a hunting rifle. The pair disappeared outside. Sensing something was wrong, the host went into the bedroom and noticed the .22 missing from the top of his bureau, where he had left it. "They got my gun!" he shouted, and ran off to find the two teenagers. A few minutes later his friend followed, then stopped cold when he got to the front door. His buddy was facedown on the walkway outside, blood pooling beneath his head. Keith was standing before the body, gripping the butt end of a rifle. John was holding the revolver.

My hand trembled over the mouse. The muscles in my legs and arms turned to sludge while the blood in my face pulsed with a stinging heat. But still, I kept reading, racing even faster over the words. The victim had a single bullet hole in the back of his head from the shot John fired; his cheek and jawbones were pulverized.

Keith and John fled, but before they left the murder scene, they emptied the victim's wallet and tossed it, bloodstained, a few feet from the body. With the cash and a stolen car, they went on a crime spree, holding up gas stations as they attempted to drive across the country. During one attempted holdup, John shot another victim, who miraculously survived. Police caught up with the pair two days and five states later after a botched robbery attempt. They were held in juvenile detention before being extradited to Rhode Island to face charges. By then, I imagined, their victim's parents were already arranging their son's burial.

Keith didn't pull the trigger, but that hardly mattered. The coroner said the body had been struck in the face as many as six times. Two of his teeth and a piece of facial skin were found on the sidewalk. A third tooth was located under his left arm.

Both John and Keith were charged as adults. The judge termed John a "cold-blooded killer" and handed down the maximum sentence—life plus forty-five years. The crime, the judge said, was "an exhibition of human savagery at its worst." Keith was tried as an adult and sentenced to forty years for accessory to murder.

———

I LEANED MY forehead into my hands, squeezing my eyes shut against the pictures that formed. The night, dark and cold with winter pushing in. Keith, his features contorted with rage, throwing his weight into the thrust of the gun stock. Steam pouring from his mouth and nose as if he were the devil himself, while his arms shook from the impact of each successive blow to his victim's face. The cracking of bone and teeth, the tearing of skin. Then his friend firing a shot to the back of the head. A single, neat hole leaking blood on the front walk. It became a living thing, grotesque and huge, growing inside me, infecting everything good I felt about Keith. The outlines had been filled in. Keith was no longer a generic, gentle inmate who trained puppies and who ducked his head shyly when he smiled. Now he was someone capable of taking another's life without a thought.

I closed the document on my computer and shut my eyes, fighting back the bile rising in my throat. Instinctively, I glanced down at Daisy for comfort—but tonight it had the opposite effect and I had to turn away. At that moment, she wasn't my Daisy but a dumb dog who gave her affection indiscriminately to anyone with a cookie in his hand. Even as I told myself I wasn't being logical, that I was unfairly transferring my disgust with Keith onto her, I couldn't forgive Daisy for living with Keith, as if she had any choice or was even capable of knowing his past. Picturing her returning to Keith on Sunday with her tail wagging as if he deserved love made my bond with her feel flimsy and cheap. The thought of his hands on her made my skin crawl. I didn't know how I could ever touch her again.

I pushed away from my desk and stepped over Daisy, willing her not to wake up. It didn't work. She stretched and followed me into the hallway, her tags jingling, then stood passively by my side. I turned away from her and toward my children's rooms. Light seeped beneath Aviva's bedroom door but Josh's room was dark. I stood, listening to the sounds of the house: Josh's breathing, congested from his allergies. Aviva moving about in her room. Music, small and strained, floated from the kitchen, where Marty sat with his laptop and a beer. I ticked each family member off on my mental list, and for a second felt reassured that each was present and accounted for. Then, an instant later, I went cold all over by this latest proof that none of us are truly safe; that bad things happen and, really, there's nothing you can do about it. You can pray to God or Allah or Gaia to protect the people you love, to keep the drunks off the road, the people with guns and murderous intent away, the tumors benign, the surgery successful, but in the end, you're just talking to yourself.

I was glad Keith would be locked away for another twenty years.

Suddenly, I was so tired. But Daisy needed to go out before I could go to bed. She waited, oblivious to my grief and anger, while I pulled on my boots and jacket and clipped the leash to her collar. Outside, in the cold, damp air, the details of the crime played out again and again. I did a quick calculation and realized that I was in my first trimester with Aviva when it happened, living two towns away, just over the state line. One life beginning, another ending way too soon. I put myself in the place of the victim, the last frame of his life occupied by the sixteen-year-old punk he'd welcomed into his house, charging at him with his own gun. Then the explosion of pain.

I lifted my face to the sky, dully aware of Daisy sniffing in the grass. There was no moon or stars visible. Just blackness. Nothing was the same. Over the past five months, I'd been collecting scraps of information like precious bits of timber in the desert and using them to construct an image of Keith that would justify my deep and growing affection for him, and that would free me to trust him with Daisy. Now there was this, and everything came crashing down.

Back in the house, I picked up the towel I kept by the door on weekends and used it to wipe the nighttime dew from each of Daisy's paws. She wagged her tail and arched her face toward mine, enjoying the attention, but I leaned away and turned my head, for some reason unable to bear the contact with her cold, clammy nose.

I just wanted to go to sleep.

I kissed Marty good night, grateful that I was married to someone who, even if he did notice I was distraught, would know enough not to question me but wait until I was ready to talk. And I wasn't ready—because saying it out loud would make it real. "I'll be up soon," he said, and bent to press his mouth against the top of Daisy's head. "Good night, sweetie-face," he said to her, then turned back to his computer, once again absorbed in the finger-picking style of a guitarist on YouTube.

In bed I shivered under the blanket and used it to wipe my eyes, which were spilling over now that I was alone in the dark. If only there was something in that document, a word, a phrase, anything that would, if not absolve Keith, at least temper what he did. If only he hadn't so *brutally* attacked that guy. If the victim had pulled a gun and Keith acted in self-defense. Or if he had stuck around and admitted what he did instead of stealing a car and going off on a crime spree like some kind of psychopath.

But nothing in that document allowed Keith a way out. The fact that he didn't strike the fatal blow was just a technicality—if that young man had died from the beating instead of the gunshot, Keith would have been the murderer.

I didn't want to think anymore. I wanted to rewind the clock to before I learned Keith's last name—no, all the way back to that late-autumn night so I could warn the party host to keep the doors locked.

───────────

AT FIVE THE next morning, I woke to Daisy's breath in my face. I knew her chin was resting on the bed and she was staring at me, willing me with her eyes to open mine. I turned my back, but that just made her more insistent. She whined and thumped her tail against my bureau, prancing in place and lifting the blanket into peaks with her nose. I sighed and got out of bed. She was ecstatic to see me upright and wagged her entire body against my legs, butting me with her head. But I pushed past her and groped my way down the stairs to switch on the coffeemaker before taking Daisy outside.

Daisy gnawed on a bone while I drank coffee in the dark and thought about Keith, what his childhood might have been like, how it would lead him to end up in prison before he was even done growing. It must have been bad. Yet what did that matter? Plenty of people overcome childhood abuse and neglect and grow up to become decent human beings.

I flipped through other murders—ones I or my newspaper coworkers had covered and ones I'd read about—to see whether any would yield insight into Keith's state of mind or unveil possible extenuating circumstances that might help me make sense of what he did.

A detective once took me into his darkroom to show me crime scene photos from a case I was covering. He pointed out the frenzied, overlapping stab wounds clustered around the female victim's groin and chest, and explained that their location, number, and pattern indicated a crime of passion—an explosion of violence against someone the perpetrator had an intimate relationship with. Premeditated murders tend to be cleaner and quicker, he said. They're more likely to be carried out with a gun, which can be deployed from a distance and without physical exertion. So, where does that put Keith? His friend did the shooting, but he threw himself at the victim with the barrel of the rifle. Was he overcome by a burst of uncontrollable anger, one fueled by alcohol? For my desperate mind, that would have been easier to comprehend than a planned attack. If only he hadn't gone looking for the gun.

Once I interviewed a high school girl while she and her family were holed up in a hotel room while police searched for her stalker. Earlier that day the stalker had chosen a home at random, broken in, and killed the mother and two young children who lived there. The high school girl was terrified that he would come for her next.

In terms of sheer atrocity, Keith's crime seemed less shocking than those two, but more deliberate than one Marty covered, in which an off-duty police officer shot a legislative aide. A jury found the police officer guilty of manslaughter instead of first-degree murder after his attorney argued successfully that his client shot the victim in self-defense while trying to break up a drug deal.

Maybe Keith's defense attorney was incompetent.

I was grasping at straws. Worse, I was categorizing Keith's crime as if I kept a personal rating system for murderers.

That morning, I went through the motions with Daisy, my thoughts mired in a stew of dread and confusion. Our morning walk was short. I might as well have been alone, that's how little attention I gave to Daisy. I felt betrayed and angry, heartsick, but mostly deeply, profoundly sad. All of the work Keith and I poured into Daisy was for each other, too, and that made him like family. As sick as I felt about what he did, knowing how long his sentence stretched in either direction left me bereft over his wasted life.

Operating on automatic, I showered after the walk, leaving Daisy outside the bathroom door while I dried my hair. There would be no playing with the hair dryer that morning. Then, I stuffed my pocket with treats, and headed with Daisy to Christina's class. It was jarring, somehow, to see the other puppy raisers behaving the same as usual with their dogs. Of course, nothing had changed for them. I wondered, had any of them learned what their inmates were in for? I was afraid to ask for fear they would tell me the obvious: that I shouldn't have overstepped my bounds as a puppy raiser and let my curiosity distract me from my work with Daisy.

I was okay in class when I focused on commands, but during the pauses when we had to stand around waiting for other dogs to execute theirs, my thoughts would snap right back to the crime. I kept searching for a loophole, something that would allow me to forgive Keith. And I kept coming up empty. After class I avoided the other puppy raisers and headed straight for my car with Daisy. But instead of going home, I took a detour to a bike path. The night before, I needed to sleep; now I needed a mind-clearing, heart-pumping walk.

I led Daisy out of the car and we set out on the trail, which follows an old rail bed past a lake and through woods. I didn't even give Daisy a chance to sniff for a place to pee, but forged ahead with my eyes to the ground and Daisy jogging to keep up. The trail curved around a narrow beach and widened slightly to a spot where somebody had placed an engraved, granite memorial bench. The person whose memory it had been dedicated to had lived a long life, judging by the dates next to the name. Suddenly I was furious, not with Keith but with the victim. Who the hell was he, flashing his gun around? Did he think that made him a tough guy? And why did he let all of those underage kids into his house to get drunk? He was just inviting trouble, and there it came, knocking on his door. If he had only left the guns locked up where they belonged, he wouldn't be dead and Keith's life wouldn't have been ruined. And what was he doing with guns, anyway? Why does anyone need a gun? I hated them! The cold air seared my lungs; I was breathing hard, tugging roughly on Daisy whenever she attempted to pause at a scent.

Then, as I realized I was blaming the victim for his own murder, I forced my mind into his parents' perspective, imagining myself taking the phone call from a police detective, telling me there'd been an incident involving my son. And then identifying my boy's body, maybe by his hair color or his clothing because his features were obliterated by blunt force trauma. What's it like to know that your child was murdered by his own gun? The child whose arrival on earth you celebrated with balloons and birth announcements? Whose very existence must have been preordained because once he was born, you couldn't imagine the universe without him in it?

I've seen what a parent's grief looks like. It is raw and primal; it is inconceivable. Once, standing by a pile of debris in the yard of a burned-out home, I watched the father of two young children who died in the house fire that he himself had survived wince in pain as he hoisted his scarred body behind the controls of a backhoe. He was supposed to take only a symbolic first swipe at the side of the house, then turn the machine over to the workers, but he refused to relinquish the seat. His face rigid, he clawed away at the husk of a home until, had it been the living, breathing monster he imagined it to be, it would have been dead from the wounds he inflicted with the machine.

My nose was running and my eyes tearing from cold and grief by the time I returned to the car with Daisy. She fell asleep immediately in the backseat. When we got home, the house was empty. Marty had taken Aviva to a gymnastics meet and Josh was next door, playing. Daisy collapsed inside her crate and I lay down on the couch. We both slept.

That night when the kids were in bed, I was ready to tell Marty, if only to release the pressure of it churning through my system. Although, looking back, I guess part of me was seeking the comfort of entering familiar conversational territory with my husband. He and I have a long history of discussing crimes, both ones we or colleagues have covered and ones we've read about. We'll ponder the perpetrator's motivation and state of mind, speculate about the choice of weapon. And Marty will crack jokes, keeping us at a safe emotional distance from the crime.

I caught him as he was walking down the stairs and followed him into the kitchen. "I found out what Keith did," I said to his back.

He turned around with a questioning look. "Oh?"

I sank into a kitchen chair, took a deep breath, and reported what I'd learned as a news story, laying out fact after objective fact. It was just too confusing to talk about how it made me feel.

"Jesus" was all he said. No wisecracks, no discussion. He'd need to let it sink in, just as I had. His reaction made me feel validated, but worse. Although Marty knew him only through me and Daisy, it seemed that Marty had grown fond of Keith as well.

———

ONE OF THE empty classrooms at religious school was converted each Sunday into a lounge where parents could pump cups of coffee from stainless-steel carafes, grab a chair, and socialize. A few weeks earlier, I'd begun bringing Daisy in to meet people and to practice her down-stays. I wandered in with her that Sunday, feeling hollow, and took a seat in one of the straight-backed desk chairs while the dog lovers in the room vied for Daisy's attention. I let her say hello, but guided her back to my side and into a down-stay after I caught her nosing around in someone's knitting bag.

"Sharron trains service dogs," one of the women was telling her husband. "Sharron, tell him what you do."

"Oh. Um." I shifted in my seat and looked down at Daisy, who was eyeing my pocket expectantly. I pulled out a few pieces of kibble and fed them to her while I launched into the now familiar spiel beginning with "She's actually trained in prison. I just have her on weekends."

When I finished speaking, the husband looked at Daisy with wonder. "Wow. And that's got to be a good thing for the prisoners, too. Think about it: they probably learn empathy and trust, what it means to care for someone who's totally dependent on you . . ."

I was nodding my head in agreement when Brett, whose

son has autism, poked his head through the doorway, "Oh, good! Daisy's here," he said. "Can Matty meet her?" Before I could answer, Brett was ushering the eight-year-old into the room. With his dark hair and eyes, Matty was a miniature version of his father, but while Brett often looked worried, Matty wore a perpetual smile that seemed to invite people into his world. "Matty! Matty! Look! Come meet Daisy. Come meet the dog." Brett tried to direct the boy's attention to Daisy. Matty scanned the room and jogged toward Daisy, flapping his arms, but veered off in the direction of the teacher's desk, where he spotted a computer. Brett corralled his son and guided him toward Daisy, who stood up to greet him. With his father holding him in place, Matty tapped Daisy twice on the head with his hand before breaking away from Brett and running toward the door. Brett took off after him, calling over his shoulder, "Next time I'll try to get him to focus. He loves dogs!" Daisy's tail dropped as she watched them go. She stared at the door with what I imagined was a mixture of hope and disappointment. She loves children.

"Down," I said, more gently than I had since Friday night, and she dropped to the tile without taking her eyes off the doorway.

By now the husband and wife and a handful of others were debating whether rehabilitation was possible in prison. I turned away from them and watched Daisy, who looked slightly miserable now, with her face tucked between her front paws. She would have been so happy if I'd let her follow Matty out of the room or if he had stayed to play with her. That was all she wanted, that connection—just like all of us. I'd been ignoring her all weekend, yet she hadn't done anything wrong. I felt rotten.

The conversations in the room merged together into background noise. I lowered myself cross-legged to the floor to face Daisy, bringing my head to hers while I stroked her ears. She looked straight into my eyes, held the gaze for a moment, and licked my nose. And a little of the ugliness that I'd been carrying with me started to lift.

———————

I DELAYED RETURNING Daisy to prison for as long as possible that evening. I didn't want to face Keith. Marty asked whether I'd be okay seeing him and when I admitted that I was nervous, he reassured me that from everything I had said about him, he seemed to have pulled himself together. "They wouldn't have given him Daisy otherwise," he reminded me.

Still, the sludge returned to my arms and legs on the drive back to the prison, and I felt jittery and weak when I pulled into the parking lot. I had to keep telling myself that Daisy would be safe, that the only thing different was that now I knew why Keith was in prison. He was the same person who took exceptional care of Daisy, and so many years had passed since he was the sixteen-year-old described in the court document. Daisy herself was proof that Keith didn't go around acting on his violent impulses.

None of that counted, though, because no matter how reassured I was that Daisy was safe, the fact remained that I had to face Keith, knowing what I did. He would take one look at me and see the fear and revulsion in my expression. I was sure he would know that I knew.

The stiff nylon of the leash bit into my hand, I gripped it so tightly walking into the reception area. Visitors crowded the small space. They stood like cattle, dumbly accepting whatever awaited on the other side of the razor wire. For some, prison is a rite of passage, the way enlisting in the military or going off to college is for others. But surely there were others in that room who couldn't believe that they were there—parents who never imagined that the prerequisite for visiting their grown son would be a clean record and a pat-down. Where did Keith's parents fit in? I scanned the crowd, looking for anyone who shared a family resemblance, who could be his mother or father. No one fit. If they were the right age, they were the wrong ethnicity, or too short and stocky. Also, anyone visiting Keith would recognize Daisy and, in all of the times I'd passed through the reception area, no one had ever called out her name. Anyway, it was clear no one ever came to see Keith from his excitement over getting permission to bring Daisy into the visitors' room to meet children. Did he even have any family?

Smitty waved me past and this time, instead of being annoyed by the dual locked doors and gates, I was thankful for them. They kept the bad guys inside, where they couldn't hurt anyone. The farther I advanced into the prison, the shakier I became. It was hard to swallow. I rubbed the area below my collarbone where my chest grew tight. I thought my knees might give out. Somehow, I made it through the final door into shift command, where I noted Keith's presence without looking at him—registered the swath of beige in my peripheral vision. I now realized it was the same uniform, if not the same articles of clothing, that he'd been putting on and taking off every day for nearly two decades. I wondered how many inches he'd put on since the murder, how many pairs of shoes he'd outgrown.

I started talking immediately, trying extra hard to act natural. My voice sounded strained to my own ears as I nervously chattered about Daisy's weekend and praised her progress. I had a hard time meeting Keith's eye and flinched when he took the leash from me, careful not to accidentally brush his hand, which I now pictured curled around the barrel of a rifle.

Pretending nothing had changed was excruciating. I had to get out of there before I made eye contact with him and burst into flames or disintegrated into a pile of ash or, more likely, started shaking uncontrollably. But before I turned to leave, I braved a quick look at Keith, half expecting him to bore into my eyes and silently mouth, "You know!" But he wasn't looking at me. He was looking at Daisy, his expression soft and gentle as he guided her to his side and fed her bits of kibble. He looked exactly the same as always.

———

AS I DROVE home, my thoughts arced back and forth from Keith as accessory to murder to Keith who had spent the last seventeen years being punished for that crime. I couldn't quite digest either, but it barely seemed real that he had been in prison for nearly two decades. What was it like for him to wake up every morning on the same thin mattress? In those first few months, he probably began the climb out of sleep thinking he was in his bed at home—until he opened his eyes and the fixtures of his cell came into focus: the dusky red steel door with the tiny window, the stainless-steel toilet just feet from his head. What was sleep like for him now, after all these years? Did he even dream of his old life? Or had he run out of material long ago? So much time had gone by since the crime. The world had changed so much. It was like he was a character from a fairy tale, locked away in the past while time moved on without him. Keith had never been on the Internet. Had never held a cell phone in his hand. He hadn't rubbed his hand against the rough bark of a tree trunk in nearly two decades, and before the NEADS program came along, he hadn't seen a dog in over ten years.

It was impossible to fathom the deprivation, the wasted years. Thinking about it filled me with despair for Keith, then I'd admonish myself for feeling sorry for him and scrabble back to the crime to justify his ruined life.

I should have known—no, I *did* know this might happen. In the same way that I had overlooked the grim reality of prison, I had used my hurried, twice-weekly meetings with Keith and a great deal of imagination to create a person with whom I was happy to raise a puppy. Now I didn't know how, or if, I could keep working with him.

All week, I kept returning to the crime, trying to reconcile the kid described in the court document with the man with whom I thought of as my canine coparent.

"I don't get it." I was on the phone with Marty, whom I'd called at work when I couldn't take being alone with my thoughts anymore. "If you're training a puppy to be a service dog, you absolutely cannot have a temper. Yeah, you can get frustrated, but you can't act on it because if you do, the only thing the dog will learn is to be afraid of you . . . wait, are you busy right now?"

"Yeah, but that's okay. The mayor doesn't mind waiting, right, Timmy?" Marty held the phone away from his mouth and in a soft, timid voice said, "No, not at all, Mr. Luttrell. It's an honor to be interviewed by you."

"Okay. Good." I laughed, at the joke and with relief that I had Marty to talk to. "So, think about it. Think of what he did. He completely lost control when he attacked that guy, and since then he's been spending every moment of his life with criminals. How could he learn to be any different? Yet, look at Daisy. She's completely trusting and smart and wonderful, so you know he's doing something right."

During Marty's silence, I heard voices punctuated by laughter coming from another area of the newsroom. When he spoke, he said, "Sometimes people manage to rise above their circumstances, whether it's through sheer will or something else. And remember, he was just a kid when it happened, and he was probably drunk. Not that that's an excuse, but you know what it's like. Kids do stupid, dangerous things."

I did know that. There was an old issue of *Newsweek* in my nightstand with a cover story about the teenage brain. I kept it there for easy reference, figuring, at the least, it would help me understand Aviva and, soon enough, Josh. The article describes how the prefrontal cortex, which is responsible for reasoning, planning, and judgment, isn't connected until the midtwenties. Teenagers rely on the amygdala to make decisions. That's the area of the brain associated with impulsive and aggressive behaviors and the reason why adolescents can be so infuriatingly blind to the consequences of their actions.

It's astonishing that any of us survive those years, including my husband and I.

Both Marty and I had a rough run through adolescence. There's no good reason why I didn't die or end up in prison before my slow-developing maturity finally delivered me safely to adulthood. I drank. A lot. Occasionally, I used drugs. I drove under the influence of various substances, some days waking to find the car keys on the floor by the bed, not remembering how I got home. And I was angry for reasons I couldn't articulate. I had an explosive temper that, when fueled by alcohol as Keith's was that night, easily could have landed me in jail. In fact, one night it did. I was locked up in protective custody for fighting with my high school boyfriend and mouthing off to a couple of police officers who found me drinking by the side of the road. But that was mild. The fear that my boyfriend would dump me as my father had my mother sent me into rages whenever I doubted his fidelity. I'd throw punches and, once, my wooden-soled clogs at his head. The only thing that kept me from assault and battery charges, I'm convinced, was my poor aim and his forgiving nature.

I didn't know Marty when he was a kid, but by his account, he was worse than I. He was a shrimp, overshadowed physically and in every other way by his brother Dennis, eleven months older, a charmer and a good student. Teachers choked on their own spit when they found out Marty and Dennis were from the same family. Marty couldn't compete, so he chose the opposite route, fighting with other boys to prove how tough he was and raining mischief on the neighborhood. He and his friend Billy were like matches and gasoline, more or less harmless when apart, but incendiary when they were together. They would roll tires down a steep hill into oncoming traffic, then run away laughing as drivers swerved and slammed on their brakes. The two boys would hop freight trains and ride them to the next town. They used sodium nitrate from the drugstore to make pipe bombs and blow up mailboxes and garden gnomes. Marty outgrew his idiocy and made it to adulthood. Billy wasn't so lucky. A few years after high school his body was found in another state, stuffed into the trunk of a car.

IN PAIRS AND in groups, teenagers can be reckless in ways that wouldn't even occur to them while they're alone. Research bears this out, with studies showing that adolescents are more likely to act impulsively and cause harm to themselves and others when they're with friends. According to the court document, Keith and John fed each other's anger in the hours leading up to the murder. It didn't seem likely that either would have done it without the other one there. But they chose to be together that night, a young man was dead, and Keith had been living a more or less friendless existence since.

The fact that teenagers are literally not in a right mind when they commit crimes was recognized by the U.S. Supreme Court in 2005 when it struck down the juvenile death penalty, calling it cruel and unusual punishment; then a few years later, the court abolished mandatory life sentences without parole for those under eighteen. In the majority opinion in the 2005 decision, Justice Anthony M. Kennedy wrote, "From a moral standpoint, it would be misguided to equate the failings of a minor with those of an adult, for a greater possibility exists that a minor's character deficiencies will be reformed."

If you think about it, all adults are reformed children. At some point, usually in our twenties, we stop acting impulsively; we mature. Most of us, anyway. When someone cuts us off in traffic, we restrain ourselves from flipping off the driver by deciding he must be late for an appointment or he's racing to the hospital where his wife is in labor. We go to work every morning even when we'd rather sleep in, because we accept that we won't be paid otherwise. Keith never got to that point of maturity—or when he did, he wasn't free to exercise adult privileges. Had he stayed at home the night of the murder, where might he be now? Would he have made it through the violent, impulsive years of his adolescence and emerged safe on the other side, married now with a couple of young kids and a steady job? Or would he be serving time for some other crime?

What about my own kids? Would they emerge intact from adolescence? I mentally prodded their characters for weak spots that might one day cause their own lives to crumble apart as Keith's did. Aviva was nearly as old as Keith was when he committed the crime. She's a good kid. She works hard; she's an honor student. But really, what's the difference between her and Keith at that age? Circumstance? Environment? Developmentally, she's the same as he was at sixteen. There have been times when she's come completely unhinged and gone after Josh with fists and fingernails. We don't need a brain scan to know that she's not working at full adult capacity at those moments.

I'm not concerned about Josh, who's so innately pacifist that he couldn't even enjoy *Shrek 2* because of the violence. But as soon as I tell myself he'll be okay, I want to look around for some wood to knock, lest evil spirits punish me for complacency. If Josh strays on the way to adulthood, it will be because he's following the wrong person. He's so quiet; the kids in the carpool plow him over with their chatter and I have to hold up a hand for silence so he can finish a sentence. Even I tend to forget he's there sometimes, he barely stirs the air. Josh fits in best when he feels he has a job to do: carrying his classmates' backpacks, pouring buckets of water on the pool slide so the other kids will go faster . . . what if he falls in with the wrong crowd and does things he knows are wrong, just so someone will finally notice him?

All week long I was distracted. I'd be on the phone interviewing parents for a work project about ways to stay involved in your child's education, and I'd wonder whether Keith's parents encouraged him to do well in school. At Thursday evening's Cub Scouts pack meeting, I found myself searching the boys' faces for signs that one of them might end up in prison one day. Not knowing what Keith was like as a child made my own kids seem vulnerable. They could be victims. They could be perpetrators.

"What if our kids end up like Keith?" I said to Marty more than once that week. I was looking for reassurance and he'd deliver by reminding me that our children, for all their faults, were good kids, and that we, despite *our* faults, were more attentive than our own parents were. He was lost in a pile of brothers and I was the last remaining shred in my splintered family, easily overlooked by a mother who was still reeling from being left alone to finish raising me. Also, times were different back then; kids roamed their neighborhoods unsupervised. We always know where our kids are, at least for now. And they're solid people who, although they drive us crazy sometimes, fill us with pride.

I don't think parents alone are always enough to get a kid safely to adulthood, though. Years ago, during those evenings around a restaurant table with friends, discussing our children, our kids were still little but their adolescence loomed like storm clouds on the horizon. Gabrielle, the most philosophical and measured of us, doubted we could do much to set our kids right if they tilted into juvenile delinquency, since we'd be the ones that they'd be rebelling against. That's why our kids need surrogate parents, she said, and confided that, like an arranged marriage, she'd already begun scouting potential adult role models for her children—she'd been secretly assessing her kids' coaches, teachers, the neighbors, even us—to identify whom she'd want her kids to turn to for adult guidance. A few years later she and her family moved away and we eventually lost touch, so I don't know how her plan worked out, but I know I'm grateful that Aviva has long chats with the woman whose children she babysits for. Over the past five years, she has taught my daughter about organic gardening and the medicinal properties of herbs while sprinkling their chats with wisdom born of her own memories of adolescence. If Aviva ever feels the need—and it's likely she already has—she can talk with her about all of those subjects too charged to bring up to her mother. I'm hoping Josh finds someone like that.

Which makes me wonder, who was there for Keith? How could he possibly have grown up normal in prison, surrounded by deviants and criminals and without the milestones that mark our progress: driver's license, first job, high school graduation, the military, college, career, marriage, parenthood. Some pass those milestones along a direct route to adulthood. For both Marty and me, it was long and circuitous. Marty enlisted in the air force straight out of high school, served four years, hitchhiked back and forth across the country a few times, worked odd jobs, and ultimately went to college on the GI Bill. He was thirty-six when we met and tells me I wouldn't have liked him when he was younger. When I'd ask why, he'd say simply, "Because I was an asshole."

For me, there were three different colleges, a year off to work, and a broken engagement six weeks before the wedding when I realized if I went through with it, I'd never figure out what kind of person I wanted to be. Terrified of being alone, I talked myself into wanting to be married and kept up the charade with my college boyfriend for three years until the moment when it was time to put the stamps on the wedding invitations. I eased him into the breakup by assuring him we'd set a new date once I learned how to live on my own. That was another lie I told both of us. After I'd ripped myself clean of him and exposed myself, finally alone, to the world, I discovered I was happier that way. Eventually he forgave me, which is a testament to his character, not mine.

Keith didn't have any of those experiences. He had to figure out how to become an adult without the benefit of any of the institutions or people that we use to steady ourselves along the way, and in an environment where he was defined not by who he was but by the worst thing he'd done. And the crazy thing is, in some respects, he managed it. The proof is in Daisy. I suspected she helped get him there. To Daisy, Keith had no past. He was just . . . Keith. The attentive, caring guy who put food in her dish and poured her clean, cold water. Who praised her when she worked and gently guided her back to task when she strayed. Who taught her new things, and rewarded her with treats and affection. He was the guy who threw the tennis ball and bit off pieces of apple for her to eat. The one breathing softly when the lights were out at night, and who was still there when she opened her eyes in the morning.

Like Daisy, so captivated by her own reflection in the sliding doors that first weekend with us, Keith only glimpsed himself— the good in himself, anyway—through Daisy. There are no full-length mirrors or plate-glass windows in prison. The only way to see yourself is through others and that image is distorted by what you did and who you have to be to survive. Most of the guys believe that's who they'll ever be, and Keith did, too, for a long, long time. Until Daisy. By responding to Keith's care and training with affection and respect, she encouraged him to work at being the kind of person who deserved to be loved. And he did—harder than he'd ever done before.

12

Speak

FOR DAISY'S SAKE, for Keith's, for mine, and for the person out there who would eventually come to rely on Daisy, I had to be a dog. I had to drop the ugliness of Keith's past back in the box and seal it up where it couldn't leach out and poison all that I knew was good in him. Except I'm not a dog; I kept returning to pry open the lid and sift through its contents. For one thing, the town where the murder took place was on my way to prison. I'd scan the houses, glancing at the front walkways as I drove past, searching for I don't know what—a bloodstain, a granite marker. A few times I'd stop in the town for a quick errand with Daisy and feel guilty that the people who were cooing over the dog may have known Keith's victim—maybe even were the victim's parents.

I told my kids what he did but left out the details, emphasizing instead the role that unattended guns and underage drinking played in the tragedy. To them, the news wasn't the bombshell it was to me, but merely a precursor to yet another lecture from their mother. I broke the news to friends, then studied their reactions for clues to how I myself should feel. Most of them just shook their heads and muttered words about it being a senseless tragedy for everyone involved. My friend Deb, however, stared at me in shock. We were in the woods, walking Daisy and Tanner, and she stopped in the middle of the path. "How old was the kid they killed?" Her eyes were filling with tears and I suddenly felt defensive, my seesawing allegiances now dipping toward Keith. "He was twenty, but Keith was sentenced to forty years! He's missed *everything* that a normal, nonincarcerated person experiences. He's living out his life in prison."

Her voice was shaky but strong when she responded. "I get that. But Keith's parents still get to talk to him. That other kid's parents will never see their son again."

And that set me to hating Keith again. Worse, I felt ashamed for defending him.

———

OVER TIME, I became more skilled at keeping Keith's crime inside that box, particularly when I was face-to-face with him on weekends. Daisy steadily reminded me of the kindness that surely existed in him. The rest of the time, particularly during the week, when Daisy wasn't with me, I wrestled constantly with it. If I thought knowing what Keith did would quell my curiosity, I couldn't have been more wrong. It just made me want to find out more—find out *why*. Eventually, I did find out more, but the question of *why* will never be answered. Not for me, not for him.

In time, as I continued working with NEADS, I requested and received permission to sit in on a few of Christy's training sessions at the prison. This also gave me the opportunity to talk with Keith about his crime.

We sat across from each other at a table in the visiting room, at first talking about Daisy. I asked questions about what it was like to be with her twenty-four hours a day, five days a week; how he trained her, and whether he ever got tired of it. He described his methods, his typical day with Daisy, and when I asked whether he got any emotional fulfillment out of his work with her, he nodded his head enthusiastically.

"Oh, yeah. I love it. It's . . . I don't know . . . I just love it. You have to understand, there's a lot of negativity in this place, and when you've been here as long as me . . ." He paused and looked up at me from across the table. "Do you know what I'm in here for?"

A prickly heat pulsed through my face, yet I felt oddly relieved to finally admit it. "Yes, I do."

Neither of us spoke for a moment. The other inmates were at the front of the room with Christy. They were teaching their dogs to tug on a rope tied to the door handle of a mini fridge.

I drew in a breath. "You're so good with Daisy. She's amazing. I don't understand how . . ." There was no sense in tiptoeing around it, so I just straight out asked, "What happened?"

Keith exhaled loudly. He leaned forward in his chair and stared down at his fists, which he held clasped on the surface of the table. When he spoke, he seemed bewildered.

"I don't know. You have to understand, I didn't know who I was back then. I had no identity. If someone said to me, 'Who are you?' I wouldn't have known how to answer."

He went on to explain that before he hit adolescence, he was a normal kid who lived and breathed baseball. His dream was to make it to the major leagues, just like his mom's cousin who played in the minors and pitched one game for the Atlanta Braves before he contracted encephalitis and died. Then things got messed up when Keith was fourteen. He found an adoption certificate with his name on it in his parents' file cabinet—and that's when the story came out that the man who raised him wasn't his biological father. Keith didn't know who he was anymore. He started getting into trouble, fighting, running away. Things got worse the next year when Keith's family moved to another region of the country for a job transfer. To Keith, the pieces of his identity were being painfully stripped away, leaving behind nothing but raw anger. The confusion, the betrayal by his parents roiled until it distilled into a simmering rage that every now and then flared up. He gave his parents more grief than he could bear to think about now and eventually wore them down. They agreed to let him move back to his hometown and live with his twenty-year-old aunt while he finished high school.

"I'd been back less than three weeks when it happened."

One bad decision, so much damage.

———————

KNOWING SOMETHING ABOUT Keith's background put me at ease, in a way. I stopped worrying as much about my own kids following a similar path. Now I had the information I needed to neatly separate his family's situation from mine. And it gave me a sense of control: We wouldn't relocate while the kids were going through adolescence. And we certainly didn't have any family secrets we were keeping from them.

Yet I still struggled with how to feel about Keith. So he hit a rough patch when he was fourteen. Many of us do, to a degree, but most of us don't help kill someone. I needed to know more. So, I brought it up again. I asked why he attacked that young man. Keith started to tell me how confused he was at that time of his life, but I cut him off. "I get that you were angry as a kid, Keith. But *why* did you do it? Did you hate him? The victim?"

"No!" Keith's voice betrayed hurt. "I didn't even know him. I'd only just met him through John." Though that night was close to two decades ago, in a rush of words Keith recounted the events with a raw horror, as if telling the story for the first time. He insisted that they hadn't planned to kill him. He and John grabbed the guns that had been left in the bedroom and were heading outside to throw them in the bushes, "to mess with him." If they'd done that to the kid's new bike, you'd call it "teasing" or, depending on the degree of malice, "bullying." At least that must've been what Keith thought. But the victim discovered the guns missing and flew out the front door in a fury—at which point Keith reacted by charging at him with the rifle barrel. And John shot him.

I didn't know whether to take his word that the murder wasn't premeditated. Time, particularly time spent in prison, has a way of distorting memories. But I wanted to believe him.

Keith described being swept up in the events that followed, carried along on the crime spree as if his free will had vanished along with that young man's life—as if the murder and everything that followed had been predetermined and he was simply acting out the role that had been written for him.

"It wasn't even real. And then those first ten or fifteen years after, in here, I was like in a fog. It was like they were happening to someone else."

"What do you mean?"

"I don't know. I was so focused on getting through each day, and I never faced up to what I did. I was blaming everyone but myself." He blamed his parents for hiding the fact of his adoption, for moving out of state, then for giving in and letting him move back to Rhode Island to finish high school. He blamed his codefendant for pulling the trigger and dragging him along on the multistate crime spree, for sucking him into the nightmare.

Yet, through all of this, his parents never turned their backs on him. Their support, even when he'd scream and swear at them over the phone from juvenile detention and, later, medium security, kept him from collapsing for good. It was what kept him going through those years of denial, until years after the murder, it finally "sunk in." As if lifting a veil, for the first time he saw himself for who he was that night: a kid who helped to kill a fellow human and then ran away. Now he thought about the victim all the time, what kind of person he would've been had he lived, what he was like when he was alive. He wondered about the victim's family and how they managed to go on each day. And always, there was the inescapable fact of his culpability. It was brutal.

He called his parents and apologized. He enrolled in college courses. Some of the correctional officers noticed the change. Captain Lefebvre did. He was recommended for the program where he spoke to students about prison life. "I started noticing all the other guys around me who were so selfish, cared only about themselves. I didn't want to be that guy. I wanted to be someone who grows up and learns here. It became totally not about me anymore. It became about everyone else around me. Making other people happy made me feel better."

Having Daisy meant he was needed for the first time in his life. It didn't take long before Keith found he needed Daisy, too. "I don't like getting caught up in that human-dog stuff, but she's almost, like, human." They were in his cell. He was going through the parole process, his fourth attempt since being locked up, and was feeling dark and anxious. He felt Daisy watching him. He looked over at her and they locked eyes, then slowly, almost imperceptibly, she nodded her head. And Keith felt less alone.

Caring for her jarred something loose that had been sealed tight inside him. His parents couldn't afford the trip to visit him more than once a year, but his mother did have a chance to see him with Daisy. There was a peacefulness to her son that she hadn't witnessed since he was a child. "Daisy really taught him to love again," she said.

WHEN CAPTAIN LEFEBVRE helped to start the prison-pup partnership at J. J. Moran, many people predicted it would be a disaster. At worst, they said, the inmates would harm the dogs; at best, the ones entrusted with their care and training would screw up and let the dogs run wild. Lefebvre nursed his own private doubts, but he never let on.

They started small, with just two yellow Labs. The puppies arrived on a cold January day. Lefebvre kept an eye out for trouble when he walked into the yard with the inmates who had been picked to train them. Word got around fast that there were puppies in the prison and a group of inmates and correctional officers clustered around the group. One of them, a hardened con who had been locked up for more than twenty years, stepped forward and spoke. In a gruff voice, tinged with higher notes of anticipation, he asked Captain Lefebvre for permission to pet Candie, one of the puppies. When Lefebvre nodded, the man dropped to his knees and pressed his face into the Lab's fur. When he finally pulled away, Lefebvre saw that his face was wet with tears.

Okay, Lefebvre thought. This just may work out after all.

And it did. The atmosphere of the prison became less charged with the dogs there to ease the tension. In group sessions with prison counselors, if a dog was there with his handler and one of the inmates started to get agitated, the dog would trot over and lick his hands or lean against him—essentially *alerting* him to pay attention to his own escalating emotions. They inspired friendly conversation between inmates and with correctional officers. The COs would come up to the guys with the dogs and ask permission to say hello. And while the guards were petting the dogs, they would talk about their own dogs, kid around that maybe they should drop them off in prison for some training. And the barriers between them—guard and prisoner—would crumble just enough to remind the other that without the uniforms, they would just be two guys, talking.

In those early days of the prison-pup partnership, the *Providence Journal* published an article about the program. Most people praised it as a way to put criminals' time to good use. But a few readers were outraged. They wrote letters and called the corrections department director to berate him for rewarding criminals with dogs. What these people didn't understand was that any rewards the inmates garnered from participating in the program are not only well earned, they extend far beyond the prison walls to society itself. The dogs teach the inmates how to locate the parts of them that want to help, not hurt. No other program comes close to doing that.

The inmates use positive reinforcement to train the dogs. If the dog misbehaves, they redirect, never punish. They mark wanted behavior by pressing a clicker and following the sound with a treat. The click cements the action to the reward, speeding up the training process and improving communication between dog and handler.

When Daisy would act up, say by breaking a stay, Keith would calmly return Daisy to her spot, then reward her for staying there. He wouldn't yell. In fact, she was so attuned to his every mood that after those first two weeks of solid togetherness, he would relinquish her to the backup handler whenever he felt gloomy or on edge for fear she would think she caused his bad mood. Seeing how well this positive training method works is something of a revelation to the dog handlers, living in an environment where punishment and violence, certainly not patient coaching, are the default methods of dealing with conflict. In prison, the dogs give their handlers real-life training in being helpful, and most of the guys, Keith among them, have discovered that they like it; it feels nice. And as a bonus, they've learned that positive reinforcement works on people, too, that in fact, it feels good to open up a little bit every now and then and offer the best of themselves to the other guys and the correctional officers. You have to wonder how their lives might have been different had they figured this out before they landed in prison.

At the same time Daisy was reintroducing Keith to what he calls the "soft" part inside of him, she was showing him how to behave in civil society. With the dogs, the inmates get practice at being members of a normally functioning environment. They're allowed to talk with people outside the prison system—people like Christy and the weekend puppy raisers—about a topic that has nothing to do with their crime.

They also get to see the culmination of their love and labor.

Halfway through the training period with their new dog, NEADS clients have the opportunity to go to the prison with Christy to meet the inmate who raised and trained their puppy. These "meet and greets" take place in the visiting room during the time usually reserved for class. All of the dog handlers attend. The guys will be in their usual places, sitting at the tables with their dogs, when, in an echo back to the puppy's first introduction to prison, the automatic door will slide open to reveal Christy and the now full-grown dog. Only this time, holding on to the dog's leash will be a man or a woman in a wheelchair, or with an uneven gait, or an autistic child accompanied by a parent. This is what keeps the inmates going through the rough parts of raising a puppy, and it's what makes it okay, in the end, to say good-bye to their best friends.

———

DURING ONE OF our conversations, Keith tried to describe what working with Daisy had done for him: "In prison you don't know who you are. You're away from the world, then I went to a training and I saw how human it all was. And when I got Daisy it started to change me as a human being. It started to bring in some positive qualities and get rid of some of the negative ones. It was almost like I was living a normal life. She was able to take me out of this place and live like a human."

13

Roll Over

THERE WILL NEVER be an excuse for what Keith did—
there were too many splits in the road that he should have
chosen along the way toward the murder—but hearing about
his struggle and regrets made it possible for me to continue
working with him. Seeing the other inmates with their puppies
reminded me, too, that there's more than one side to each of us.
The question for me was the same one we ask ourselves all the
time about fallen public figures: Is it possible to judge a person's
achievements separately from his or her transgressions? Or will
the bad always overshadow the good? To me, with Keith, the
answer was clear: we had a dog to graduate.

———

UNLIKE KEITH, I knew from the very beginning that I needed
a dog in my life. I just didn't realize how much until I began to

notice the way that simply being with Daisy changed the way I thought. After every encounter with a stranger who asked about Daisy's vest, after every training class and field trip, I felt lighter. I was nicer, not just to the people around me but to myself. Those inner voices that snipe and bitch at me throughout the day found positive things to comment on instead.

And really, Daisy couldn't have come into my life at a better time, because my self-confidence was about to suffer another blow: unemployment.

Every organization I've worked for has had mass layoffs— usually multiple rounds. It always plays out the same way. First there are the rumors. Then, a week or a month later, the ax falls. The employees walk around skittish, like hunted prey, whispering to one another. Whenever the boss calls someone into his office, the rest of us pretend to be busy with work. Until the door opens again and we look up from our desks and try to interpret the expression on our coworker's face for clues to our own fate.

I worked mostly from home at my latest job but I'd been through enough bloody corporate massacres that I was hyperattuned to the warning signs. Our company lost a few big clients when the economy collapsed and things looked grim enough that on a Wednesday in January when my boss's voice sounded strained on the phone, I felt the hair on the back of my neck stand on end. "What's wrong? Is it bad news?" I asked. He was silent for an uncomfortably long time.

"I can't talk about it. We'll talk next week," he said.

I didn't tell Marty about the conversation. There was no sense in having both of us lie awake all night. If we were a different type of couple, we would have talked through my concerns and come up with a plan, or at the very least, it might have been a relief to offload some of my fears to him rather than bear them alone. But that's not how we operate. When it comes to sharing my worst fears with Marty, I prefer to bury them. Bringing them into the open has a doubling effect, makes them grow like a cancer that spreads when exposed to air. He worries enough as it is. So many nights, even when our lives seem to be humming along smoothly, when we're both employed and the kids seem relatively happy, something will wake me in the middle of the night and I'll find Marty's side of the bed empty and cold. Usually I sink back into sleep, but sometimes it's as if he's left a residue of panic behind that has tendriled over to me from the rumpled sheets, and I'll spring out of bed, alarmed, and search through the house until I find him, playing his guitar softly. Sometimes he'll tell me what the dream was about: our children in danger and he helpless to save them. But more often, he doesn't. Why worry both of us?

So, every night after the phone call with my boss, at two, three, four o'clock, the fears that had been bubbling in my subconscious all day would roil up and surge into full-blown terror. I'd fling open my eyes and stare, panicked, into the dark, picking over the evidence, replaying the conversation in my head, slowing it down, speeding it up, turning it this way and that, probing it for any possible explanation other than I was about to lose my job and, with it, half our household income. We already lived from paycheck to paycheck. Every month we somehow managed to pay our bills and the fees for the kids' music lessons and other activities, but there was never anything left over. Aviva would be applying to colleges in less than two years and we hadn't managed to put anything away for her or Josh's education. The likelihood of me finding another job in this economy was slim and the income from the freelance work I did on the side wasn't even enough to cover the bills, let alone tuition. And how much longer could Marty hold on to his job in a dying industry? He was a newspaper reporter, for God's sake! We'd have to sell our house. Maybe my mother and stepfather would let us move in with them. It would mean uprooting the kids, but at least we had them to take us in an emergency.

And while I worried about our future, shame scraped away at my thinning confidence. Every stupid question I'd asked during a meeting, every great idea I failed to come up with but someone else did, revisited me as a burning failure. There were three writers in my work group and Hal was judging us against one another. If any of us were to go, it would be me or Wendy because we were the last to be hired. I'd been in the job longer, but she had greater seniority with the company. She also had skills from her previous positions on the web side of the operation. And she was taller than I was. And younger and blond and capable and nice. She was so nice. I was starting to hate Wendy.

─────────

WORK MAKES UP roughly one-quarter to one-half of my identity, with most of the balance taken up by my kids. If the work vanished and with the kids growing away from me, there'd be only a deep, black void spreading in all directions. I'd be adrift, lost.

That weekend, I spent a lot of time just looking at Daisy, absorbing every aspect of her: her silky ears, one puddling on the floor beneath her head while she slept on her side; her muzzle with its shimmery highlights like velveteen; the dark perforations where the whiskers grew; the dusky black triangle above her mouth, as if some of the color from her nose had drifted south and clung like soot to her fur.

Staring at her face is like slipping beneath my down-filled comforter on a freezing night. Warmth seeps into my body; I lose myself to her. Sometimes on walks, I'd look straight down at her. From that vantage point, the top of Daisy's head is a blunt arrow, her body undulates like a caterpillar's, her paws paddle the road as it streams by. Looking down from above flashes me back to a warm summer evening when Aviva was seven or eight. We were racing each other down the sidewalk toward a Chinese restaurant. When I glanced down to check her progress, to modulate my pace to equal hers, I saw the whole of my daughter right there at my side; the hair on the top of her head glinting auburn in the slanted sunlight, her legs and elbows pumping wildly; her plastic sandals flashing hot pink against the pavement that moved beneath us. My heart was so filled with love for that child at that moment that I nearly stopped breathing. We raced past the music store, past the check-cashing store with its yellow and green Brazilian flag in the window, and before we reached the restaurant, I slowed my pace just a bit so Aviva would pull ahead and win, but not so far that she would move beyond my protective reach.

Now, with her gaining distance from me and with Josh soon to follow, and my job perhaps being peeled from my grasp, I didn't know how to steady myself but for Daisy. But then, on Saturday, Aviva surprised me by asking to come to Christina's class. "Really? You might be bored," I said, pleased that she wanted to be with me while at the same time testing her commitment.

She assured me that she wouldn't be, that she wanted to see what class was all about. Maybe she sensed something was weighing on my mind. For all of our arguing, Aviva is remarkably attuned to me. On the drive over I described the class and gave her a verbal cheat sheet of the dogs she might expect to see there: Elsa, the little black Lab; Reba and Ripley, the two Australian shepherds; Frankie and Sally, both yellow Labs; Sutton. When we arrived, I pointed Aviva toward the chairs at the front of the room and watched her walk over and choose a seat by herself, away from the handful of other observers. Every now and then during class, I'd glance over to check Aviva's body language, afraid I'd find her slumped in the chair with her arms folded tight across her chest. But each time, she was sitting up straight, watching the action unfold in the ring. Whenever a puppy would do something adorable, say, pounce on the toy squirrel Christina dragged by a long string in front of the dogs to test their stays, I'd catch Aviva's eye and she would clasp her hands together in a precious gesture and mouth, "That's so cute!"

Toward the end of the class, Christina announced that we would be working on stranger greetings. She had us line up with our dogs along one wall and waved Aviva and another visitor over. "We need some strangers," she called out. Aviva placed an index finger on her chest and raised her eyebrows. "Yes, come on over and meet some dogs." Aviva rose uncertainly and I smiled encouragingly as she made her way stiffly to Christina, who flung an arm around her shoulder and walked her to the first dog in line.

Christina instructed us to keep our dogs still while the "strangers" walked up to say hello. She told the two volunteers to stand before each dog and pet them only when they were calm and instructed by their handlers to "Say hello." When Aviva reached us, Daisy looked from me to Aviva and back again, excited by this unexpected visit from her weekend sister. "Hello. May I pet your dog?" Aviva asked me, playing the part of a well-mannered stranger.

"Why, yes you may," I said. "Daisy—Say hello." Daisy launched herself at Aviva, wiggling and licking; I had to lure her back to my side with a treat while Aviva moved on and continued down the line of dogs. Having Aviva included in class this way made me disproportionately happy. It affirmed that no matter how far she pulls away from me, she'll still stop and look back to make sure I'm still with her. And that in the greater scheme, my family, not my job, is what gives me a sense of purpose . . . now, if only I could earn a living off our kids.

MY VOICE SOUNDED twisted and squeezed when I answered the phone at eleven o'clock Wednesday morning, the time of my weekly check-in with my boss. Hal got right to it. One-third of our division was being laid off, including me. My tears were splashing into the telephone receiver before he'd finished his sentence. "But you'll be okay," he said.

"What do you mean?" I reached for a tissue from the box on my desk. He forced an upbeat tone to his voice when he told me he had arranged for me to do contract work for another division of our company, which ran a program for the Department of Defense. I'd be doing the same type of work that I did for our corporate clients, only for military members and their families who were dealing with the toll of multiple deployments to combat zones. I'd have to work exclusively from home and I'd lose all my benefits, including the company's contributions to my 401(k), but we still had health insurance through Marty and I'd earn my higher freelance rate so our income wouldn't drop by too much. I wouldn't have to worry for now. When I hung up the phone, I was completely overcome by relief and sorrow. I was one of the lucky ones, but the fact remained, he chose Wendy over me.

I waited until Marty had eaten dinner and was settled in after work before telling him I was laid off. He drew in a sharp breath like he had been struck. "But we'll be all right," I said, echoing Hal's assurances to me, and told him about the work I'd be doing for the military. Even so, it was a while before he recovered, and that night when I woke up at three o'clock, his side of the bed was empty.

ON FRIDAY, I huddled in my jacket for warmth while the prison gates made their achingly slow progress on their tracks. It was early February and the cold front that had settled in seemed in no hurry to move along. I hurried through the frozen courtyard into shift command, where Keith was waiting with Daisy. My nose and eyes felt raw from days of crying. I looked at Keith, standing there in the same clothes he wore every single weekend, the creased yet unhemmed pants, the shirt collar threadbare. We were both rejects.

"Daisy? You ready, girl? Okay, say hello to Sharron." He said the same thing to her every weekend, and when he walked Daisy over, I cradled her face in my hands, looked her in the eye, and said my line.

"Why, hello there! It's so good to see you again!"

It was true. The minute she wiggled up to me, I felt relief from the shame of losing my job. She didn't judge and find me lacking. Yes, I was the one cast out, the one my boss deemed most expendable, but I still had Daisy. And with her, a whole crowd of people who were counting on me. My work with her would allow me to prove my worth.

Keith was holding out her food and paperwork to me, ready to pass the baton for the weekend. And on Sunday, I would pass it back to him. Together we would continue to hand it off, back and forth, until we had completed our mission. Because of Daisy, there was still plenty of work to do.

———

BY MY LAST day at work, Daisy and I had become regulars at Christina's training class. I kept going to Dave's monthly sessions, so with five classes a month of training, along with regular outings with Daisy and, often, other weekend puppy raisers, I was becoming more confident. As a bonus, I'd finally found the companionship that I had been craving. The field trips felt like the playgroups I had brought my children to when they were toddlers. The adults would trade tips and sometimes the conversation would shift to weightier topics until one of us had to correct a puppy or race a dog outdoors when it began waddling in circles, sniffing the ground. The social structure built around my children may have been weakening, but Daisy was handing me the tools to start building a new one.

In addition to my field trip friends, Daisy introduced me to new people everywhere we went. Just as she brought a dose of humanity into the harsh environment of prison, Daisy made the world a friendlier place. When I was with her, I belonged. Daisy was my membership card, my secret handshake. No, she was more than that. Daisy was a small planet with her own gravitational field, and clinging to her leash, I was her moon. Daisy was irresistible. She was beautiful to behold and she was where no pet dog would be: considering the selection in the shampoo aisle of the drugstore, bumping open the door and strolling out of the stall in a public restroom. People just *had* to talk with me about Daisy and to let me know about their own dogs.

One day I was standing in the hallway at religious school, waiting for Josh, when I saw one of the other mothers. She glanced right at me without a flicker of recognition. This was the same woman who would usually practically bodysurf her way across a corridor packed with children to get to me. I was baffled at the cold shoulder until I realized—I'd left Daisy at home that day. Being ignored stung, but it was a lasting lesson on how service dogs can help people who too often feel invisible be noticed.

Once, I was driving through Boston traffic with Daisy in the backseat, sniffing the air through the lowered window. I stopped at a red light and heard someone whistling and calling out. In the next lane, two well-groomed young men in a shiny SUV were smiling at me. I whipped back to face forward, flushing in embarrassment. I wasn't sure whether to be flattered or angry. But mostly I was confused. It'd been a long time since anyone flirted with me (unless you count the inmates in minimum security—and I don't). Maybe I was having an exceptionally good day? I resisted the urge to peek at my reflection in the rearview mirror when I heard a horn. I turned to glare at the two men in the SUV. The driver smiled. "We like your dog!" he said, gesturing toward Daisy. "She's beautiful!" The dog. Of course.

In stores and other public places our steps activated a soundtrack of kissy noises and cries of "A dog!" With each aisle we turned down, couples would nudge each other, shoppers would do double takes, people would smile or just stare. Children would insist to their distracted parents that there was a dog in the store and demand to know why, until the parents would finally look up from the labels they were squinting at and see us. If the parents were close enough to read Daisy's puppy-in-training patch, they'd tell their child that the dog was learning to help people. Others assumed I was the one being helped, and a few times I overheard parents telling their children that I was blind. I always turned my back when I heard that for fear the kid would ask why I had my reading glasses on and a shopping list in my hand. People around town got used to seeing Daisy. Once, walking into a restaurant, we ran into a family I barely knew. They greeted Daisy—not me—by name.

As I brought Daisy to public places more frequently, I became more aware of the effect that dogs have on humans, especially ones who are broken—physically or in spirit. People I would have avoided sought me out and spilled their stories, and I felt richer for the connection. A homeless man who helped me and Josh find a public restroom smiled mischievously when he confessed that he preferred dogs to humans, and gave me the name of the best park in the city for dog watching. A young father told me how his dog had helped his daughter withstand her cancer treatment. A confused, elderly woman cornered me in the laundry soap aisle of the supermarket to tell me about her orange and white dog, Ginger, who had died decades earlier, then hunted me down two aisles over to tell me that she got it wrong, Ginger was actually a cat.

And with every encounter, I marveled at how with Daisy, I'm somebody. People want to talk with me. Now I know how it feels to be a celebrity—not one of the trashy sex tape ones, but somebody beloved, like Oprah or Tom Hanks. If Daisy does that for me, imagine how she'll help someone whose disability has made them invisible or, worse, unapproachable.

The spotlight has never called out to me, but there have been times throughout my life when I've been warmed by its glow. The first time was when I was pregnant with Aviva. People would smile warmly at me when my belly and I bobbed into view. They would stop to talk about their own pregnancies. Once, at a work event, I was leaning back on my heels to counterbalance the medicine ball under my maternity blouse when a man I didn't know caught my eye from across the room and charged through the crowd, hands held out in front of him. When he reached me, he apologized even while patting my belly. "I'm sorry. I just have to do this." It was good training for early motherhood, when the babies attracted all kinds of strangers who would reminisce about their own children's infancies.

Pregnant bellies, babies, dogs—for so many of us, they tap into a deep well of joyful memories. People are drawn to what makes them happy, and it feels good to be the source of those positive feelings, even if it means enduring a stranger's hand on your stomach.

While Daisy helped keep me from falling too deeply into despair when I lost my job, she brought some relief to Marty, as well, who, with his brothers, was near frantic about his parents' health. Nana and Pop raised seven sons—seven "perfect" sons, Nana always joked. They sold their suburban house a few years ago and moved into a cramped two-bedroom apartment in a sprawling 1970s-era complex in the same town. Nana dubbed the new digs "brick city" for its acres of identical redbrick buildings, separated by parking lots and concrete walkways. The advantage of brick city was that it was maintenance free—no lawn to mow when it's ninety degrees out. If the roof leaks, it's management's problem. But after the move, Nana and Pop's world shrunk along with their surroundings, and they began a rapid decline into old age, with its accompanying infirmities and concerns. This decline was a fresh source of endless rounds of plotting among the siblings and their wives to get Nana and Pop into assisted living.

Until recently, Pop had kept busy in his retirement by playing pool at the senior center and driving older adults to the supermarket and medical appointments. Nana, who never learned to drive and whose job for over three decades was being a full-time mother, spent her time on friends and church. And with thirteen grandchildren, there was usually at least one who needed babysitting. When Aviva and Josh were younger, and I had to travel for my job, she would move into our house to help take care of the kids.

My parents-in-law are devout Catholics who never missed Sunday mass until recently. Yet, when I came into their son's life, the Jewish girl who would raise their grandchildren in the Jewish faith, Pop called me a mensch, Yiddish for a good person. I loved Marty's parents for that, for their gift of acceptance without question.

Boy, when viewed from behind, those twenty years since we first met went by fast. And each successive one has wrung just a little more from my once vibrant mother- and father-in-law. Now Nana had stopped cooking and many days she couldn't be roused from her bed. When anyone asked her why, she looked truly perplexed and would answer, "I don't know. I just feel blah." Her memory was slipping. Pop was as mentally sharp as when he was a Boston newspaperman, but his body was failing in alarming ways. We'd visit every week or two and each time we arrived, Marty would stop on the way to the apartment to inspect his father's Ford Crown Victoria for new scratches and dents. A few times we found the car with its front tires resting on the parking barrier and its nose pointing toward the sky like a barge that had run aground.

Visits left us depressed. Sometimes the only sound in the room was Marty rocking back and forth in a creaky, upholstered swivel chair. It set my teeth on edge. Josh would wrap himself in Nana's fleece throw and eat from the candy dish while Aviva sat with a smile frozen on her face, answering patiently each time Nana asked what grade she was in and whether she had learned to drive yet.

The first time I brought Daisy to brick city with us, I didn't know how Nana and Pop would feel about having a puppy in their home. Pop especially could be grumpy. Also, back when he was holding down two jobs and raising seven kids, he was known to drive various family pets to outlying farms and speed off without them.

I led Daisy into the apartment and closed the door behind us while Marty and the kids hugged Nana and bent to kiss Pop, who rarely got up from his easy chair these days. Daisy wagged her tail, hoping to be noticed. Pop didn't say anything, but Nana rested her hands on her thighs and bent down toward Daisy. "Now who is this?" she asked. Daisy shimmied her entire body and attempted to reach Nana's lowered face with her tongue. I kept a tight grip on the leash to keep her from head-butting my mother-in-law.

"It's the *service dog, Daisy!*" Pop bellowed from his easy chair. "Marty told us about her last time he was here. *Come here, Daisy!*" Pop is a small man, but his voice can be startlingly robust. I led Daisy over to him, and without permission she did a "My lap" and cleaned Pop's glasses.

Marty and I moved in to pull Daisy off, but Pop, squinting open his eyes, cupped Daisy's head in his hands. "Daisy. You're a good girl, aren't you, giving Pops a bath?"

From then on, Daisy was the focus of our visits to brick city. She would say hello first to Nana, then visit Pop in his easy chair with a "My lap." After her hellos, I'd lead Daisy to the center of the room for the dog-and-pony show, minus the pony. We'd show off her commands. Pop would watch from his easy chair and Nana would marvel, "I just can't believe this dog! She is so smart! I tell everybody about her, you know." When a couple of Marty's brothers started to refer to Daisy as "Daisy, the Wonder Dog" and "the Fourteenth Grandchild," we knew that Nana was indeed bragging about her. We were also pleased to realize that she remembered the commands that Daisy had mastered and would point out when I skipped over one.

Always, at some point during the visit, Pop would call Daisy over and ask for her paw. Then he would bend low and stroke her head while speaking softly to her.

I know Nana and Pop appreciated our visits, but I also suspect they were in some ways a burden, if only because we asked about their health and every once in awhile, when we worked up the nerve, floated the idea of moving them to an assisted living facility. Daisy, on the other hand, carried no such freight. She was, pure and simple, a delight to be near; she made people feel good about themselves. It's the reason why service dogs do so much more for their human partners than the tasks they perform. It's the way a child feels understood just by sitting next to a gentle dog. It's why Keith became a better person for having taught Daisy, and what helped make it possible for me to stick with the program after I found out what he did.

SIX MONTHS HAD passed since that first training class when Christy had wondered whether I would be bringing Daisy to a NEADS graduation ceremony. Graduations are held a few times a year, and the trainers like the puppies to attend at least one as an audience member so they'll be familiar with the experience when it's their turn to graduate with their human partners. The ceremonies are held in a hotel ballroom set up with a stage and rows upon rows of chairs. They span two or more hours and are packed with people and dogs, including former and current graduates, their families, volunteers, and people who support NEADS or simply love dogs.

Finally, by the spring graduation in March, both Daisy and I were ready. The event was held at a Sheraton, right off the high-way. Josh helped me find a spot in the parking lot, which was already crowded with cars sporting WOOF and paw print decals. Daisy pressed her nose into the ground the second I let her out of the car, and she kept it there all the way to the front entrance and along the carpeted lobby. I eyed the floor nervously and looked down at Daisy, wishing there was a way for me to peer directly into her bladder. She had been too distracted to "Better go now" outside. I was fishing out my wallet for the five-dollar suggested donation in lieu of an admission charge when Daisy caught sight of another dog and headed toward him. It felt like

that first day in Christina's class, with people and dogs everywhere and Daisy determined to personally meet each one. I
dropped the money into a container shaped like a fire hydrant,
grabbed a program to share with Josh, and lured Daisy back
to my side with a treat. In the ballroom, rows of chairs faced a
raised platform flanked by screens. An enormous American flag
served as a backdrop to the stage, where a woman was speaking
into the microphone. The place was nearly jam-packed, but Josh
and I found a couple of empty seats and settled in with Daisy at
our feet. When the speaker wrapped up, the room erupted into
applause, startling Daisy, who rose to her feet and tried to bolt
out into the aisle. I blocked her with my leg and stuffed treats
into her mouth until the applause died down. The same thing
happened with the next speaker, and the next, until we had before us an instant lesson in conditioned response, because after
just a few more rounds of applause followed by food reward,
Daisy learned that clapping is a precursor to treats, and would
raise her face expectantly at the sound.

Finally, it was time for the graduates to take the stage. The
ceremony itself wasn't as you would picture it: no "Pomp and
Circumstance." No dogs in gowns or mortarboards (which,
I'll admit, was a great disappointment to both me and Josh).
NEADS trains client-dog teams year-round, so, often by the
time they take possession of their diplomas, client and dog have
been living and working together for months.

Each team is introduced with a slide show featuring highlights of their two weeks of training at NEADS, followed by
the clients' often stirring accounts of how their new dogs have
transformed their lives. One mother spoke about her autistic
son's tendency to run off into crowds. Now, before outings, she

tethers their big yellow Lab to her four-year-old, and if the boy tries to bolt, the dog drops to the ground, anchoring the boy in place. Their dog has given her peace of mind, and her son a companion.

Several of the graduates were combat veterans injured in the line of duty in Iraq and Afghanistan. When introduced, each climbed the ramp or steered his wheelchair up to the stage and took the microphone. While theirs dogs gazed out at the audience or simply lay serenely beside them, they would describe the IED or mortar attack that cost them limbs or shattered bones. Some suffered debilitating migraines and memory lapses. They spoke about the depression that made staying in bed an attractive alternative to facing another day. Then they would look down at their dogs in their official red service vests and, in voices that cracked with emotion, talk about their four-legged battle buddies, the ones who restored their faith, who gave them a reason to get up in the morning (if only to be let out); who soothed their frayed nerves; who brought them peace.

I was wiping tears from my eyes when Josh nudged me. He was pointing at the floor. I looked down. Daisy wasn't there. Yet I was still holding her leash in my hand. I dropped to my knees and followed the leash with my eyes. It continued along the row of seats behind us and disappeared under the chair of the person sitting directly in back of me. Daisy's hind end, tail wagging, was poking out from under it. While I was getting teary-eyed listening to the speakers onstage, Daisy had decided to pay a social call to a dog two rows back. I tugged, hand over hand, dragging Daisy back under the chairs until she popped out from under my seat, blinking up at me. It wasn't easy, shaking off the humiliation of having my dog misbehave in a room full of

Weekends with Daisy 241

trainers and puppy raisers. I stared fixedly ahead, pretending nothing had happened, and tried to refocus on the graduate on the stage. He was thanking everyone who helped to train his dog, including the prison inmates.

I looked around the room expecting to see inmates. Now I realize how ridiculous that was, as if the corrections department would load up a van of prisoners and march them in, shackled together, to see their dogs graduate. But at the time I didn't think it through. I had been focusing on how integral their role is in the training process—how essential Keith's work with Daisy was—and they wouldn't be there to receive accolades. The inmates aren't even mentioned by name when the puppy trainers and weekend puppy raisers are singled out for recognition, just referred to as "the inmates from" J. J. Moran correctional facility or Northeastern Correctional Center, or wherever. Although that, too, made sense when I realized how painful it would be for their victims to see them acknowledged for their contribution.

After the graduation ceremony, on the way back to the prison, I kept thinking about what Keith had missed. When I met up with him in shift command I tried my best to paint a picture, describing the room, the people, the dogs, all the while hoping the guard would let us have a few more minutes together. Keith laughed at how quickly Daisy grasped the applause-equals-cookie equation.

"Hopefully that will be her up there someday soon," he said.

"Oh yeah," I answered. "I have no doubt about that. Not a doubt." I should have found some wood to knock.

14

Uh-oh

WINTER FINALLY BROKE and spring settled in for real. The dogs went slightly bonkers, rolling in the fresh grass, snorting up newly unlocked scents. Daisy suffered selective hearing loss, most acutely with the words "Come" and "Heel."

In May, Daisy turned a year old. She had the look of a yearling—full-grown but not yet filled out. She was always waiting for the next command: When I moved, she did. When I stopped, she stopped. When I glanced down at her, she would stare back up at me, searching my face, ready to spring into action. If I went too long without paying attention to her, Daisy would poke her nose into my leg to remind me that she was there, ready, waiting, wanting to do something for me. If I still didn't respond, she would trot off and return a few seconds later bearing a gift: Aviva's flip-flop (just in case I was wondering where it was), the kids' dirty socks, which they were always leaving around the house or stuffed into their sneakers.

On the Friday after her birthday, I arrived in shift command to find Keith smiling. "Daisy passed her twelve-month evaluation—Christy took her up to NEADS and said she looks real good."

"She went up already?" I was surprised once again by the reminder that for five days of each week, I had no idea what was happening with Daisy. When the dogs are a year old, Christy takes them from the prison back up to NEADS for a few days of assessments. The dogs' hips are x-rayed and Christy takes them on field trips and does obedience work with them. It's an important rite of passage for the dogs. And for the inmates, too, judging by the relief in Keith's voice.

"Yeah. Her hips checked out okay. And she did real well for Christy." He smiled again. "It'll probably be just a few more months now. Then she's off to the big leagues."

———

I WAS CONFIDENT enough in Daisy's training that Josh and I decided to take her on a train. She had already seen plenty of them—I would bring her to the station, where we'd walk along the platform killing time until a train pulled in. Then I'd feed her a steady stream of treats as it hissed and clanged to a stop. On several of these excursions, I led her up the steep, narrow steps into a car, and then we walked along the aisle and out the other side. For this, our first train ride, Daisy readily jumped aboard but I hadn't anticipated how little legroom there would be. When I led Daisy into our seat with the "Through" command, she slipped in and backed right out again, like a horse stubbornly refusing to stay in the stall. I stood in the aisle, considering the situation, when Josh nudged me with his elbow. "You're blocking everyone." A knot of people had formed behind us, so I gave Daisy a little push with my knees and stepped in behind her so she couldn't pop out again. Josh had ducked into the seat across the aisle and, just like his older sister was wont to do, was staring out the window, pretending not to know us. Just the weekend before, he'd told me he was starting to get embarrassed being around Daisy in public, and probably wouldn't be accompanying us on any more outings for fear people would think she was his service dog. The prospect of riding on the train into the city was too enticing for him to turn down, but judging by his behavior at the moment, he was regretting his decision.

Daisy, filling the space between the seats, turned her head and met my gaze with a pleading look. "Good girl, Daisy," I said. I guided her onto the floor in a down-stay and sat on the seat, arranging my legs awkwardly around her body. When the train lurched forward, she gazed up at me again and I offered her dog cookies and praise. Eventually she fell asleep, the best possible outcome for any new adventure, Kerry had told us during orientation.

The weather had been warm and the sky clear when we stepped on the train, but thunderclouds had collected in the sky over Boston and fat raindrops were splattering the windows when we pulled into South Station. We hurried off the train and were rushing toward the building along with the other passengers when lightning cracked the sky and a thunderclap jolted through my skull and elicited screams all around us. I glanced warily at the steel beams supporting the train platform roof, then down at Daisy, who seemed as intent as I on reaching the building. "Let's run," I called to Josh, and we broke into a jog, Daisy picking up her pace to match mine.

The thunderstorm lasted only twenty minutes or so, leaving dazzling sunshine and warm temperatures in its wake. Down in the subway, a train screeched up to the platform and we led Daisy onto the car, where she sniffed the shoes of the riders closest to her. I kept watch on her tail, which looked so vulnerable among all of those feet.

We spent the afternoon walking around Faneuil Hall Marketplace, chatting with friendly strangers, watching street performers. Daisy met gussied-up horses harnessed to fancy carriages. We wandered among baby strollers with balloons tied to their handles. Daisy ignored spilled French fries (with my help) and puddles of ice cream. Everywhere, pigeons stood their ground until the last minute, when they'd register our approach and run, heads bobbing, out of the way.

The three of us were beat when we took the subway back to South Station and boarded the train. This time, Daisy scooted easily between the seats. She was asleep before the train pulled out of the station. The train conductor, a virile-looking guy in his thirties, came by for our tickets. A few minutes later he returned and perched himself across the aisle to chat with the three young women in the seats in front of us. After a few minutes of shameless flirting, the conductor turned to Daisy. He cocked his head to read her vest. "What's the dog for?" he asked. I gave him the standard reply, telling him that Daisy was being trained to help someone who is disabled and that depending on the dog's strengths, she might go to a person who has trouble walking or who uses a wheelchair, or maybe a child who is developmentally delayed. The train conductor's attention was still on the three young women and it seemed he was only half listening, because when I got to the part about developmentally delayed children, he looked at Josh and said, "Oh! Is that your dog, buddy?"

Josh, being polite, smiled and told him yes before the conductor turned his full attention back to the women.

About thirty seconds ticked by before Josh sat up straight as though he'd been slapped. "Wait a minute!" he said, grabbing my arm. "Why did he say that? Does he think I *need* Daisy?"

The conductor was teasing one of the women about her age. He rose, slapping his leg, and strode up the aisle, announcing the next stop. The women leaned into one another, whispering.

"Yeah, Josh," I said. "He probably does. But so what?"

Josh was silent while he considered this. His fear that someone would think Daisy was his dog had been realized, but ultimately he must have decided "so what," because he didn't mention it again and he kept going on field trips with us.

———————

THE NEXT DAY was Memorial Day and we left the house early to watch our town's parade. There on the sidewalk in the center of town, Daisy had a job to do. Everywhere she looked, there were pieces of candy on the sidewalk to pick up and deposit into my outstretched palm. And every second, another roll of Smarties or a Starburst arced through the air and clattered to the ground. The littlest Girl Scouts—the Daisies—were tossing handfuls of candy into the crowd as they marched by. And my Daisy had never been busier, scurrying from Tootsie Roll to lollipop, trying to keep up with the storm of sweets.

And now she was handing me candy. Lots of it. I passed

some along to the kids who were stooping to pick up their own pieces and shoved the rest in my backpack for Josh and Aviva, who were marching in the parade—Josh with the Boy Scouts, and Aviva in a gold-plumed hat and playing the flute, with the high school band.

Daisy and I had been together for nine months by Memorial Day and I was feeling pretty confident and proud of both of us. The morning was gorgeous—sunny and warm—and as if anyone needed their mood lifted, Daisy made everyone that much friendlier. I had long conversations with fellow townspeople whom I'd seen around but never spoken to before. Marty was nearby, shooting photos and talking with people he knew.

The procession marched out of sight, the music growing fainter as it made its way to the World War II memorial up the street. I spotted Josh with his troop and glimpsed Aviva, who was mostly blocked from view by a taller flute player. We sat in front of the town library. Daisy took up two levels, her hindquarters resting on the sidewalk and her front legs on the street. She did that on the stairs at home, too, like she can't make up her mind between steps. After a peaceful fifteen minutes, the procession reappeared up the street, the marching band gradually growing louder until it clattered to a halt in front of the World War I memorial near our spot. When the final notes of a stray instrument drifted away and the only sounds were of parents shushing their children and the occasional calls of a chickadee, the parade sergeant at arms barked out a command. The members of the honor guard responded in unison, holding up their rifles and cocking their triggers. The little kids jammed their fingers into their ears and I realized a second too late what was about to happen. All at once, the members of the honor guard squeezed their triggers. The children screamed and giggled as gunshots cracked apart the silence. Daisy's reaction was instantaneous. She bolted in the opposite direction of the shots, nearly yanking my arm out of its socket, desperate to get away. Her eyes were bulging, their whites showing. I ran with her, my backpack bouncing on my shoulders, toward the parking lot behind the library. We stopped and Daisy dropped to the ground, trembling. I dug treats out of my pocket, but she wouldn't take them. This was bad. Really, seriously bad.

I looked around desperately, spotted a stick on the grass, and picked it up. "Wanna stick? Wanna stick? Get the stick!" I made myself sound joyful. I ducked and squealed like Rumpelstiltskin, keeping my voice high and happy to snap Daisy out of her terror, until finally, blessedly, she seemed to forget about what had happened ten minutes earlier and was caught up in my joy, dancing gleefully, and trying to wrestle the stick out of my hand.

BACK AT THE prison late that afternoon, my throat closed up a bit when I described to Keith what had happened. I didn't know how to tell him about her reaction to the twenty-one-gun salute without saying the word "gun," "rifle," or "shots." Those words made me uncomfortably aware that Keith had been involved in murder. I ended up stumbling over all three, then quickly reassuring Keith that Daisy had recovered nicely. "And she didn't even react to the thunderstorm the day before," I told him.

Keith lifted his arm casually in the direction of a driving range beyond the prison and mentioned that Daisy had a similar reaction to someone setting off fireworks there. When she tried to bolt, he called her back into position and kept walking as though nothing had happened. Before I left, he said he'd be on the lookout for more signs, but by next Friday when I returned to pick up Daisy, he said they'd had a quiet week.

I decided not to worry.

On Saturday evening, Daisy was keeping me company as I separated mail into piles to recycle, toss, and keep when Josh called out from the other room where he'd been flipping through the television channels. Daisy followed me into the living room. "It's the parade!" Josh pointed to the television, where the local cable-access station was playing footage from the Memorial Day parade. Daisy stared at the television, lowering her tail as the marching band approached the camera and grew louder. She stiffened, then ducked her head away from the television and spun around to leave the room. Through the television speaker, we heard the sergeant at arms call out his command, followed by the efficient clicks of the rifles being cocked. Alarmed, I watched Daisy flatten herself to the ground and army-crawl toward the doorway. I scrambled for the mute button on the remote, but it was too late. Daisy bolted just as the gunshots sounded.

My shame was so deep that I'm pretty sure it was being produced in my bone marrow right along with my blood cells. We were so close to the end, and now her career as a service dog was in jeopardy. I had managed to give Daisy a Bad Experience.

DAISY WOKE UP when I pulled off the highway toward the prison. I pulsed the control for the back window and she pushed her snout through the crack. I did not want to face Keith; in fact, I was dreading it. A couple of months earlier, the weekend before the NEADS dogs started their seasonal flea and tick treatment, I had returned Daisy to prison with a small battalion of ticks (a fact I wasn't aware of until Keith mentioned it in an overly casual voice the following Friday). In April, Keith had noticed her favoring her right leg. A visit to the veterinarian was arranged and Daisy was diagnosed with Lyme disease. Tucker had had Lyme disease and I knew it was easily treatable, but Keith, with his limited life experience, later told me that was the worst day of his life since he'd been in prison. He'd been afraid Daisy was going to die. And now this.

For the hundredth time that weekend, I berated myself for sitting too close to the honor guard. It's not like I didn't know there'd be a twenty-one-gun salute. My kids had marched in every single Memorial Day parade in my town since Aviva was in kindergarten—ten parades! I just didn't think it through, and that was my problem. I never think. I was really starting to hate myself.

Maybe I was imagining it, but Daisy seemed overeager to return to prison. She probably couldn't wait to get away from me. I'd let bad things happen to her. I threaded one of Daisy's ears between my fingers, taking comfort in the velvety softness while I watched for Keith through the window. A lean figure across the prison yard walked purposefully in the direction of shift command while others milled about. When he got closer, I saw it was Keith, wearing gray gym shorts and dazzlingly white sneakers instead of his usual slacks and button-down khaki shirt. His mind was probably still on the basketball court.

Inside shift command, I handed him Daisy's leash and the folder with her weekend paperwork. "I put this in the report," I said, indicating the folder, "but remember I told you about the parade last weekend?" I didn't wait for him to respond. "Well, our local access station was showing it on television and when Daisy heard the"—I swallowed hard—"gunshots, she panicked and ran from the room."

"Oh." He stood up straighter, alert to learn more. "That's not good. How did she react, exactly? Did she cower?"

"She did. She slunk out of the room with her body low to the ground and ran into another room. She was just lying there in the dark, trembling." My throat was tight and my voice pitched higher than usual.

Keith looked down at Daisy, who lifted her face to him.

"I feel terrible." I stared down at his sneakers. They were New Balance.

"Don't." Now he was reassuring me. "Remember? She had that bad reaction to the fireworks I told you about? I'll talk to Christy when I see her Tuesday. I'll find out from her the best way to deal with it." He asked Daisy to stand, then turned back to me, this time with a lift in his voice. "Hey, I need a new challenge, anyway. She picks things up so quickly, and we're so close to the end of her training now that I'm running out of things to teach her."

Once again we had switched roles. Now he was the one reassuring me that Daisy would be okay. Some prison inmates survive incarceration by finding religion. Others devote themselves passionately to lifting weights. Now that I knew what Keith had done and how long he'd been in prison, it was clearer than ever that his salvation was Daisy. He believed in her and because of that, he believed in himself.

THERE IS NO precise point in the training process when a dog is ready to leave its inmate and start training with its human match. Some have the confidence, maturity, and skills to be placed when they're sixteen months old, some at eighteen months. If a dog is strong all the way around, Christy will begin searching through the client applications soon after the dog passes its twelve-month evaluation. She will consult with the NEADS client coordinator to find the applicant whose needs and lifestyle mesh most closely with the dog's strengths and unique qualities. Then she'll introduce the dog to the human. She can usually tell right away whether the match will be successful.

The fluidity to the process was a good thing because it allowed for extra time to work on Daisy's sound sensitivity. But not having a precise end date to the training also prolonged our uncertainty about Daisy's future.

DAISY'S FEAR OF loud noises became a real-life lesson in how to think like a dog—a skill that Dave tried to teach us during a training class at a shopping mall. He had us stand with our dogs in a semicircle at the foot of a "down" escalator so he could watch them react to the sight of him descending. We looked at him skeptically until he explained: "To us, it's just a person coming down an escalator, no big deal, right? But a dog doesn't know about escalators. What they see is a tiny person floating in the air and gradually getting bigger and bigger." Knowing this ahead of time allowed us to look for signs of distress in our dogs and distract them with treats. Or, if necessary, lead them calmly away from the source of their anxiety. Through these exercises, and others, I became more adept at seeing the world through Daisy's eyes and got more practice tamping down my own emotional responses. Calm person equaled calm dog. And it worked with children, too.

My newly honed skills were put to the test in June, on the day that Aviva turned sixteen. Our first stop that morning was the Department of Motor Vehicles so she could take the exam for her learner's permit. We were sitting on a hard wooden bench, waiting for our number to be called, when the door opened from the parking lot and one of Aviva's schoolmates walked in with her mother. We said hello and I was about to comment on the coincidence that the two girls were applying for their learner's permit on the same day when I remembered they shared a birthday. I swear, it was two, maybe three summers ago that we discovered that fact, except it wasn't. It was eleven years ago, the month before kindergarten started. The girls were playing in the sandbox at a local park, exchanging their vitals: favorite color, favorite food, when they found out they had the same birthday.

Now here they were, about to drive cars.

Aviva jumped up when her number was called, and roughly fifteen minutes later, after scoring a passing grade on the computerized test and smiling for the camera, she was waving a sheet of paper at me: her brand-new learner's permit. We gave her picture a critical review on the way to the car ("It's adorable!" I said. "My hair looks poofy," she said), then we drove straight from the DMV to the parking lot of a nearby high school for Aviva's very first driving lesson. We switched seats and I showed Aviva how to adjust hers. When she was comfortable she looked over at me with a huge smile on her face.

That's when I had an out-of-body experience. My daughter was behind the wheel and I was in the passenger seat. The world had flipped inside out.

"Okay? What do I do now?" Aviva put her hand on the emergency brake.

I gestured behind me. "Get back there in the booster seat, where you belong. If you're good, we'll stop at McDonald's for a Happy Meal."

She laughed nervously. And I took a deep breath and guided her, step by step, from releasing the emergency brake to pushing in the clutch and letting it out slowly. Both my and Marty's cars have manual transmissions, so Aviva had no choice but to learn how to work the clutch and stick shift. The car bucked violently, then stalled. Aviva looked at me, alarmed. "What did I do?"

"It's okay." I reassured her by confessing that I was so inexperienced when I bought my first car with a manual transmission, that I drove it home down a four-lane highway without taking it out of second gear.

She relaxed, then wiggled slightly in her seat and looked straight ahead. "Okay. I think I'm ready to try again."

Eventually, Aviva was able to move the car forward without stalling the engine, shift it into second gear, and drive around the school. Throughout that hour, I kept myself detached and my voice calm, just as I did with Daisy, even as I silently pressed my foot into an imaginary brake and strangled the armrest. The past ten months with Daisy, of learning to be patient, to hold back my reactions and to learn forgiveness, prepared me for the passenger seat better than sixteen years of motherhood.

This was a rite of passage for me, too.

15

Keep Going

THE NEXT WEEKEND, I joined fellow puppy raisers for a trip to the Boston Museum of Science. We were in a small alcove furnished to look like a typical American living room, and a storm was brewing. It didn't matter that it was fake, Daisy's terror was real. A television in the corner was playing a mock weather report on an endless loop while lightning flashed behind curtained windows and thunder boomed from invisible speakers. A lamp flickered and the room went dark. A moment later when the lights came on again, I followed the leash in my hand to a spot underneath the wooden bench where I sat. Daisy was lying there, trembling.

It was as if a switch inside Daisy's brain had been flipped on during the parade, and there was no way to turn it off again.

At the Museum of Science, the situation with Daisy continued to deteriorate. I managed to coax her out from under the wooden bench before the recording loop reached the thunderstorms again. Her tail was low as we hurried through the Theater of Electricity, but before we reached the lobby, a group of kids at an interactive exhibit forced a metal disc to shoot high up a pole. It clattered back to the base with a ringing retort. Daisy jumped about as high as the disc. I quickened my pace for fear she would drop to the ground and I wouldn't be able to get her back up. She followed in a slouch. We made it out of the electricity area and into the museum lobby, where a museum employee on a Segway whirred toward us, smiling. Daisy was completely undone. First the thunder, then the clanging metal disc, now an exceptionally tall human being with wheels for feet. The whites of her eyes were showing as she pulled me through a nearby doorway that led us into the Natural Mysteries collection room. She dropped to the floor, panting, elbows bent and tucked in close to her body. It was quiet in there, but the surroundings were anything but calming. Stuffed animals glared down from high shelves, teeth bared or wings held aloft. Every now and then Daisy lifted her gaze to check that the lynx and birds of prey hadn't moved any closer, even though it was clear from their poses that they were about to attack.

Michelle, one of the puppy raisers, found me sitting on a bench, staring miserably at Daisy. "Leave it!" she told her dog, Frankie, who was wagging her tail, trying to rouse Daisy. Christina has a strict rule against letting dogs say hello to one another when they're on leash, and Michelle, who was on her third NEADS puppy, had the protocol down pat.

I told Michelle what happened. "I thought she'd be okay with the thunder, because she's heard it before and never had a bad reaction," I said, remembering our jog amid the lightning bolts from the train to South Station. Michelle pulled a high-value dog treat from her bait bag and held it just out of reach. "Daisy, stand!" Daisy tucked her head between her paws and pretended to be hard of hearing, vision impaired, and scent challenged. Michelle and I exchanged glances. Daisy's mental state was pretty bad if she wouldn't take chicken jerky. Michelle had another idea. "Okay, then. Let's see if Frankie has better luck. Frankie, say hello to Daisy." Frankie, delighted by the opportunity to break Christina's rule, dropped to the floor and nuzzled Daisy's ear. She flipped onto her back and pawed at Daisy, sneezing once for good measure. Daisy turned her face away. First the refusal to take a treat, now she was ignoring a friend. Daisy loved dogs, maybe even more than food. Michelle's boyfriend joined her and they sat nearby and talked while I sat alone, staring at Daisy, willing away the hot pressure that was building behind my eyes. The world is an unpredictable place, punctuated by backfiring cars, thunderclaps, and rumbling trucks. A service dog has to be unflappable, otherwise he puts both himself and his person in danger. Like this, Daisy would not make it as a service dog. She would fail. I would fail. Keith would fail.

Eventually, Daisy stirred. I don't know what did it: the passage of time, becoming familiar enough with her immediate environment after spending a good thirty minutes in the natural history room, or maybe it was Frankie's overtures that finally reanimated Daisy, but when I stood up to coax Daisy to her feet, she raised her rump in the air and treated herself to a long, luxurious stretch. "We'll be in the cafeteria," I whispered to Michelle, and hurried Daisy away from the lynx and hawks and toward the lobby, where I kept a wary eye out for the wheeled museum employee. We made it to the cafeteria without incident and settled ourselves at a table near a mother and her young children. Her baby leaned over in his high chair and waved a spoon at Daisy. Daisy thumped her tail against the floor in response, her frazzled nerves once again seemingly restored to normal.

Keith looked deflated that evening when I told him about the incident at the museum. "But she was back to her old self when she saw the baby in the cafeteria. Her tail was wagging, she acted happy . . ." This time I was the one trying to reassure Keith that it wasn't as bad as it seemed. Of course, neither of us believed it. On top of everything else, our efforts to fix Daisy were constrained by long separations and prison walls. Under normal circumstances, we could come up with a coordinated plan to desensitize Daisy and fine-tune it as we went along, but this approach seemed patched together and unwieldy.

For the inmates, the most stressful period of training is the very end, when they've taught their dogs everything they can and all that's left to do is wait for the dogs to go back up to NEADS to be placed with clients. That's when their thoughts turn darkest; if anything can go wrong, it will because that's the way the fates have played it for them their entire lives. They're terrified their dogs will suffer a career-ending injury on a weekend, or get caught in a door and start balking at entranceways. It's like those movies where the police detective is killed in a shootout when he's just days away from retirement, or the fighter pilot volunteers for one last mission before finally returning home from the war, and the plane goes down in a fiery crash.

I just couldn't let that happen to Daisy.

The next Saturday I told Christina about the incident in

the museum. She dug around behind her desk and found a re-cording of a thunderstorm. She popped it in her boom box and played the rumbling, crashing soundtrack at low volume while we took our dogs through their paces. With the exception of a pony-size mastiff who drooled even more than normal during class, none of the dogs, Daisy included, seemed distressed by the sounds. Christina suggested I attempt the same at home by finding a similar recording online to play at low volumes while Daisy was in the room. As with the train at the station, I would gradually desensitize her to sounds.

After class Elsa's puppy raiser, Lisa, and I decided to find more conditioning opportunities for Daisy at one of those pop-up carnivals that appear in an empty field overnight and are gone two days later. Christina had told me about an especially high-value treat—a specially formulated sausage roll that, once opened, had to be refrigerated. She was so enthusiastic about it that I began to think of it as the crack cocaine of dog treats. I bought some at a pet store and tucked it into my backpack, unopened, in case of emergency. Josh and I met Lisa in the parking lot of the carnival. Josh wanted to check out the rides, so we made our way past the food vendors, with Lisa and I issu-ing a steady stream of "Leave it"s as the dogs sniffed at spilled popcorn and oozing packets of mustard on the ground. So far so good.

The ride area was partitioned off by portable metal fences. To Daisy and Elsa, it must have seemed like we'd entered a strange new land where large, groaning objects spun and whirled over-head while humans screamed. If I were a dog, I'd be concerned. Elsa was exceptionally low-key and seemed unimpressed by the commotion. Daisy was trying to keep calm. She lifted her gaze warily and kept her tail tight against her rump. Her ears were folded against her head. Josh headed toward the scrambler. It was early in the day and there wasn't yet a line. He picked a cherry-red car and climbed aboard while I watched.

Josh was three years old the first time he went on a carnival ride. Aviva, at seven, took his hand and led him up the ramp to the dragon roller coaster—a kiddie ride that glided along gentle hills and valleys on an oval-shaped track. They picked the first car and I chewed on my thumbnail while the carnival worker lowered the safety bar and tugged it slightly to make sure it was secure. The ride lurched forward and Josh grabbed on to the bar with both hands, alarm crossing his face. The dragon followed its circuit across the track and each time my children came into view, Josh was grimacing in terror, eyes fixed straight ahead and hair blowing back while Aviva leaned toward him, her lips moving, trying to comfort her little brother.

Now he was on the scrambler alone, flying toward me, then careening away, trying to hide his smile each time we made eye contact. Later in the summer, we'd be sending him off to overnight camp and Aviva to Central America for the volunteer trip. We were all learning to overcome our fears. If only Daisy could.

When Josh staggered off the ride to rejoin us, Daisy sniffed him all over and licked his face. This seemed to distract her from the commotion that threatened to unhinge her. Josh and Daisy had their own private language, which included a special greeting. He would kneel in front of Daisy, say, "Shake, shake, touch," and she would offer him first one paw, then the other, then finish by touching her nose to his. Though I wouldn't allow myself to linger on Daisy's eventual departure, every now and then I would ask Josh whether it was going to be hard for him to say good-bye. Josh, always thoughtful, would pause and say yes, it will be hard, but it will be worth it because he knows she's going to help make someone's life better. I was never sure whether he was parroting me or he really meant it, but knowing Josh, who seemed to come to this earth prepackaged with an acute sense of empathy, I tend to think it was the latter.

A few rides later, feeling confident, we led the dogs through the midway, refusing the barkers' offers of beanbags and basketballs to toss. We were walking past a dart game when a player hit the target and popped a balloon. Daisy flinched and bolted to the end of her leash. I dug into my bait bag, pulling out dog biscuits to feed her, since the sausage remained buried deep in my backpack. She took the pieces carelessly, nipping at my fingers. That's called taking treats with a "hard mouth," a sign that the dog is agitated. "Just keep walking," Lisa said. "Pretend like nothing happened." I did, but a group of boys around Josh's age had exploding caps and started slamming them to the ground, setting off a volley of miniexplosions just as we approached. Just like at the museum, each successive sound built on the last one until Daisy was helpless with anxiety. She dropped to the ground and slunk ahead, pulling me to a patch of grass where she pressed her muzzle between her front legs and stopped moving entirely, save for a steady trembling.

I threw myself on the ground next to her and unzipped my backpack. But when I felt around for the sausage and pulled it out, I saw the wrapper was a thick, impenetrable plastic, absolutely impossible to open without a knife. Lisa and I dug at the wrapper with our fingernails and our car keys while Daisy lay trembling and Elsa leaned forward, watching with interest. The plastic stretched and puckered but wouldn't tear. I wanted to fling the damn thing at a tree or smash it under a rock, but finally, we managed to poke a hole in the wrapper large enough to fit in a finger and scoop out some sausage. Elsa stood up, nose trembling in the direction of the meat. Lisa held her back while I offered the glob of sausage to Daisy. Daisy lifted her eyes in interest, paused, then looked away from the sausage. My heart sank.

Lisa handed me Elsa's leash and took Daisy's from me. She stood up. "Daisy, let's go," she said in a high, happy voice. Daisy shifted her eyebrows up without making eye contact with Lisa, then down, all the while keeping her head flat on the grass like a turtle's. Lisa worked at Daisy for a while, trying out different tones of voice, going from high and happy to commanding. Daisy wouldn't budge, she just lay there, still trembling, acting like she wished she were invisible.

Lisa took in the activity around us. The spot where Daisy collapsed was between the carnival rides and the midway. Clawing, roaring metal monsters ahead of us, bursting balloons to the right. "Let's try leading her away from the noise," she said, pulsing Daisy's leash toward the quieter direction. "Let's go," she said. I couldn't believe it. Daisy rose to her feet. Her shoulders were hunched and her tail tucked, but she was moving. She followed Lisa. Josh and I scrambled to our feet and headed away from the carnival, toward a small pond that lay at the bottom of a slope.

Lisa and I settled on the grass while Josh explored the banks of the pond. Daisy and Elsa lay on their sides in the grass, wiggling toward each other until they were close enough to touch muzzles. We were so relieved that neither Lisa nor I had the heart to scold the dogs for breaking the rules.

KEITH WAS CONCERNED. Even when Daisy acted herself, he worried constantly that she'd fall apart at any minute. The signs were all there. She avoided the visiting room because Christy had dropped a metal pot behind her to test her reaction to the sudden, violent sound. The prison block itself was a cacophony of slamming doors. So even when Daisy was calm, Keith knew that all it took was a single, sudden noise to send her scurrying for cover. And this was the dog who was so smart and obedient that everyone thought she was a shoe-in to graduate.

It would have been easy to blame me for Daisy's fear of loud noises—God knows I blamed myself. But Keith never suggested that it was my fault. Instead, he approached it as a puzzle that he and I could solve together. The easy thing would have been to quit trying, to tell Christy that this one couldn't be saved, but I'm sure that thought never crossed Keith's mind. If anything, his old fear of Daisy failing made him dig in his heels harder.

Keith, out of other ideas, decided to change his approach. Instead of staging loud sounds and feeding Daisy treats as they happened, he ignored her. Keith realized that Daisy, being so exquisitely attuned to him, anticipated loud, violent noises before they actually occurred. She'd pick up on his tone when he plotted with another inmate to drop a book or other hard object and would go into defensive mode. Her anticipation of loud noises was fueling her reaction to them.

"We need to get her confidence back," he told me one Friday night in shift command. He explained that he was using a sort of reverse psychology on her. He'd put her in a down-stay in the block, with all of its echoes and slamming doors and metal, and hold her leash down with his foot so she couldn't bolt. "I won't let anyone pay attention to her. She can't go to anyone else for comfort because that just reinforces her fear." When someone dropped a book or slammed a door, Daisy would look up to Keith for his reaction. He wouldn't look back, just kept doing whatever he was doing: reading, playing cards, or talking with the other inmates. Eventually, Daisy took her cue from Keith. She started to relax.

I began using the same approach on weekends. It's similar to the strategy we'd use with our kids when they came crying to us with a minor injury. We'd kiss the boo-boo and send them on their way without another word about it. It worked with them, and at last it seemed to be working with Daisy.

———

ON A WARM Saturday in July, I urged Daisy into the backseat for our drive into Logan Airport. In a couple of hours, Aviva would board a plane alone to Miami, where she would meet her tour group and travel on to Costa Rica for ten days. There, they would help rebuild roads and pathways in a remote village that had been devastated by floods.

Marty hoisted Aviva's bag into the back of the car. "I see you packed your bowling ball collection," he joked, trying to lighten the mood as Aviva slid in next to Daisy, who provided a furry barrier between her and Josh. Aviva snapped, "I need everything in there." I kept my mouth shut. I had peeked into her duffel bag the day before. Among the hiking boots, bug spray, and malaria medicine (just in case) was a blow dryer and an electric hair straightener. She would be staying in the rain forest. When she came back into her room with her packing list in hand, I pointed out to her that she would have to carry that heavy bag up a river in a canoe and on a jungle trek before reaching their hut—where there may or may not be electricity. She reminded me that they would be spending a night in Costa Rica's capital city on either side of the trip and there would most certainly be power outlets there. "Besides, everybody's going to hate me anyway. They'll hate me more if I have frizzy hair." I sucked in my breath to argue, but instead let it out slowly. Since Daisy, I've been better at gleaning the actual meaning behind my children's words. With Daisy, I'd read her body language in the context of the circumstances so I could address the underlying issue. In this case with Aviva, I knew her concern with her hair was entirely irrational, especially considering that she is neither vain nor shallow. Which told me it was a cover for her anxiety about the trip. And who wouldn't be anxious? She didn't know any of the other kids, she'd be traveling alone for the first time, and she didn't know what awaited her once she got to Costa Rica.

Later, I slipped one extra item in her duffel bag: the Mommy Amulet. When Aviva was little and afraid to fall asleep, Marty and I would pull her bed into the doorway each night so she'd feel closer to us and her brother across the hall. Our move to a new home was our chance to break that habit, but we needed a substitute. I dug through my jewelry box and found a pewter disk embossed with three prancing horses—a gift from my father. This, I told Aviva, would protect her while she slept. We pinned it to the underside of her pillow, and every night I would "power it up" by pressing my palms against it. At some point over the years—I don't know when—the Mommy Amulet found its way back to my jewelry box. I guess Aviva decided she didn't need it anymore. On this trip, though, so far from home, I didn't want to take any chances. I powered it up and tucked it in Aviva's duffel bag with a note letting her know it was fully charged.

DAISY POKED HER head over the backseat and thumped her tail against Josh while an airport security worker opened the back of our car and gave it a cursory check for explosives. "Hey there, puppy," he said, smiling before slamming the hatch shut and waving us on. We found a spot for the car and trooped through the parking garage into the elevator.

"Daisy, Nudge," I said, pointing to the button. Daisy sprang up and pushed it with her nose. Josh and Marty laughed and Aviva rolled her eyes but fought to contain a smile.

The check-in line was chaotic and long but Daisy stayed calm despite the rumbling wheeled suitcases, the periodic crackling announcements over the PA system, the dull thud of luggage being picked up and dropped to the ground every few feet as the line advanced, and all the other sounds that fill an airport on a typical Saturday. While we waited, Josh knelt by her side and massaged her ears while Aviva hugged her carry-on bag, silently radiating anxiety.

After we got Aviva's boarding pass, she joined the security line and the rest of us followed her progress outside the roped-off section for as long as possible. When we reached the final bend in the line and said good-bye, Aviva knitted her eyebrows in concern when I swiped at my eyes and she told me not to cry. We all hugged her, even Josh, a moment so rare I wish I had captured it on camera, and then she bent down to kiss the top of Daisy's head. Daisy whipped her tail back and forth in return.

"I'll miss you!" she told Daisy, sounding like a child but looking like a young adult.

We stood and watched Aviva's back while she removed her shoes. The fluttering in my stomach briefly quieted when I saw her speak to the young woman in line next to her. "Oh, thank God, she's making a friend," I said as much to myself as to Marty. Then, Aviva walked through the metal detector and, except for one last sighting of the top of what may have been her head but could have been another petite brunette, she was gone.

Aviva was five days old the first time we were separated. She was at home with Marty and I was gone less than a half hour, but I felt as if I had left behind a vital organ. I had that same sensation when we left the airport, knowing my child still existed, but quite definitely apart from me.

AVIVA DIDN'T HAVE access to the Internet or a cell phone while she was away. We were completely cut off from each other. It was excruciating, having her so far away and not knowing whether she was happy and making friends. Fortunately, I had Daisy, who was a comfort, not just because she was a warm, affectionate dog, but because she was a good reminder of the value of leaving your home and having new experiences. It's a sure path to growth and maturity. Daisy did it every Friday while Keith stayed behind. Now it was my turn with Aviva.

NEITHER DAISY NOR Josh were with us ten days later when Marty and I waited at the airport for our daughter's homecoming. We stood outside the gates, quietly speculating on her state of mind. We figured she'd hate us, but couldn't decide whether it would be for sending her into the jungle to dig ditches, or because she had to come home. "Oh my gosh!" I looked at Marty. "We sent her to Mr. Travers and didn't even realize it!" We were laughing over that, calling it "Señor Travers's Trabajo en el Campo" and wondering how to say "Sledgehammer Acres" in Spanish, when the first wave of travelers appeared. We scanned the crowd, skipping over the men, briefly stopping at the small, slender young women before finally we spotted her. Aviva was waving to us, smiling. Marty and I looked at each other, surprised. Marty spoke out of the side of his mouth: "There must have been a mix-up during the layover in Miami. They sent us the happy girl."

"Good, let's keep her," I whispered back.

The Massachusetts Turnpike stretched ahead through the dark, bringing us closer to home, and all the while Aviva talked more to us than she had all summer. She described the friends she'd made, the bags of sand she'd hauled, the mud that had sucked the boots off her feet. As the only fluent Spanish speaker in the group, she took on the role of translator, which gave her stature with the villagers and her peers. It was better than I had hoped for. As difficult as it is to go off into the unknown—or to be the one left behind to fret and worry—it's only by taking that risk that you discover just how capable you are. I like to think Daisy demonstrated that for Aviva each weekend, even if neither of them realized it.

———————

EACH WEEKEND, I added trips to Daisy's itinerary, ever conscious of our dwindling time together. Now that I knew Keith had been locked up for more than half of his young life, each new experience of Daisy's that I recorded on the weekend report had me wondering about the last time—if ever—Keith had done the same.

Sally's puppy raiser, Dawn, hosted a get-together on her poolside patio. Five NEADS puppies were in attendance and Lisa was determined to get all of the dogs into the swimming pool. Most of the dogs took to it right away. Daisy wasn't so sure about it at first. The largest body of water she'd been in was a small woodland stream. Daisy was five months old when Josh, Marty, and I brought her for a walk along a wooded trail that wound around a lake. In one spot, a stream flowed down a hillside, splashing over rocks and emptying into a small pool. Daisy heard the water before we saw it. She stopped, her tail held straight out behind her. She lifted her face and sniffed in the direction of the gurgling sound. Marty and Josh kept walking, but I led Daisy off the path and to the stream. She pricked her ears and stared intently at the moving water, following its progress over the rocks and into the pool. She poked her muzzle into the flow, then pulled away, snorting and sneezing. She tentatively dipped a paw in the water, quickly withdrawing it when it touched the surface. She tried again, more boldly swiping at the spot where the stream spilled into the pool, then reared back and pounced into it, surprised that instead of pinning that weirdly moving ribbon of silver to the ground, she was swallowed up by it. Daisy clambered out of the water and shook her body. I shielded my face from the muddy spray and before she could make another try at catching the stream, I led her, running to catch up with Marty and Josh.

"Daisy! Look what I have!" I threw a dog toy into the pool.

Before Daisy could react, Frankie launched herself into the water and Elsa flew in after her, soaking my shirt. Daisy wheeled away from the splashes and trotted toward the grass, watching over her shoulder.

Next, Lisa stripped down to her bathing suit and waded into the water, holding a tennis ball. "Come on, Daisy! Get the ball!" She waved it high above her head, teasing Daisy with it. Daisy paced the sides of the pool, looking from the water to Lisa to the ball. "Ready?" Daisy stopped pacing and reared back, shifting her weight toward her haunches. "Go get it!" Lisa tossed the ball, then screamed and covered her face with both hands as a waterspout erupted next to her when Sutton and Sally simultaneously hit the water in a race to seize the ball. Daisy, excited by the other dogs, paced faster, turning sharply when she reached the ends of the pool. Lisa waded over to the steps and tried to coax Daisy in that way. I wasn't wearing a bathing suit, but I did have on nylon shorts that would hold up to water if it became absolutely necessary that I go in. And it was beginning to look absolutely necessary. I stepped gingerly into the pool and walked tippy-toed down the stairs, holding my arms out like broken wings and shivering like a wimp.

"If I can do this, you certainly can, Daisy. You're a Lab, so start acting like one!" I told her. Daisy had stopped pacing and locked in on me to watch my progress into the pool, and now, without hesitation, she followed me in and launched herself off the steps. She paddled a couple of feet, her head skimming the surface like an otter, clamped her jaws around the tennis ball, turned around to swim back, and bounded up the pool steps, flinging water off her coat. Everybody clapped and cheered. After that, we couldn't keep Daisy out of the pool. She had overcome her fear. My hope was that every new frontier Daisy conquered would weaken the power that loud noises held over her. For the first time since the parade, I felt hope in Daisy's future.

———

THE NEXT DAY at the prison, I described Daisy's accomplishment to Keith, letting him know that once she got past her reluctance to go into the water we could barely keep her out of the pool. He nodded his head in agreement—"Daisy loves to go in the pool"—then smiled sheepishly as he caught himself. "Well, it's not a *real* pool. We have a little kiddie pool for the dogs so when it gets really hot they can go in there and cool off." He gestured toward the prison yard behind him. I pictured him in his prison uniform, standing next to a plastic aqua-blue pool patterned with smiling cartoon fish. I could have burst out laughing or crying, either one. When was the last time he swam? He still would have been a kid, obviously. Later, back in his cell, would he smell the chlorine from Dawn's pool on Daisy's fur and remember the sensation of propelling his body, weightless, through water? Did swimming pools hold the same magical appeal for him as a kid as they once did for me?

I spent the summers between ages nine and eleven in South Florida and spent almost every waking moment in the water. I learned to swim the first day of the first summer when I jumped recklessly into the apartment complex pool after my cousins, then learned too late that I was in the deep end and sinking like a stone. It would be my third near-drowning. The first time, I was six, hopping along the shallow end of a community pool in my ruffled bathing suit when the bottom dropped off sharply and I was underwater. I gazed up at the rippling clouds in the sky and, figuring it was the last time I'd see them, calmly thought, *Good-bye, cruel world.* Then my older brother Steve was there, dragging me back to the shallow end. The second time was a year later when a counselor at Brownies camp reached off the dock from which I'd just jumped to yank me, sputtering, up from the silty bottom of the lake and told me to stay in the little-kid area from then on. This time no one was coming to the rescue. By instinct, I flapped my arms and kicked my legs until I broke the surface and dog-paddled safely to the side. After I caught my breath, I hoisted my dripping body out of the pool, elated, and jumped in again and again.

If trying out new things didn't matter, we wouldn't send our kids on volunteer trips to foreign countries or lure dogs into swimming pools. But every novel experience we have teaches us about the world and ourselves, it builds our confidence and helps us tackle ever more challenges. But where did that leave Keith? If a dog needs to get out into the world every week in order to grow up confident and well adjusted, what about people like him, who come of age in prison?

Every time I started to feel sorry for Keith, though, the memory of finding out what he did returned with a sickening rush. His victim never got to finish growing up. Keith was where he belonged . . . except—and I kept going back to this—someday he would leave prison and rejoin society. How would he manage to keep his own head above water, let alone contribute in any meaningful way?

One of the other inmate handlers, Steve, once described how it used to tear at him to send his dog out each weekend. Steve had been locked up for almost forty years when he got his first dog to train. Rugby unleashed emotions in Steve that were entirely foreign to him, and powerful. During the week, he'd work with Rugby and everything around them faded into background noise; no one else existed. Then the weekend would come and Steve would be alone like before, only now it hurt. He'd become frantic with anxiety about his dog. Part of the prison parking lot was visible from the sliver of window in Steve's prison cell. On Fridays, after he handed Rugby's leash to the weekend puppy raiser, he would sprint through the yard back to his block, race up the stairs two at a time, and shut himself in his cell, where he'd kneel on his cot in front of the window in time to watch the car drive away with Rugby riding in the back. All weekend, he'd think about Rugby, wondering what he was doing, hoping he was okay. And when Rugby was due to return on Sunday evening, Steve would again kneel on his cot, watching and waiting, and his heart would leap when the car came into view.

Over time, as he watched his puppy grow and gain confidence, letting Rugby go on weekends became a little bit easier for Steve. He began to appreciate the value of his dog's excursions because he understood intimately that prison was no place to grow up. And, after four decades of the same thing day in and day out, Steve said he lived as a free man vicariously through his dog.

Sometimes after I dropped off Daisy, I'd imagine Keith reading my notes on the weekend report and inspecting her fur for pine sap, the odor of fried food or woodsmoke, or other evidence of how she spent the weekend. Eventually, Keith will be freed from prison, but he won't have the measured, thoughtful introduction to the wider world that Daisy benefited from.

He will be hit with it all at once, and although I'll never make peace with what he did, it's in everybody's best interest that his reintegration into society is an easy one. I hoped that every experience I gave to Daisy would in a small way become Keith's, too—would somehow help prepare him for his future.

WE HAD BARELY recovered from sending Aviva away for ten days when it was time to bring Josh to Boy Scouts camp. It was like double majoring in letting go. Daisy rested her head on Josh's lap during the forty-five-minute drive north. It would be Josh's first time away from us, not counting visits with relatives. His brand-new footlocker was in the trunk of the car, packed with clothes and towels, a Red Sox T-shirt for sports night, bug spray, sunscreen, juice boxes, and bags of cookies, chips, and fruit snacks, just in case he got hungry between meals (my idea). He wore his uniform, the shirt swallowing him up (the clerk at the Scouting store had picked out one several sizes too large so it would last through the years).

We found Josh's troop and, with Daisy, followed the other boys and their parents along a wide wooded trail to the campsite, a collection of canvas tents on wooden platforms surrounded by towering pines. Inside each tent was just enough room for two metal cots, each topped by a thin mattress of blue ticking. I caught the eye of my friend Mary, whose son, Matthew, we had decided earlier, would be bunking with Josh. Matthew was the only boy in the troop as soft-spoken as Josh. If the other boys ignored them, they'd have each other, we figured.

"If it were me staying in one of those tents, I'd be running back to the car, crying," I whispered to her.

Mary laughed. "I'd beat you there."

We left when the boys were called down for their swim test. Josh was stoic when we said good-bye, though he knelt down in the dirt next to Daisy and hugged her around the neck. She stood up to back away, then wagged her tail as if to apologize for resisting. Dogs don't like to be hugged.

On the ride home, Daisy stretched out on the backseat, her head resting in the spot where Josh had been on the trip over. As I did so often, I marveled at that dog and the place she occupied between my family and Keith as witness to, and sometimes facilitator of, our growth. Somehow, this dog in her blue training vest was a living reminder to keep learning and trying.

I RUBBED DAISY'S ears while Keith waited to be buzzed into shift command that evening. Daisy spotted him outside the window and lifted her haunches, propelled into a stand by the movement of her tail. I was afraid I'd forget to mention it, so as soon as he stepped through the door I asked whether he minded if I came for her the following Saturday morning rather than Friday.

"No, that's fine. I'll be here." He laughed at the absurdity of the statement. "You can always find me here."

Whenever I had to pick up or return Daisy at other than the usual time, I would ask Keith if that was convenient for him. He always looked surprised and just a little bit uncomfortable at the question. An officer once overheard one of these exchanges and admonished me. "Just tell him when you'll be here," he said, as if by asking, I was upsetting the power differential between inmate and civilian. But that seemed rude, so I still asked. It would have been different if I could have explained why to Keith, which in this case was because I had to pick up Josh at camp on Friday night. But we're not allowed to talk about our families, or anything personal for that matter, so in the absence of being able to explain *why,* all that was left for me to do was to be extra polite.

———————

MARTY WAS STILL at work on Friday when it was time to pick up Josh from camp, so I drove there alone. Matthew's parents, Dave and Mary, were getting out of their minivan when I pulled up.

"Ten bucks says Matthew's still wearing the clothes I dropped him off in," Mary said as we slipped through the gate past the administrator's cabin.

"We plan to tie him to the roof rack for the ride home," Dave told me.

"I don't care what Josh smells like. I just hope the other boys didn't turn him into an indentured servant." I was imagining my son stuffed in a footlocker all week, let out only to do the other boys' chores, when I noticed two boys in baseball caps headed down the lane. They looked vaguely familiar, but Josh didn't like to wear hats. I turned my attention back to Mary and Dave, who were speculating on the condition in which we'd find our kids. When I looked up again, the boys were walking toward us with purposeful strides, like small army generals patrolling their troops. They waved and as we got closer, I saw that the boy on the left was Josh.

"What? *That's Josh!*" I said. The hat, the confident stride, the sense of *belonging* that he projected . . . it was disorienting. Then he was right there, smiling up at me, grabbing my arm, and the words just poured out of him. He and the other scout had been dropping something off at the office for their scoutmaster when they spotted us. Now he wanted to give me a tour of the camp. After I got our hugs and kisses in, I followed Josh, surreptitiously checking him over for signs of neglect. He looked good. And happy. He brought me to the waterfront to show me where he took swimming lessons and earned his first-aid merit badge. We wandered into the camp store, where he introduced me to the caretaker's dog, an ancient Lab mix named Sampson. I bought him a T-shirt with the camp's name and we carried it up the trail, past a boulder, which Josh told me was said to be haunted by the spirit of a Boy Scout who wandered into the woods and was never found. Finally we reached his troop's campsite. He continued on to his tent when one of the Boy Scout leaders pulled me aside to tell me what a great kid I had. I smiled to myself as he described the way Josh would keep the campsite tidy, picking up the litter and cleaning the bathrooms when the other boys goofed off. That's my boy, fitting in by finding a job to do.

When the sun went down, the campers and their parents found seats in a makeshift amphitheater carved into the side of a hill and overlooking a lake. Josh sat with his troop several tiers down from me. There were skits and corny jokes, then the story of Taunkacoo, the Native American spirit who wanders Camp Resolute in search of one boy from each troop who most exemplifies scouting. Later, it was explained that the boys chose the Honor Scout by casting ballots for the camper who was most trustworthy, loyal, helpful, friendly, courteous, and kind.

A drumbeat sounded over the lake, then gradually grew

louder as Scouts in Native American costume bearing flaming torches paddled silently to the shoreline in canoes. A hush fell over the crowd as the costumed Scouts landed their canoes and crept up from the beach and through the amphitheater, tapping the chosen boys on the shoulders. One of the boys who rose from his seat wore a baseball cap. I could barely make him out, just the cap, bobbing behind the torchbearer in the flickering light. I didn't want to jinx it or be exposed as a mother who cared too much about this sort of thing, but I couldn't help it. My shy little boy, so often overlooked by teachers and coaches, drowned out by louder, more insistent children, was quite possibly about to be officially recognized just for being himself.

"Is that Josh?" Mary asked.

I was craning my neck to see over the rows upon rows of silhouetted figures. "I can't tell."

The boys assembled on the stage to receive their Order of Taunkacoo Honor Camper award while those of us in the audience were asked to stand. I strained on tippy-toes so I could see the gathering below, but it was too dark to make out the faces of the boys.

"These campers have given to you their unselfish service," the Scout narrating the ceremony said. "Look at them. Learn from them. Pattern your lives after them." One by one, he called out the Honor Scouts' names. And when he got to Joshua Luttrell, my boy stepped out of the shadows to receive his award, his face briefly illuminated by the firelight.

Man, letting go of my kids was hard, but it was proving to be so worth it.

———

THROUGHOUT THE REST of the summer, Keith and I continued to work with Daisy on her sound sensitivity. Little by little, Keith and I started to see some success. One night our neighbor lit a small armory's worth of fireworks in the street in front of our house. He had given me advance warning, so I drew the shades and sat on the floor with Daisy, listening to rockets whistle and explode outside the window. I talked to her and fed her a mixture of biscuit pieces and the high-value sausage, and she soaked up my affection as if nothing was happening outside. Lightning storms came and went without any reaction from her, and I continued to play the recording of thunder at low volume. Keith kept me updated, reporting that she seemed to be making progress, both with the classic desensitization method of spending increasing amounts of time in the gym, and his ignoring her when she looked for his response to loud noises.

IN EARLY SEPTEMBER, Christina announced at the end of her training class that an evaluator from Therapy Dog International would be available the following Saturday to test dogs for TDI certification, which some nursing homes and hospitals require before allowing therapy dogs in to visit patients. A TDI-certified dog has to be trusted in any situation amid any kind of distractions, including loud, sudden noises. TDI certification is not a requirement for service dogs and earning certification wouldn't mean Daisy would graduate, but it would be a good litmus test. If she were to pass, I'd know she was that much more likely to make it through the program.

The next weekend I showed up at Christina's training school with Daisy, Josh, and our next-door neighbor Catherine. During the testing, the kids would act the part of noisy crowds, hospital patients, and, of course, children. Another puppy raiser brought her niece.

We stepped inside and were greeted by the familiar scent of cleaning solution and dog. Josh and Catherine were diverted by the vivid orange and pink of a Dunkin' Donuts box, and I led Daisy to the sign-in area. A scowling woman behind a make-shift desk handed me a form to fill out. All of the stress hormone I was pumping out in anticipation of Daisy's test must have caused my brain cells to curl up in defeat. I don't know how else to explain why I became incapable of completing the TDI test form. Worse, I didn't even realize that I wasn't filling it out properly. I'd walk Daisy up to the desk and hand the form to the TDI woman only for her to call me back, flicking the blank section with the back of her hand, her scowl deeper than before. Finally, on my third try at filling in all the blanks, she said in a voice that could have eviscerated a cow, "Why don't you try something new this time? Why don't you try *reading* the form before you give it back to me?"

The good news is, she wasn't the one testing the dogs. We could hear that happening behind a high wooden room divider on wheels. One at a time, a handler would lead in his or her dog and stand by passively as the assessor said hello, patted, then brushed the dog. Another dog would be brought in while the assessor gauged the tested dog's reaction. Then the assessor would yell, "Crowd!" and Josh, Catherine, and the weekend puppy raiser's niece would run into the testing area to mill about. "Medical equipment!" the assessor would say after a minute or two, and the kids would run off to the sidelines and return with a walker, a wheelchair, and an IV pole. Things got a little ugly during this portion, but only among the children. The problem was, there was only one wheelchair and all the kids wanted it. The puppy raiser's niece, who at nine was the youngest of the group, kept making it to the chair first and would zip around the dog with an expression of malicious glee on her face while Josh and Catherine glumly wheeled an IV pole or stomped around behind a walker. Catherine negotiated a take-turns agreement . . . which the niece immediately breached. Between tests, Josh and Catherine would return to the Dunkin' Donuts box while the niece played with the dogs (and likely plotted the fastest route back to the wheelchair).

I was filling out the TDI form for what I hoped was the final time when a loud crash rang out from behind the wooden divider. Daisy started to dart for safety, but Christina, who was standing by, swept the kids away from the Dunkin' Donuts box, broke off a piece of blueberry muffin, and popped it into Daisy's mouth in one smooth motion. I stared at Christina, aghast. The dogs weren't allowed to have people food. She saw my expression and pointed to Daisy, who had settled back down to chew, her fears erased by this unexpected treat. "Hey, desperate times call for desperate measures." Even though Daisy's performance on the TDI test wouldn't factor into her becoming a service dog, it was troublesome to think that she might associate the evaluation with a loud, scary noise; that her fear could carry over to the final assessment, the one that would count.

DAISY WAS THE fifth dog to be tested and Christina used the fear-erasing blueberry muffin four times while we waited for Daisy's turn. The dog handlers weren't allowed to bring any treats—freshly baked or otherwise—into the testing area. Food would only cloud the results. I used the trick of forcing my mind to go blank so Daisy wouldn't pick up on my anxiety. She sat by my side, the leash clipped to her collar (Gentle Leaders aren't allowed during testing, either), and peered up expectantly at the assessor, waiting for permission to say hello. Instead, the assessor greeted me and we shook hands while Daisy watched. Then the handler stooped to pat Daisy's head and back. Daisy brushed the floor with her tail and opened her mouth in a happy pant, but stayed rooted to the spot. Next, the assessor inspected her ears and paws, and ran a brush through Daisy's coat. The assessor instructed us to walk away on a loose leash and turn right, then left, then do a U-turn. Daisy, so accustomed to these sorts of exercises, loped easily alongside me. We returned to our spot and the kids were called in. Daisy turned to me with a pleading look, hoping I'd let her off leash for a game of tag. I looked straight ahead, pointedly ignoring her. The assessor asked the kids to retrieve the medical equipment. The three of them bolted out of the testing area. There was a brief skirmish at the wheelchair between the niece and Catherine. Catherine won. She presented the wheelchair grandly to Josh, who hopped in and happily spun around for a minute before surrendering it to Catherine so she could have a turn. I smiled to myself.

The assessor called the kids out of the testing area and while they were leaving, she picked up a metal dog bowl and dropped it behind Daisy. Daisy gazed expectantly up at me, waiting for me to magically produce a bite of muffin. I knew then we were safe. Daisy passed the TDI test with flying colors.

On our way home we stopped at a restaurant to celebrate. A group of teenagers seated nearby made a huge fuss when they realized there was a dog under our table. Josh, Catherine, and I tried to stifle our laughter as the first one to spot Daisy pointed her out to the others ("There, no, over there, look, you can see his tail . . ."). When we got up to leave, I called Daisy out from under the table, where she had snoozed the entire time, exhausted from the TDI test, and turned her to face the teenagers. "Daisy?" I said. She looked up at me. "Take a bow." She slammed her chest to the floor and popped up again while the kids at the table punched each other in the shoulders and clapped their hands.

Yes, we liked to show off.

───────────

IT'S POSSIBLE THAT my feet never made contact with the ground on my way into the prison that Sunday night to return Daisy to Keith, I was feeling that buoyant.

"Oh, that's good news," Keith said, his voice full of emotion. I had just finished telling him about the TDI test and he was clutching Daisy's leash and smiling at me with an open, hopeful expression. He reminded me of Daisy when she was waiting for her next command, all anticipation and enthusiasm. It was in direct contrast to the Keith of a few months earlier, who thought Daisy would flunk out of the program because of the parasites. Seeing him like that made me understand just how vital a sense of hope is.

"It doesn't mean she'll definitely pass, but I'm telling you, she barely reacted to that bowl being dropped. She was like, 'Okay, now's the part where I get my muffin, right?'"

Keith laughed. "She'll pass. She's got to pass. She works so hard. She's a fighter. And, you know what I think? I think there's a plan for her. She's meant to be with a child. You should see her in the visiting room. There's always a crowd of kids around her and she just loves being around them. That's what's meant for her. That's her plan: to be with a child."

I smiled at Keith. "I think so, too."

We both knew that it was Christy who would decide whether or not Daisy was fit to become a service dog. When Daisy went up to NEADS for her final training, Christy would have her all to herself, without me or Keith or Christine or Dunkin' Donuts helping, and she'd be able to tell just what this dog was capable of.

Neither of us knew for sure when Daisy would leave the prison for good, but we were pretty sure it would be soon. Most NEADS dogs leave the prison at fifteen to sixteen months. On September 18, Daisy would be sixteen months old.

There was a man who showed up at Christina's training class every now and then with his service dog, Waldo, a black Lab with a regal bearing. Bob used a power wheelchair. One time Bob showed us how with a single phrase, "Free time," Waldo transformed from a steadfast professional who you'd trust with your infant to a galloping goofball, giddy with the joy of being a dog. It was clear from watching Bob's face that he got as much out of watching Waldo enjoy himself as he did having Waldo by his side.

I'd been thinking of Bob and Waldo a lot since we met, as well as the people I saw during graduation and my own experiences with Daisy, how she introduced me to a friendlier world and helped me locate a kinder, more patient person within myself.

I knew Keith had witnessed firsthand the effect of service

dogs on their people, because he'd seen it when clients came back to the prison to meet the inmate trainer. And I learned later that just as Daisy helped me to become a better person, she did the same for him, but in a more profound way.

Keith's skin was still boyishly smooth when he first went into prison. It wasn't until nearly two years later that he finally had enough facial hair to scrape off. Every time the guard came around with a razor, Keith would take it because he figured the more often he shaved, the faster the beard would grow. He wanted to look older. His sole goal in life was to get through each day, and to do that he had to appear tough. It was, plain and simple, a matter of survival. Fifteen years later, he had it down pretty well—and then he got Daisy. As he put it, "She made me soft, but in a good way."

Rhode Island Department of Corrections director A. T. Wall described prison as "a grim place where hope is in short supply." He's also someone who knows the value of hope, that being able to visualize a future allows a person to do what's necessary to meet it, arms wide open. He also knows the value of dogs. Fiddling with his watch, which bears the image of his own beloved yellow Lab, the late Chumster, he once told me, "It takes a dog to humanize a person."

With Daisy, Keith found himself acting spontaneous for the first time since he was a kid. Silly nicknames would fly out of his mouth. He'd call himself "daddy," have her "speak" to "grandma and grandpa" during his allotted phone call to his parents. He thought of Daisy as his girl and his baby. But more than that, through Daisy, he rediscovered his capacity for empathy.

"You have to find the sensitive side of you because you have to be sensitive to what the dog is feeling. And you can't help it, but that's going to change you as a person," he told me once.

Learning from Christy and being around the other guys in the program, the ones who, like Keith, were trying to rise above their environment by taking college courses, was like stumbling on an oasis of normalcy. Keith started to speak differently, to carry himself straighter. With Daisy, he lived something approximating what he called a "normal life, to live like a human."

He saw a future for himself.

16

Better Go Now

THE ANNIVERSARY OF my first weekend with Daisy passed and I could feel the clock running out—on her training, on her chances, and on our time together. Like a marathoner carb-loading the day before a race, I packed our weekends with training scenarios and outings. Josh and I took Daisy apple picking, where she rode in the hay wagon and wound her way with us through the corn maze. Marty got in extra wrestling sessions and Aviva would make a point of checking on the progress of Daisy's puppy skin, nearly filled in now. Josh and I went to the Museum of Work and Culture, where I posed her next to mannequins of nineteenth-century factory workers bending over looms. Josh and Daisy played endless games of hide-and-seek during our last days together. He'd bust out in laughter when, after calling Daisy from a stay, she'd race through the house and cover his face with kisses after finding him crouched behind a chair or under a table. At night, not wanting to leave her, I'd lie on the floor next to Daisy and bury my face in the scruff of her neck, breathing in her scent, feeling her warmth, etching each moment in my memory.

I told Christy and Dave and anyone else who would listen that if Daisy failed, I would take her. But truly, I wanted her to pass. Now when people asked me how I'd ever cope with giving up Daisy, I'd think first of Keith and I'd worry about him, alone again, without her.

———

TWO OTHER PUPPY raisers and I brought our newly TDI-certified dogs to visit a nursing home. Our first stop after signing in at the front desk was the activity room, where we met a staff member who proudly introduced us to her therapy dog, a small furry mixed breed named Oliver. Oliver was outraged by this invasion by a trio of Labrador retrievers in matching capes. So he barked. A lot. Our dogs tilted their heads at him and carried their tails higher, possibly considering whether they should return the sentiment. Before they could make up their minds, we retreated to the hallway, where a shrunken man in a suit and fedora lurched unsteadily up to us behind his walker and asked for directions to the exit. I looked around helplessly. Before I could answer, a woman in a wheelchair approached me. "Excuse me! What do you have there?" she demanded.

I turned Daisy to face her. "This is Daisy. Would you like to pet her?" I asked. The woman's face softened and she told me that she would like that very much. I got Daisy's attention and pointed to the woman's lap. "Visit!" I told her. Daisy responded by resting her chin on the woman's thigh. Daisy closed her eyes while the woman stroked her head and talked wistfully about her childhood dog, Peppy. To her, and most everyone else we met that day, our dogs forged a path through the tangled under-brush of their memories and led them back to their own long-dead but forever-beloved dogs. We went from room to room, hearing about Blackie and Rex, King and Taffy.

Between rooms, the man in the fedora would flag us down and pleasantly ask for directions to the exit. At one point, the dogs whipped around in unison, their noses pointing down the corridor. We followed their gazes to an unattended food cart where Oliver was on his hind legs, helping himself to the remains of that day's lunch. "That's a *therapy* dog?" Lisa asked.

"No way did that dog pass the TDI test," I grumbled.

On our way out, we passed the man in the fedora. This time he was slumped over, asleep on a bench in the foyer, just five feet from the exit.

"Oh, look!" Lisa whispered. "He was *so close!*"

I WAS STILL thinking about him after taking Daisy for a final visit to Marty's parents to say good-bye.

Marty had been threatening to stop bringing her over ever since February, when we caught Pop slipping her a candy con-versation heart. He was so sly about it, we never would have noticed except for the clicking against Daisy's teeth. Pop had been leaning forward in his easy chair, picking through the bowl of candy hearts, reading each one before returning it to the bowl. Apparently, he was searching for the proper sentiment for Daisy, who was sitting at his feet. And apparently, he found it because suddenly Daisy was trotting across the room, working her jaws. Marty and I looked at each other. "Pop!" Marty's voice was sharp. "Did you just give her something?"

I aimed for damage control: "Oh, we're not allowed to feed Daisy people food," I said apologetically while chasing Daisy down and holding my palm under her chin. I ordered her to drop it. Daisy thrust out her tongue and deposited a wet, pink candy heart in my hand. I could just make out the letters. It said "I love you." Pop looked away without saying a word.

This time Pop pulled a bowl of potato chips onto his lap. Daisy had positioned herself behind his easy chair, which was odd, but I figured there was an interesting scent back there. As we described the kids' latest activities and Marty squeaked in the upholstered rocker, varying his answers to Nana's repeated questions, sometimes adding new details, sometimes keeping them brief, Aviva was bending herself into contortions, trying to get my attention without actually using her voice. What she was trying to tell us, I learned after we left, was that when Marty and I weren't looking, Pop was sneaking potato chips behind him and into Daisy's waiting mouth.

In the car on the way home, Marty was livid and said Pop's behavior was just one more reason why his parents couldn't be trusted to live on their own. I saw it differently. To me, Pop was giving Daisy something to remember him by.

About a hundred times each weekend I was struck by the magic this dog spun everywhere she went. In the nursing home she waved her tail and the ugliness of the present vanished into thin air, leaving the residents free to fill the space with the most beautiful parts of the past. In brick city, she rooted around until she found Pop's essential self, a rule-breaking mischief-maker too often buried by the laments of old age. And soon enough she would become a service dog—I hoped—to a person who desperately needed a little magic in life. That I got to be a part of it was both a privilege and a blessing.

———

IN MID-SEPTEMBER CHRISTY sent me an e-mail. She had chosen the date that Daisy would leave the prison for good. It would be after class on the last Tuesday of the month. We'd have only two more weekends together.

I closed the e-mail and swiped at the tears before they could fully form. In an odd way, I was relieved. I'd been dreading this news, but at least now I knew when it would happen. Yet still unanswered was whether Daisy would be matched with a client and become a service dog. That all happened behind the scenes and was up to Christy, who would evaluate Daisy more closely at NEADS. I wouldn't know whether Daisy would become a service dog until after it happened. If it did at all.

———

ALL YEAR LONG, starting with Daisy's first weekend with us, I had been snapping pictures of her and uploading them to my computer. They were scattered among various files, so I started searching through them for shots to print out. My plan was to make an album chronicling Daisy's twelve months with us so that the person with whom she was matched could see how she looked at various stages of puppyhood and get a sampling of the different types of experiences she had growing up.

But before I could do that, I needed to find suitable prints for Keith. I'd send them out for processing, then, because I assumed photo albums weren't allowed in prison, hand these in a stack to the officer on duty, probably on the day I brought Daisy back to prison for the final time.

One by one, I clicked through the photos, passing over those that included me or family members, which was against prison rules. I smiled and teared up as each image opened into a memory of the past year: Daisy playing in a spring snowstorm; Daisy running up the yard with a red ball in her mouth; Daisy on her hind legs, staring intently out the dining room window during a visit to my mother's house. When I had a representative selection, I turned to the formal portraits. Back in March, a photographer invited puppy raisers to bring their dogs to Christina's training school for a free photo session. He had draped a thick white sheet of paper along a backdrop and onto the floor to create a seamless canvas on which to pose the dogs. The photographer captured Daisy in playful and serious poses, with and without her cape. I wanted Keith to have a five-by-seven—a sort of official portrait of his dog. I pored over each shot, weighing each against the others. The picture had to be perfect, it needed to capture her potential as a service dog while retaining the essence of her nature. I wanted him to remember her as happy yet confident. Finally, I settled on a picture that I hoped would make Keith feel nothing but good every time he looked at it. In it, Daisy is proudly wearing her cape. She is facing the camera, but her gaze is directed just off to the right of the frame. Her mouth is slightly open, indicating that she is focused, but calm. She looks like she's anticipating her next command and she just can't wait to carry it out.

———

MY LAST WEEKEND with Daisy wasn't a weekend at all. I took Daisy out midweek so she could accompany me and Josh to a doctor's appointment—something she hadn't been able to do on a weekend, and an important exposure. The medical assistant called Josh's name and the three of us stood up. The assistant, a stout woman in lavender scrubs, looked down at Daisy and muttered, "I don't like dogs. I'm scared of them."

I assured the assistant that Daisy was harmless, that in fact she was being trained to help someone. The woman kept glancing at Daisy while she took Josh's blood pressure and recorded his weight and height. Daisy acted the perfect lady, and the assistant started to relax. When she escorted us to the examining room, she asked to pet her. I smiled to myself. Another heart won. Later, the woman taking Josh's blood in the lab wouldn't let us leave until we had seen the photos of her own dog. Back in the waiting room, we validated our parking ticket and entertained the other young patients and their parents when I had Daisy "Fetch" it from the machine and hand it to me.

Throughout those final days together, my hyperawareness of Daisy's presence had the effect of slowing down time, allowing me to absorb every moment with her. During playtime, she'd careen around the backyard with her ears flapping and her tongue hanging out. She'd drop to her belly to catch her breath, then resume running circles on the grass.

Gratitude for her, for what she brought to me and my family—and to Keith—filled me to overflowing.

AND THEN IT was time. Josh asked to come with me and I couldn't say no, even though I knew having him there would make it harder for me. Daisy, of course, had no idea this was our last trip back to J. J. Moran. She slept all the way. Josh played with the radio while I let my mind drift, forcing myself away from thoughts of Daisy whenever I felt the pressure of tears building behind my eyes.

We pulled into the lot and my voice was tight. "Okay. Say good-bye," I told Josh. Then I dared look at his face and saw tears skimming down his cheeks. That's when I lost it. I became an instant crying wreck. The three of us together for the last time. I got out of the car and stared hard at a leaf on the ground. I couldn't bear to watch Daisy lick Josh's tears; I needed to re-gain my composure before I brought her back to Keith. When I knew I couldn't delay it any longer, I gently pulled Daisy from Josh and walked into the prison, wiping my eyes and ducking my face so the guards wouldn't see. I clutched a fat envelope of pictures for Keith.

Keith was already waiting for me in shift command. Other than the weekend paperwork, we're not allowed to give the in-mates anything directly, so I held the envelope up and told him I'd leave it for Captain Lefebvre to pass along to him. Except I could barely get the words out, I was crying that hard.

Keith thanked me—for the pictures, and for being Daisy's puppy raiser with him. His tone was gentle as he told me I did a good job with Daisy and he couldn't have done it without me, that we worked really hard to get her to where she was. I don't remember handing Daisy's leash to him, but somehow she was already in position, flush against his right leg. In a few minutes, I'd be leaving the prison for the last time. In a few days, Daisy would leave the prison for the last time. Who knew when Keith would get out, even with time off for good behavior and maybe parole it would still be years. I did know that on paper, he was only halfway through his forty-year sentence. He'd be returning to his cell, alone. Yet there he was, reassuring me and thanking me. I couldn't speak. I stole one last glance at my sweet puppy, my Daisy, and fled.

Josh and I were silent on the way home. We returned to our quiet house, to life without her. Aviva wanted to know if we'd get another NEADS puppy. Josh wanted to know if we'd ever see Daisy again. I didn't have solid answers for either one of them, just "maybe" and "I hope so."

Daisy's stuffed lamb was on the floor. I deposited it in the dog toy basket. Then I washed and dried her food and water bowl and brought them down to the basement for storage. Later, Marty found me sitting on the floor upstairs, dismantling the crate. "I should have done this months ago, when she first outgrew it," I said to him.

"No, not really," he said. "It's like the kids' bedrooms. I'm not going to turn Aviva's room into my music studio the second she moves out. You have to let everyone sit with the change before you take those drastic steps, you know?"

Which reminded me, as much as it hurt to let Daisy go, in a way, I was grateful for the practice of seeing her on to the next stage of her life, because in a few years, I'd have to do the same with my children. I only hoped their father and I prepared them as well as Keith and I did Daisy.

17

Say Hello

THE NEXT MONTH, while we waited to hear about Daisy's fate, I thought a lot about what our year together had given us. On the surface, little had changed since Daisy left, but deeper in, we were all a little different, a little bit nicer because of her. Aviva and I didn't fight as much, I think because my work with Daisy taught me to better read the unspoken messages behind my daughter's words. I'd still lose my temper, but not as frequently. Daisy gave me lots of practice—especially during those pre–Gentle Leader walks—of breathing deeply through my frustration to keep calm. My judgment remains clear when I'm in control of my temper, and the neat thing is, it's much easier that way to notice the qualities in my daughter that I admire and respect.

Josh, who accompanied me on so many field trips with Daisy, couldn't help but become aware of the obvious disabilities and the invisible hurts that so many of us struggle with. His growing confidence, I'm sure, was due in some part to the realization that our lives are what we make of them; the important thing is to keep trying. At one point, Christy asked in an e-mail how exactly Josh taught Daisy to play hide-and-seek. I didn't know the details, so I asked, transcribing Josh's instructions in a reply. When I hit the Send button I looked at Josh, who was smiling at the thought of another child experiencing the thrill of being "found" by Daisy.

Watching Daisy wait patiently to say hello to a nursing home patient or a homeless person, then wiggle up, ecstatic to meet a new friend, was a lesson for all of us. Daisy saw through the wheelchairs, the old age, the unusual behavior, to the humanity that exists in each one of us. She helped us acknowledge the burdens so many of us carry—and the strengths that allow us to go on.

A month after our final good-bye to Daisy, I opened the mailbox to find a letter announcing that Daisy had passed the program and been matched with a nine-year-old autistic boy named David. The news forced me to let go of that last stubborn shred of hope that she'd be my dog. I cried, but mostly I reveled in her triumph.

———

THREE WEEKS LATER on a Saturday afternoon we were running around, frantically searching for keys and cell phones after deciding at the last minute that Marty and I would take separate cars up to NEADS because it was the quickest way to stop the negotiations about what time we'd return home.

We were going to see Daisy.

"Let's go." I grabbed the photo album with the yellow cloth cover (the shade that best matched Daisy's name, in my opinion) and instinctively patted my pocket to make sure I hadn't forgotten the treats.

The invitation to meet David and his family had arrived shortly after the letter announcing Daisy's match. Daisy and David would be among three service dog–client teams at the meet and greet. I was so excited, I could barely contain myself. Aviva slid into the passenger seat and was still pulling her door shut when I let out the clutch and the car lurched up the driveway.

Before I could stop myself I blurted, "The last time I was this excited was when we were getting ready to pick you up at the airport from Costa Rica." I clapped my hand over my mouth too late, afraid that Aviva would be insulted to have Daisy placed on equal footing with her, but she turned to me with a huge smile on her face.

"Mom! That's so sweet!"

We found our way up to NEADS with the help of Ian the GPS man, who guided us off the highway and onto the winding country road I remembered from traveling to the orientation eighteen months earlier.

I found the driveway and Marty and Josh pulled in right behind us. My heart was pounding in my chest as I parked and the four of us picked our way over the lawn toward the slate-blue house where the clients live during training. We followed a wheelchair ramp and found ourselves welcomed by a couple of women—volunteers—who urged us to help ourselves from a table laid with platters of cookies and other freshly baked treats.

I didn't see any dogs. The only other person in sight was a large man hovering in a doorway. Marty stepped over with his hand outstretched and introduced each of us to him as Daisy's weekend puppy raisers.

"Oh! Hey! That's my son's dog!" The man, David Sr., grabbed each one of our hands. He noticed me peering around him, trying to glimpse whether perhaps Daisy was in the hallway.

"They're around here somewhere. I think they went over to the main building. They should be here soon," he said. While we waited, Marty and I peppered him with questions, asking how the training was going, whether David was excited to have Daisy. He told us that he stayed at the client house with David at night while David's mother, Lisa, trained with him during the day. While we spoke, Cindy Lopez from the puppy house walked through the room with an eight-week pudgy black Lab wearing a tiny NEADS cape. While Aviva and Josh were saying hello, the door opened and a family walked in with a yellow Lab, followed by the weekend puppy raisers Justin and his wife, Melanie. I hadn't realized it, but Nellie had been matched with an autistic boy at the same time as Daisy and they were here to meet her new family. I excused myself to say hello to them. While we spoke, Captain Lefebvre, carrying a gift bag filled with books about trains for the little boy paired with his namesake, stepped through the door. It took a moment to recognize him out of uniform.

That group had disappeared into the living room of the house and I had turned back to David Sr. when there was another commotion at the door. A woman wearing a pink NEADS sweatshirt led a small dark-haired boy into the room. They each held on to a leash. Behind them, waiting for the pair to cross the threshold, was Daisy. She was wearing the red service dog cape with a matching collar and Gentle Leader.

Josh nudged me and I sucked in my breath, wanting nothing more than to launch myself into the air and wrap my arms around that dog. Daisy was staring straight ahead. She hadn't looked past everyone's legs yet.

"Here they are," David Sr. was saying. "Lisa, David, these are the people who took care of Daisy on weekends." I tore my eyes from Daisy.

"Hi, I'm Sharron," I said, and introduced the rest of the family. I struggled to keep my tone even, I was so excited. Daisy raised her head and perked her ears when she heard me. Our eyes locked, and just as she'd done fifty times before in shift command, she folded her ears tight around her head and whipped her tail back and forth. The pressure was building behind my eyes again, but I forced myself to turn away from Daisy to the people holding her double leash. The little boy, David, was watching me with a somber curiosity. David's mom glanced down at Daisy, who looked like she would pop out of her skin, she was trying so hard to contain herself.

"It looks like she remembers you," she said. My entire face smiled then. It was the same thing that Keith had said when Daisy was just a puppy.

"May I say hello?" I asked.

"Daisy? Say hello." The words were barely out of Lisa's mouth when Daisy was right there, slamming her body against my legs. The four of us fell on her and she was wiggling and licking and dancing between me, Josh, Marty, and Aviva, attempting to greet each of us simultaneously. Our family had been reunited. But it would be only for the moment. The tears pushed through and the ones Daisy didn't lick from my face spilled onto her fur.

It's quite possible the folks at NEADS would have had to call for the Jaws of Life to pry me off Daisy, but soon enough, she took care of the matter by stepping away from me to lift her snout in the air in the direction of the refreshment table. That nose again.

Marty asked David's mother about their training. She started from the beginning, when they met Daisy for the first time, describing how Christy brought Daisy in to see them. When Christy asked Daisy to say hello, Daisy bypassed Lisa and walked right up to David. From then on, the two were inseparable. I smiled to myself, remembering Keith's gut feeling that Daisy was meant to be with a child.

David's disability is very low spectrum autism, which means he functions at a high level but has difficulty connecting with other children. "He doesn't know how to play," his mother told me, "but now David throws the ball for Daisy and Christy taught him how to play hide-and-seek with her." Josh caught my eye and we smiled at each other.

David's family applied for a service dog for several reasons. They hoped that the dog would serve as a social bridge for David, connecting him with other kids who would be more likely to look past his disability and see him as a potential playmate. The dog would also give David something to talk about with other children while keeping him calm in stressful situations. Daisy had already proved her value there. His mother said she was astonished when during a training session, David was able to walk out of a video game store without throwing a tantrum. It was a first. "I was bracing for it, but when Christy said it was time to go, David just said, 'Let's go, Daisy,' and out he walked!"

While we talked, David Sr. was showing his son the photo album we had made for him. He took it from his father and brought it over to me. The album was open to a picture of six Labrador retrievers in blue capes posing in front of a fireplace. Someone had taken it during a field trip to a senior center and one of the puppy raisers e-mailed me a copy. I had captioned it "Which one is Daisy?"

"Can I guess?" David asked in a soft voice.

"Of course! But it's not easy so it may take you a few tries." He nodded solemnly and peered down at the photo. Five of the dogs were yellow, and Daisy was nearly identical to three of them. The only sure thing that gave her away to me was her blue-striped leash, but that was long gone now and David had never seen it.

"Is this her?" David had placed his pointer finger on the dog closest to the camera: it was Daisy.

"David!" I said. "You got it right! You picked out Daisy from all of those dogs." He stared up at me and raised his eyebrows.

"Yeah," he said, and looked over his shoulder at Daisy, who was now on the floor licking her foot. "That's because I love Daisy."

AVIVA LEFT EARLY with Marty, while Josh stayed behind with me. On the ride home, we were both mostly silent, absorbed in our own thoughts. There was so much going through my mind, but the only one I wanted to talk with at that moment was Keith. I wanted to tell him about the day, about David picking Daisy out among all of those yellow Labs. I wanted him to know how wildly happy it made me to see that dog again, and about the strange mixture of pride and loss upon seeing her in the official red service dog vest. To describe how it felt at the end of the visit to watch Daisy walk away flanked by David and his mother.

But of course I couldn't do that.

SOON ENOUGH, THOUGH, David's mother would travel with Daisy to J. J. Moran to meet the prison inmate who trained her son's service dog, and Keith would experience the same momentary bliss of reunion as I did. He would talk to David's mother and receive confirmation that all of his hard work was worth it because now there was a little boy in the world who felt less alone. Soon enough, the door to the visiting room would slide open to reveal Daisy in her red vest, no longer a little puppy full of promise but an adult dog, promise fulfilled.

Epilogue

SIX MONTHS AFTER Daisy said good-bye to us, she returned to my house, this time with David and his family. She came for a playdate with Holly, my latest NEADS puppy. Daisy and Holly hit it off right away, maybe because they sensed how much they had in common: they are both Labs, though Holly's fur is lighter than Daisy's, with a thin, dark line running down the middle of her muzzle like a zipper. Holly sleeps in the crate Daisy once occupied, plays with her old toys (except for the orange barbell Daisy won for musical sits—that went to her new home). And there's one other connection that seals their bond: Keith.

I didn't know which inmate I'd be working with when Dave sent me a photo of Holly and asked whether I was ready for a new puppy. My partner could have been Nellie's handler, or maybe one of the backups had been promoted to primary trainer. I braced myself to start all over again not only with a new puppy but with a new coparent. I may have visibly sighed with relief when I walked into shift command to pick up Holly for the first time and saw that it was Keith holding on to her leash.

"Looks like you're stuck with me again," I said to him.

"I was gonna say the same thing about me," he answered.

———

DURING THE PLAYDATE, David was enamored of Holly, who, Keith pointed out during one of our meetings in shift command, looks like a baby harp seal, with her enormous brown eyes and smooth, round head. When David kneeled to hug her, Daisy pranced around on the edge of jealousy before solving the problem by goading Holly into play. The two dogs raced around the backyard until they were flat on their stomachs, legs and tails and tongues stretched out for maximum cooling effect. Daisy wiggled closer to Holly and poked her with her muzzle. Holly poked back and suddenly they were back on all four feet, pouncing on each other and racing around and around, in one giant circle.

———

I'LL BE FOREVER grateful to Daisy. She helped me transition into the next phase of my life—the one I was dreading that Mother's Day in the supermarket when I first spotted a NEADS dog—the one where the children grow up and leave the house and the generation ahead of us grows old. Aviva has her driver's license now and has saved up to buy her own car. I'm about to retire as her personal chauffeur and truth is, I'm kind of happy about it. Josh is five months away from becoming a teenager. His bar mitzvah tutor has pointed out to me that his voice cracks sometimes when he sings his prayers, meaning he really is becoming a man. (I still read to him, though. Don't tell anyone.)

It's not easy, letting kids go and moving on, but it's not quite as hard when you're prepared. Daisy was my practice run—the year of readying her for the future, a compressed, simplified version of the last sixteen with my kids. Tucker served the same role at one time, ushering us into family life. When Marty and I brought her home for the first time, we joked that she was our training wheels for parenthood. If we got her through the puppy stage, we could try again with a real baby. We learned self-sacrifice, self-discipline—the importance of tiring out a young one so we all could sleep—qualities you need in abundance when you have infants and toddlers.

Daisy had a different job. When I applied for a NEADS puppy, I thought I was getting a rental dog, the cure for my Canine Deficit Disorder. That someone with a disability would ultimately benefit was just a fortunate by-product. I couldn't have anticipated the ways in which that puppy would pick up where Tucker left off. Learning to read Daisy, and understanding that Daisy was always reading *me,* forced me out of my own cozy but narrow perspective. I wish it were a requirement of all parents—particularly parents of teenagers—to train a service dog. Practicing empathy with Daisy made me a better, more patient mother and, quite frankly, kinder to myself. Developing Daisy's strengths and working around her deficits—the fear of sudden, loud noises will always be there, but now she can manage it—allowed me to do the same for myself. My family will never be that tightly knit, freshly scrubbed unit that takes Disney cruises and eats every meal together. Dinnertime will always sneak up on me, but as long as my kids are happy and challenged, as long as they don't starve—which they won't—I'm doing an okay job.

Just as my year with Daisy had to come to an end, I'm getting used to the idea that the era of daily parenting will, too. When it hurts, I recall the early lessons of puppy training when we learned about object exchanges. That's when you offer the dog a more desirable object so it will let go of the one it has in its mouth. You might swap a cookie for a stick, say, or a tennis ball for a child's flip-flop. Daisy grasped the concept right away. Keith never had a problem with trading what he had for something better. For me, it took much longer, but I've finally learned that to get the reward, you have to let go.

Acknowledgments

YET ANOTHER WAY dogs are magic: without Daisy, I wouldn't have so many people to thank. Above all, I owe an enormous debt of gratitude to my gifted agent, Sorche Elizabeth Fairbank, who spotted the real story of Daisy before I did, coaxed it out of me, then applied her considerable savvy to find it a loving home at Gallery Books. I wish I knew what I did to deserve Sorche so I could keep doing it.

I couldn't have been in better hands than with my editor at Gallery, the talented, warm-hearted, and quick-witted Abby Zidle. Abby saw the potential in Daisy and deftly guided me through drafts to final copy, all while keeping me laughing. Many thanks to Gallery's Vice President and Publisher Jennifer Bergstrom for falling in love with Daisy. I promise to keep you both supplied with cute puppy pictures.

I am utterly grateful for the writer's organization Grub Street, a treasured resource in the heart of Boston.

The staff and inmates of the Rhode Island Department of Corrections were hugely helpful in aiding my understanding of the puppy program and the culture of prison. Special thanks to Director A. T. Wall, retired Deputy Warden Kirk Kaszyk, and Deputy Warden Joe Jankowski for submitting to my interviews; Tracey Zeckhausen, who got the wheels moving; Deputy Warden Robert Clancy for giving me access to (almost) everything I needed; Correctional Officers John Smith (Smitty), Anthony Del Signore (Del), Louis Cesario, and Joe Souza for making me feel at home in the most unlikeliest place. Joe gets an extra thank you for his care and devotion to the pups.

To the inmates past and present who care for and train the dogs, thank you for giving me a peek into your world. Special thanks to Steve and Steve, Ron, Dennis, and of course, Keith.

To Mike and Megan for opening your home to me and answering all of my questions with extraordinary insight and candor. You are a remarkable couple.

I'm deeply indebted to Deputy Warden Nelson Lefebvre (congratulations on your promotion!) for embracing my ideas and never wavering in his support. Deputy Warden Lefebvre cleared the trail for my reporting missions inside the prison; sat for long interviews; and proudly shared his scrapbooks of the puppy program. I was told several times throughout this project that without Lefebvre, there would be no puppy program at J. J. Moran. After seeing all he did, I have no doubt this is true.

John Moon at NEADS was an early supporter of the book and deserves many, many thanks for his help and chats. Also at NEADS, Cindy Lopez, Cindy Ryan, Christy Bassett, Jennifer

Banks, and Dave Hessel allowed me to lurk in the background while they went about their jobs. I thank them and Kerry Lemerise, now of Guiding Eyes for the Blind. You all deserve high-value treats and belly rubs for putting up with my requests and answering my questions.

To my fellow puppy raisers, I love our classes and field trips and I am grateful for each one of you. There is no one I would rather be with when the (puppy) shit hits the fan. Christina Rossetti of Alpha Dog K9 made dog training more fun than I think is legal. Thank you for teaching me so much.

Dr. Alan M. Beck, the director of the Center for the Human-Animal Bond at Purdue University's College of Veterinary Medicine, offered information and invaluable insights into the relationship between people and their dogs. Helping me to understand juvenile justice and the effects of incarceration on teenagers were Dr. Donna M. Bishop, professor in the College of Criminal Justice at Northeastern University; and Joshua Dohan, director of the Youth Advocacy Division of the Committee for Public Counsel Services in Massachusetts.

To Lisa, thank you for giving Daisy a loving home. David, thank you for being Daisy's boy.

Friends and family pulled me through months of talking, planning, writing, and fretting. Thank you to Chelsea Lowe for her early support; Deb Lane for giving me deadlines and the occasional gut check; Francine Puckley Mathieson for being my writing buddy and helping me push through paragraph after paragraph simply by sitting with me while we worked on our manuscripts; Dan Chase for resurrecting several days of writing from a dead hard drive; and Crystle Chase for her overall enthusiasm and, of course, for being Holly's person. I owe double thanks to Meredith Albright for taking my author photo and for insisting I stay at her house so I could write, undistracted. If not for her and my father David Kahn, who lent me his apartment, it's possible I'd still be on chapter 7. Dad, I'm sorry I drank all of your beer.

Jan Gardner, I'm so grateful to know you. I suspect everyone else lucky enough to have crossed paths with you would say the same.

The depth and breadth of my gratitude for my mother and lifelong fan, Lenore Goldstein, are boundless. I don't know how you put up with my mishegas during this project. Thank you for not disowning me. Supporting me alongside my mother was my stepfather, Irv Goldstein. To my brothers, Craig and Steve Kahn, thank you for being even more excited about Weekends with Daisy than I was, if that's even possible.

Puppy kisses for my Aunt Carole Kahn who, with her German shepherd, Misty, introduced me at a very young age to the magic of dogs.

Finally, my abiding love goes to Aviva, Josh, and Marty, who accepted this endeavor with good humor and grace. It's one thing to have your life disrupted by an endless parade of puppies, quite another to see it displayed in the pages of a book Thank you. You guys are everything to me.

Photo credits

6, 10, 11, 12, 19: Courtesy of Barb Lawton

21: Courtesy of Ty Bellitti Photography

22: Courtesy of Ruth Anne Bleakney

16: Courtesy of Anne Lefebvre

7, 8, 13, 23: Courtesy of Jack Hurley

All other insert photos courtesy of
Sharron Kahn Luttrell